WAR AND AMERICAN THOUGHT

War
and
American Thought

**FROM THE REVOLUTION
TO THE MONROE DOCTRINE**

Reginald C. Stuart

THE KENT STATE UNIVERSITY PRESS

Library of Congress Cataloging in Publication Data

Stuart, Reginald C.
  War and American thought.

  Bibliography: p.
  Includes index.
  1. United States — History, Military — To 1900.
2. War — Public opinion. 3. Public opinion — United States. I. Title.
E 181.S9   973   81-19358
ISBN 0-87338-267-6   AACR2

for Penni and Jonathan

CONTENTS

ACKNOWLEDGMENTS

In the course of researching and writing even a modest work, academic authors incur many more debts than can ever be repaid. Only the most direct contributions can be acknowledged. Early phases of this project came together in a paper delivered at the 1976 annual meeting of the Canadian Historical Association in Quebec City, Quebec, Canada. This subsequently appeared in the Association's *Historical Papers* as "The American View of War: The Revolutionary Perspective." I am grateful to the Association for permission to reuse much of that article and to my commentator, Don Higginbotham, for encouragement.

As the project developed, the University of Prince Edward Island provided financial support for summer research trips through the Senate Research Committee. The University also provided a paid sabbatical leave during which the book was completed. My close colleague in the History Department, Professor Thomas Spira, patiently read the manuscript at several stages of development, including the entire final draught. His expertise in European history, his penetrating observations, and his editorial experience helped me to avoid pitfalls and smooth out the manuscript.

During my sabbatical year, the University of Virginia transformed the legends of Southern hospitality into reality. Professor Martin Havran, Chairman of History at that time, proved a warm personal and professional host, providing introductions to stimulating colleagues, access to copying facilities, and use of secretarial assistance. The Alderman Library supplied a wealth of material, and many of the resident historians enriched my work through conversation and criticism of portions of the manuscript. In particular, Robert Rutland, editor of the James Madison Papers, gave generously of his time as a reader and friend and permitted free access to the materials in his charge. William Abbot of the George Washington Papers read several of the earlier chapters and made a similar contribution. Merrill D. Peterson read the entire work, presenting comments on points general and specific. Finally, Laura Nagy of the Kent State University Press deserves mention for her patient editorial work on my style.

Other acknowledgments must go to the many librarians who have been invariably helpful, the American Philosophical Society in Philadelphia which provided a timely grant during my sabbatical year, and to all my friends and colleagues, especially Lawrence Kaplan, who have donated time and encouragement to my efforts. Quotations from the Adams Papers are from the microfilm edition, by permission of the Massachusetts Historical Society. A portion of Chapter 3, delivered first at the 1978 meeting of the Organization of American Historians, appeared as "War Powers of the Constitution in Historical Perspective," *Parameters*, 10 (December, 1980).

Finally, my wife deserves recognition for her support and assistance throughout this project. She understands how consuming such work can become, and became involved through typing the final manuscript, as well as assisting in portions of the research. Any errors or omissions remain entirely my responsibility, but she, and others, must share in any credit which this book attracts.

INTRODUCTION

Armed conflict litters the American past, even though Americans believe themselves to have been historically pacific. Viewed through a patriotic lens, all American wars have been justified struggles in self-defense, initiated only after unprovoked aggression. But the record reveals that Americans have fought both offensive and defensive wars, and many that can only be labelled aggressive, and even expansionist. Further probing suggests that in all cases, these conflicts arose from the ambitions and policies of politicians and leaders who conceived of themselves as thinking and acting in the national interest. War, like peace or trade, has been used as an instrument of policy, although American mythology has maintained that Americans always rejected Carl von Clausewitz's dictum to this effect. American military systems, devised and justified for self-defense, have also been utilized in the aggressive pursuit of national interests. The myth of American uniqueness has obscured how much Americans have been part of the Western world in this regard.

This book probes the attitudes toward war of the Revolutionary generation, focusing upon politicians and political leaders. But it also seeks to draw together the views of other elements in American society from the colonial period to the early 1820s. Generations are not discrete. They overlap in an untidy manner. Yet it is safe to say that in 1783, for the men in power, the Revolution and the colonial heritage were the primary determinants of their world view. The same could be said for 1800, or even 1812; but by 1820, the Revolution was an inherited experience for most Americans. The colonial past had faded into vague impressions gleaned from the printed page and the often selective memories of elders. Few prominent Americans knew what it had been like to be alive in the British Empire of the eighteenth century, or to fight for independence. The vast majority of Americans by 1820 had known only a sovereign United States.

Studies in the history of ideas can too easily disembody thought from experience. Once the amalgam of attitudes toward war that Revolutionary Americans held has been established, this book traces how these attitudes interrelated with military and foreign policy, politics, and the events of the Revolutionary and Early National periods of American history. The emerging republican ideology and national policies as defined and pursued by the Revolutionary leaders are therefore significant topics. And the book develops along chronological lines to show how ideas interacted with events. This is the most convenient and persuasive method for demonstrating how attitudes toward war changed over time. Almost all of the events discussed have received extended treatment by historians. But these events have not been interpreted from the perspective of evolving American attitudes toward war.

Just as attitudes toward war intertwine with republican ideology in the years following the American Revolution, so do both of these philosophies relate to burgeoning nationalism. By the late colonial period, the common elements of American national-ism existed, including a certain loyalty to America as a place. But the emotional commitment to America as an idea was in embryo form only, nurtured by the imperial crises and the Revolution which would follow. By 1783, the United States enjoyed political independence, a geographic identity, a distinct form of govern-ment, and a heritage of accomplishment against great odds. The movement for constitutional reform carried this nascent nation-alism forward, spread it further among the population, and gave it a solid institutional base along with the republicanism which provided its ideological impetus. This process continued to the War of 1812, which aroused an emotional commitment to the United States that had not been seen on a wide scale before.

The Revolutionary generation discovered that it had created an independent nation and embarked upon a course that challenged many of its ideological and moral precepts. For example, republican thought dictated that monarchs, through their political irresponsibility, were the principal cause of war in the world. But the Americans found that domestic, foreign, and even human impulses were equally dangerous as generators of conflict. By facing the problems of independent nationhood, the Revolutionary generation confronted the issue of relating means and ends in achieving ambitions and protecting rights.

The Revolutionary leaders found also that people and nations are often violent, irrational, and difficult to deal with. As a result, force often seems necessary to defend the state, protect its citizens and its vital interests, or even to pursue what are perceived as rights, although these may be little more than ambitions. When the Revolutionary leaders embarked on their course of republican independence, they came to believe that their country embodied worthy values. What began as an experiment resulted in a nation cherished for its own sake. Committed to national survival, the leaders modified their moral ideas and used force not only in self-defense, but also to protect and expand both trade and territorial control. Once they had begun such projects, these men found it occasionally difficult to justify morally both means and ends. Although their developing nationalism led them away from attitudes and values they held in great esteem, they did not abandon their principles either readily or utterly. If events and circumstances challenged their sense of restraint, their civilized temperaments and habits of mind remained barricades against excess.

Apart from this, the Revolutionary leaders are intrinsically interesting because they drew upon a heritage which prized restraint in all things. The English writer H. G. Wells argued that without a supreme act of will over its destructive passions, mankind would obliterate itself in future wars. Wells understood the truth of Herbert Spencer's comment that most men would rather die than think. But the leaders who emerged during the Revolutionary generation preferred thought to death and confronted fundamental problems in human social organization and intercourse. To a remarkable degree, these men believed that reason can control emotion, and that goodness of heart can be welded to rational analysis. This led them to conclude that progress is possible, despite mankind's dark nature and history's bleak record. Their venture in independence embraced such ideals, which subsequently became part of America's national-republican ideology.

As the Revolutionary leaders applied reason to restrain passion while developing national policies, they found themselves guides of a weak state during one of history's great whirlwinds. The international European imperial struggles of the eighteenth century yielded to the crusades for liberalism and democracy which erupted out of the French Revolution. And these in turn quit the field to Napoleon and his bid for personal mastery of world affairs. Throughout, these tumults threatened to upset the American experiment in independent republicanism. The Revolutionary generation variously employed diplomacy, neutrality, embargoes on trade, and even warfare to remain at arm's length from European politics.

The Revolutionary generation was guided by what can be termed a "limited-war mentality." This sensibly sought to control rather than eliminate armed conflict. The origins, development, and application of this mentality constitute the principal themes of this book. The Revolutionary generation drew its ideas from many sources and assumed that war was normal, even inevitable, in human affairs. Progress in controlling this kind of violence was possible only through successive curbs on its use. This generation therefore tried to apply the tenets of the *jus ad bellum*, which argued for patience and forbearance before sovereigns resorted to force of arms. The Revolutionary generation believed also in the *jus in bello*, a set of humane rules which sought to limit the brutality of war on noncombatants and soldiers alike. To be just and moral, wars could only have the redress of genuine grievances and the establishment of peace as their objectives. Wars of conquest, by contrast, were morally forbidden. Finally, the Revolutionary generation believed that, although force could be used to pursue state policy objectives, it must be accompanied by caution and restraint. Force was, after all, an instrument, and not an end in itself. These ideas were complex and proved enormously difficult to apply in foreign and military policy, but the Revolutionary leaders nevertheless made that effort of will that Wells considered essential for the blissful future of humanity.

It is unsurprising that the Revolutionary generation failed to achieve peace by these efforts. Noble ambitions often fail in a world of power. Perhaps too, as Arthur C. Clarke has suggested, war is a function of mankind's current stage of biological evolution and will not be abandoned until we move onto another plane. The Revolutionary leaders, although they would have found this thought sensible, did not counsel or practice despair. Rather, they attempted to reconcile the antitheses of war and civilization so that the latter could be defended without succumbing to barbarism.

Some word on the definitions of "war" as used in this study is required. The term refers in general to the armed clash of states and their societies. "Limited war" refers to the restricted use of armed forces to achieve specific objectives short of prostrating the antagonist state. In democratic societies, limited war usually results from the sanction of popular majorities in elected assemblies, but equally as often the recommendation to employ force comes from the executive authority, whether the state is monarchical or republican. As a rule, ideological fervor is absent in such conflicts, although it may exist within individuals or segments of the population. Further, these conflicts are fought with standing forces, augmented by volunteer and militia units. Finally, the broad mass of society and its components remain relatively untouched by the war in question. In short, the term "limited war" refers to the overall character of a conflict, rather than specific acts or attitudes found within it.

This contrasts with the concept of total war, especially as it has developed in the twentieth century. Here, utter defeat of the enemy, perhaps accompanied by the establishment of an altered world order, provides the primary sustaining force to the war, whatever its immediate causes. The bulk of society becomes involved, under close government control, both in actual fighting and in producing the goods and services which support the war effort. Although total war is customarily associated with industrialized societies, this need not be so. Ideological fervor is also a feature of total war, and has punctuated conflicts throughout history. Despite attempted definitions, wars are complex affairs. Even the most sensible and defensible generalizations cannot be applied procrustean fashion.

Scholars considering American attitudes toward war have usually argued that liberal ideology dictated a rejection of war as an instrument of national policy. By inclination and experience, Americans were anti- or non-Clausewitzian, at least were so until the atomic age. But this generalization does not apply to the

Revolutionary generation, and may not even apply throughout the American past. At the very least, American attitudes at any given moment are complex, not homogeneous. This study therefore provides a foundation for reassessing American attitudes toward war in general, as well as among the members of the Revolutionary generation. That is why the final chapter ventures so far beyond the eclipse of the Revolutionary leadership. As with so much research, this study represents a beginning, rather than a final word, on the subject considered.

1

LEGENDS AND LEGACIES:
THE OLD WORLD AND THE NEW

Historical legends have obscured the historical legacies which shaped the Revolutionary generation's approach to war and peace. By the latter half of the eighteenth century, American views of war reflected European ideas inherited from the classics, from clerics, and from contemporary Enlightenment philosophers and political polemicists, as well as from colonial experience with European and aboriginal adversaries alike. Eighteenth-century ideas about war cannot be found in any single source. As with mercantilism, American thought on war was a composite that grew and metamorphosed throughout the seventeenth and eighteenth centuries. And as with mercantilism, this thought emphasized understanding and shaping of the broad forces at work.

American and European ideas on war closely intertwined. The cultural and political threads, the events, the problems, the needs which shape national characteristics, or the thought of a generation such as that which lived through the American Revolution, are all too complex to be wrenched from contemporary context. Throughout the colonial period Americans continuously imported ideas and methods, developed others spontaneously, and constantly synthesized approaches to deal with their immediate problems and conditions.[1] Because they remained Englishmen in so many ways, it is difficult to determine what was distinctly American about American attitudes toward war. This problem compounds because not only ideas, but also continental events and morality influenced early American thinking. English colonials were simultaneously Americans, Englishmen, and western Europeans. American uniqueness in attitudes to war must in some respects be treated as a legend, rather than as a legacy. The Revolutionary generation was a part of its age.

Thomas Jefferson asserted that generations were discrete. Individuals think of themselves as distinct from those who preceded them, or will follow. But generations are untidy collections of individuals who are rough chronological contemporaries sharing common habits of mind and behavior. Such individuals can differ drastically on particulars, such as conducting foreign policy, voting funds for roads or salaries, or electing a town clerk. And generations overlap chronologically. Although all were part of the Revolutionary generation, in 1760 George Washington was twenty-eight, John Adams twenty-five, Thomas Jefferson seventeen, James Madison nine, and Alexander Hamilton five. But this group, and many of their contemporaries who had reached at least the age of young manhood when the Anglo-American difficulties began in earnest, shared many qualities and attitudes, which justifies treating them collectively. For example, they all supported the quest for independence, the Constitution of 1787, and republicanism. They had well-educated and well-read minds immersed in the history and philosophy of their time, and they possessed liberal moral and political viewpoints, broad human compassion, and enlightened social perspectives. They all agreed on the need for social and political experimentation, and were guardedly optimistic about future human progress.[2]

The elusive nature of intellectual history complicates the task of grappling with the form and nuances of their views of war. We can trace their lives and reconstitute their libraries and reading habits. But we cannot assert with utter confidence which works were necessarily influential. When they cited such authors as Hugo Grotius or Emmerich de Vattel, was this because those men challenged and shaped their thoughts, or because the authors confirmed a preconceived idea?[3] Precise linkages between thought and action are difficult to establish. But regarding war, the generation's colonial experience, its expectations, and the literature and practices of the time all pointed in one broad but unmistakable direction. Thoughtful men of the eighteenth century accepted war as both normal and inevitable in human affairs. They believed that some conflicts were justified by the laws of

God and man and some were not, and they elaborated criteria for drawing such distinctions. They also believed that although war led to brutality, waste, and destruction, humane and restrained conduct could render it compatible with civilization. Finally, they believed that war was an instrument of the policy pursued by sovereign authority.

In addition, the Revolutionary generation greatly desired to reconcile idealism with reality. Educated and reflective, these men focused upon political balance, individual reason, and social order and improvement as preferable to political imbalances, individual passions, and social chaos or stasis. Although the power of scripture and canon law had declined as moral guidelines for human behavior after the Reformation shattered the ostensible unity of Christian Europe, secular tenets arose to take their place. War seemed the antithesis of civilization, yet given its inevitability, restraint in war was the key to a harmonious coexistence between mankind and military conflict. In this respect, the members of the Revolutionary generation were at one with the currents of the eighteenth century.

The international state system which emerged following the disintegration of the feudal order and the wreckage of the Religious Wars was another important formative factor in the matrix of ideas about human conflict which wafted around the Revolutionary generation. The rise of absolute monarchies coincided with the development of a complex, shifting international political system, even as the English colonists settled along the North American coast and pushed into the interior valleys. As monarchs and their advisers monopolized military and diplomatic power, they became convinced that the survival of each state was essential for the survival of all. The resulting balance-of-power system, although imperfect, prevented any single state from gaining ascendancy in European affairs. Within such a context, interest groups and monarchs sought to employ national force to further interests and ambitions.[4] Ideals such as morality, rationality, humanity, orderliness, and loyalty were secondary in such a maelstrom, but were not utter strangers. Despite its provincial origins, the Revolutionary generation was entirely familiar with this broad development in western history in the seventeenth and eighteenth centuries.

The Revolutionary generation also observed that war itself had acquired the trappings of civilization and learning. Officers became more professional military men than mere aristocrats in uniforms. War departments became more bureaucratic. Fortifications and gunnery became more scientific. Military manuals and memoirs appeared, many of which were republished in the American colonies.[5] The English colonists were on the fringes of these changes in the nature of war, but were still conversant with them because of colonial membership in European civilization. So the Revolutionary generation, as much as the monarchs of the time, knew that troops were useful for self-defense in a predatory universe, for pursuing ambitions and interests, and for maintaining domestic order.[6]

These threads interwove through the seventeenth and eighteenth centuries to produce the limited-war mentality in western thought. Calling this age one of limited war can be overdrawn, but there was nevertheless a remarkable thrust toward restraint and control of military violence coupled with the realization that wars were inevitable, necessary, and even useful. The fury and destruction of the Religious Wars had left deep scars which reminded scholars and statesmen alike of what could happen if war's anarchic tendencies ran to excess. The limited-war mentality was thus a conscious response to previous conditions, even as it drew upon ideals and humane aspirations, such as vestiges of chivalry and Christian precepts.[7]

This mentality was a fragile edifice. Painstakingly constructed, its gossamer web trembled whenever musketeers assembled or cannon roared. Europeans often ignored this frame of mind when warring against peoples they considered inferior — the Irish, aborigines in Africa or America, or infidels. But they generally accepted its guidelines when fighting against one another. Once the French Revolution unleashed patriotic spasms reinforced by the themes of the early Romantic movement, however, the web of restraint lay in tatters. By 1793 a new age of ideological war had arrived for Europeans. But the American Revolutionary generation and its leaders continued to conceive and develop policies with the aid of the limited-war mentality. The American Revolution and the concomitant war for independence, despite stressing democracy, individual rights, and egalitarianism, insulated Americans to a large degree from developments in Europe. The

Revolutionary generation retained the ideals of the limited-war mentality, even as it adopted new systems for political and social organization.

European behavior in war shifted in the late eighteenth century, but American attitudes remained much the same. Until the shift in Europe, the continental and American versions of the limited-war mentality were quite similar. Men accepted the inevitability of war, and whether in Versailles or Boston, believed that force was an instrument of policy. And although the Enlightenment in both Europe and America radiated a pacific aura, most of its spokesmen sought only to curb excess, recognizing that war would probably never be eliminated from human affairs. Westerners saw mankind as a mixture of conflicting good and evil tendencies, and optimism and pessimism were therefore inescapably intertwined in the limited-war mentality.[8]

Christian and secular thought alike condoned the use of violence under proper circumstances and direction. Hugo Grotius, to take one of the principal legists who codified laws of conduct in war, stated that "so far from anything in the principles of nature being repugnant to war, every part of them indeed rather favours it. For the preservation of our lives and persons, which is the end of war . . . is in no way dissonant to the principles of nature."[9] Grotius presented a broadly held view of the time. Even the pacifists with plans for universal peace produced no other buttress save collective force if reason and adverse moral pressure failed to dissuade the unscrupulous from aggression.[10]

Eighteenth-century thinkers fell into a syllogistic trap regarding the origins of war. On one level, the economic, dynastic, and political differences of nation-states could be advanced as the cause of conflict. But most of these states were monarchies. Therefore, monarchs lay at the heart of war. A corollary suggested that war was never in the interests of the people, only of monarchs. If the people ruled, as in republics, so Montesquieu and others suggested, there would be no wars of aggression. Therefore, the path to peace led through republican revolutions.[11] Because it drew from this tradition, the Revolutionary generation had little faith in the notion of the teachable tyrant. They tended to accept the view that monarchs caused conflicts and the more radical among their theorists, such as Thomas Paine and James Madison, urged republican revolutions as the way to avoid war. In time, Americans learned the error in such reasoning. Some of the more sober, like Alexander Hamilton, understood it all along. They were not surprised when the republican zealotry of the French Revolution easily transformed a war of national self-defense into a crusade to reshape Europe.

When colonists migrated to America, they brought this limited-war mentality with them. The first British overseas empire developed in a world of enemies. War was integral not just to wilderness survival, but to life itself, not to mention further expansion and prosperity. This was why military concerns and forms played so large a role in early American history.[12] Colonial clerics dwelt upon the link between war and human flaws. The Puritans especially spun sermons which argued the links between earthly and ethereal realms. While sin existed, there would be conflict.[13] A poem published in 1762 put the case succinctly.

> But War, alas a Judgment sore
> Brought into th's World by Sin:
> When Sin advanc'd on this our Shore,
> Wars soon did then begin.[14]

Benjamin Franklin believed firmly that avarice and ambition often shaped human affairs, and if societies neglected their defenses, they did so at their peril.[15] The plea for military deterrence rang repeatedly through early American history.

The colonials had ample evidence to sustain such pleas. European politics, pirates, Indians, colonial rebellions, and neighboring French and Spanish settlers all mounted assaults at one time or another. Even as the settlements grew more secure, the imperial struggles migrated from Europe to present further danger. By the time the Revolutionary generation appeared, war was a commonplace event.[16] And this led directly to the moral and legal right of self-defense. The justice of defensive war had ancient roots in the Old Testament, but it ran right through Christian thought. By the eighteenth century, classical, clerical, and secular writers had amassed a considerable body of literature on the subject. Formally, this was the *jus ad bellum*, which sought to identify the circumstances under which a sovereign power could resort to force and remain within the laws of God and man. In practice, self-serving definitions and the decline of the Church diluted the force of the *jus ad bellum*, but it nevertheless identified three types of just wars: those against the enemies of the church, which wars the church commanded; those wars in self-defense, which required no explanation; and wars fought to punish for wrongs received when redress was refused, which permitted great scope for self-interested maneuvering. Even semantic trickery could excuse assaults on neighbors or rivals.

The *jus ad bellum* suffered too from vestiges of the holy-war tradition, which dated to the Old Testament. It survived to the eighteenth century, reinforced by the Crusades, the Reformation, and the Religious Wars spawned by the Counter-Reformation. Europeans tended to distinguish between civilized and savage enemies, and between Christian and non-Christian opponents. Civilized precepts most frequently applied among Christians. There at least, Europeans maintained that the purpose of war was to establish right through a trial of arms before divine judgment. The *jus ad bellum*, despite its subjective nature, and despite forces working against it, was an important pillar of the limited-war mentality.[17] International legists discarded the holy-war tradition almost completely while drawing heavily from the *jus ad bellum*. Such authorities differed in detail, but agreed upon fundamentals. Just wars could only be waged in self-defense and had to have peace as their objective. The injured party must have genuine grievances and have made sincere efforts to petition for redress. If this failed, a final plea was to be made, and war formally declared, exonerating the appeal to arms as a last resort. Holy wars, wars of conquest, and wars of ambition were widely condemned, but some authorities cautiously accepted preventive attacks if foreign aggression seemed certain and imminent.[18]

Hugo Grotius, although he wrote before the limited-war mentality became widely established, provided a foundation for all the formal work on war and peace in the seventeenth and eighteenth centuries. The plagiarism of later writers was a tribute to his influence.[19] For him, just wars were always defensive. Sovereign powers had a right and a duty to deter, prevent, and punish aggression.[20] Grotius reflected the increasingly secular nature of international relations of his time. And the Revolutionary generation read widely in Grotius and his successors, such as Emmerich de Vattel, to discover a common foundation for judging the behavior of states and statesmen. They observed that princes accepted no superior but force, and that ambition and greed frequently displaced noble or humane interests. The fear of retaliation was a more effective deterrent than the possibility of moral condemnation or divine displeasure. The best hope for avoiding war lay in the defensive character of its justification.[21] Grotius and the others disputed the common cynicism of the age, which Frederick the Great put directly: "That war is virtuous which is waged to maintain the authority of the state, preserve its security, aid allies, or check an ambitious prince who plots contrary to your interests."[22]

The widespread citation of the *jus ad bellum* reflected a hope, a noble ambition which its champions knew struggled at a great disadvantage. The emphasis on law and the legal training of many statesmen of the time, including the Revolutionary generation, helped. But the monarch, or sovereign authority, had the sole prerogative in war and peace, and those who urged restraint had to argue against merchants petitioning for letters of marque and reprisal to gain redress for losses, scheming courtiers and advisers, and personal ambitions on the part of the prince. But the prince was responsible for his people. Injuries did occur, and sometimes war was the only method of redress.[23] Men formed societies for mutual benefit. Courts could adjudicate disputes over property lines or a broken contract, but no equivalent existed if the Spanish seized English territory or the French confiscated the vessel of a Boston merchant. National courts ostensibly dealt with such problems, but customarily defended national interests. War was therefore both coercion and a method of arbitration.[24] Even the philosophers, with their pacifist reputations, agreed with such logic. For Montesquieu, "the object of war is victory; that of victory is conquest; and that of conquest is preservation."[25] As with Montesquieu, the Revolutionary generation did not dispute the right of a society to defend its interests and survive, even at the cost of war.

The *jus ad bellum* was more than a naïve hope, an archaic assertion, or a pious self-delusion. Despite its limited impact on sovereigns, it was an intellectual instrument whereby thinkers and statesmen harmonized war and civilization. It blended reason, order, and common sense to exert restraint on a ruler's impulse toward war for ephemeral or trivial reasons. If the best hopes of the legists and philosophers remained unfulfilled, their arguments nonetheless formed an important part of a barricade against international chaos during the seventeenth and eighteenth centuries.

The English colonists carried this tradition with them when they embarked for the American wilderness. War appeared continuously in their lives, provided a sporadic impetus toward intercolonial cooperation, and helped to lace the colonies and mother country closer together. It was a cement of empire.[26] But the colonists actually took part in two sets of wars. First, there was the intermittent battling with the natives, part of the white conquest of the American wilderness which lasted for nearly three centuries. The *jus ad bellum* meant little in the Indian wars; the natives' lack of Christianity, their apparently primitive society and beliefs, and their savage ways, all made them seem inferior to Europeans. War against fellow Europeans, on the other hand, called for more formal justification based upon genuine grievances. Here was the second set of conflicts — the imperial-commerical struggles of the colonial era. "Just" grievances were rarely difficult to find, or manufacture, because the colonials participated in imperial wars to further individual political ambitions, to pry open new markets, to follow the lure of glory and plunder, to secure new territory for settlers and speculators, to strike at the hated papists and the French, or simply to fulfill an obligation to the crown. Generalizing about American attitudes towards either set of wars in the colonial era is therefore dangerous.

The *jus ad bellum* was most frequently voiced by ministers in sermons. Their arguments did not appreciably alter from early settlement to the 1760s and 1770s. They detailed a wide range of items which could justly be defended by force — God's precepts, freedom of worship, friends, neighbors, allies, inheritances, and the empire. They provided a framework within which colonists could make a morally justified choice regarding a resort to arms, against whatever enemy.[27] The basic criterion was unprovoked aggression, producing injuries which an attacker refused to redress. The civil magistrates were responsible for defining the just war, although they invariably had clerical support. Local leaders often took the initiative when crises arose, but neighboring colonies did not necessarily follow suit. On one occasion the Connecticut council determined that Massachusetts was waging an unjust war against Indians, and therefore did not merit assistance.[28] Usually, ministers exhorted their congregations to support the state, and urged that soldiers were God's instruments both to protect natural rights, the commonwealth, and peace, and to punish errant enemies.[29] The Puritan clergy of New England, while militant, always emphasized the concepts of the *jus ad bellum* on such occasions.[30] They also defended the imperial cause and the international balance of power.[31] Even those absorbed by the regeneration demanded by the Great Awakening took time out to condone the British cause during the French and Indian War.[32] Finally, the New England ministers held forth an ancient view of war as a trial by combat before God. Thus victory only affirmed the righteousness of the cause.[33]

The Revolutionary generation did not learn about the *jus ad bellum* from dusty New England sermons. But this tradition survived in many places, including colonial charters and patents, the literature of the legists, and instructions and circulars to colonial governors.[34] Whatever the merits of individual cases, ministers of state had scant difficulty justifying a resort to arms. This seldom seemed more blatant than when colonials fought Indians.[35] But special interest groups urged imperial wars as well. During the limited war of Jenkin's Ear, for example, Americans envisioned mercantile opportunities, glory, and booty when they volunteered for the Cartagena expedition. They sailed to find only miserable death from disease, the arrogance of British officers, and no glory or plunder at all. In Pennsylvania, the Quaker oligarchy clung to its pacifist heritage while its opponents exploited mercantile ambition to trumpet the just wars of the Crown and the necessity of defenses as springboards to political power.[36] During the French and Indian War, land speculators, commercial interests, and frontier traders all saw profit if the French were expelled from North America. Tinges of a Protestant crusade emerged, encouraged by the fervor of the Awakening and the fact that the enemy was both French and Catholic. A recruiting ditty for a Maryland volunteer company played upon such ideas:

> No Popery nor Slavery
> No arbitrary Pow'r for me.
> But Royal George's Righteous Cause
> The Protestant and British Laws.[37]

The mixture of colonial motives at every war reflected ambitions, a sense of duty, religious perspectives, imperial pride and jingoism, and provincial pretentions. All found comfortable refuge behind the *jus ad bellum*.[38]

The *jus ad bellum* dealt with the causes of a war up to the point of its declaration. The responsible sovereign had to reflect upon the injuries done to his person, kingdom, or citizens, and petition redress. If the aggressor spurned such entreaties, the sovereign could then embark on a policy of force to obtain restitution. But a war justly declared would not remain just unless it were properly and humanely conducted, with peace as its primary objective. Forbearance, tolerance, and restraint were the principal guiding precepts. They had to remain the characteristics of the just war once armies assembled, marched, and fought.

This was the fellow traveller of the *jus ad bellum*, the *jus in bello*. According to its guidelines, the sovereign must protect the innocent, be humane toward the enemy, and curb needless slaughter and destruction. Such admonishments could receive highly subjective interpretations. But the Religious Wars pulverised the moral unity of Christian Europe, wrought vast destruction, and left a profound impression on Europeans. The advent of regular armies placed all soldiers in the same moral category, and the shared values of the officer corps in all countries reinforced the impulse to exercise greater restraint. Civilians could generally expect humane treatment through the age of limited wars, and prisoners were usually spared. Sir John Hawkins epitomized the view when he wrote, "we live in an age when humanity is in fashion." Not all subscribed to this fashion, but articulate men believed sincerely that they were making progress in restraining war's worst abuses through the continued exercise of their own civilized standards.[39]

Prudence and self-interest probably did more than conscience to maintain this civility in wartime. Sovereigns also defined objectives carefully to avoid upsetting the balance of power and employed their martial resources to achieve their goals as economically as possible. The general absence of ideological fervor in conflicts from roughly 1648 until 1793 also contributed to this age of limited war. Professional armies were closely controlled and severely disciplined, even when the troops lived off the land.[40] The Count Saxe believed that towns no longer required fortifications since war was "carried on with more moderation and humanity."[41] Montesquieu urged that nations

should do one another as little harm as possible during war, and
the rising bourgeois capitalists applauded. Wars could bring
advantages, but they could also be disruptive and expensive.[42]

Those reflecting upon war knew that it had an internal
dynamism that could overcome this sense of restraint. For
example, Cornelius van Bynkershoek, one of Grotius's successors,
argued that, since enemies were condemned criminals because of
their actions, they could be treated at their captors' discretion.[43]
Princes and statesmen betrayed one another with abandon. Wars
rarely began with formal declarations, and on the fringes of
European civilizations, especially against savage enemies, the *jus
in bello* was a stranger. Pacifism remained confined to small,
hounded, and utterly ineffectual sects in the larger society.[44]
Civilized ideals had their limitations, but did not fail completely.
The *jus in bello* was uneven because men picked and chose to suit
circumstances and ambitions, and because they distinguished
between civilized and savage enemies.

Colonial Americans confronted such problems more frequently than most Europeans because they lived in a frontier wilderness
and waged two sets of wars. There was no line down the Atlantic
Ocean that divided limited from unlimited war.[45] When such
distinctions occurred, they related to circumstances and to the
enemy in question. Old World forms and methods of warfare
transferred easily to the New World setting. Oliver Cromwell
invited New Englanders to help attack New Netherland, but "you
shall not use cruelty to the inhabitants."[46] William Hobby, a
minister in Reading, Massachusetts, could preach that "an holy
War in the Romish sense, is but a Bastard begot by the Devil upon
Lust and Cruelty."[47] On the other hand, isolation permitted wide
latitude in the exercise of military powers, as when the Virginia
assembly declared an unlimited war on the Pamunkey Indians in
1644.[48] And when New England sallied forth to assail the French,
holy-war rhetoric found easy expression. As William Pepperell's
expedition departed for Cape Breton in 1745, minister William
McClenachan saw it as a Protestant crusade for righteousness.[49]
The French and Indian war recalled for some the pattern of the
eternal war against Satan and sin, and in certain respects was the
climax of the colonial experience with military affairs. This
conflict would establish British supremacy, lead to a conquest of
the wilderness, and expand an Anglo-American empire with the

New World as its center of gravity. National ambitions, as well as religious and ideological passions, could generate a crusading atmosphere.[50]

From the mid-seventeenth to the mid-eighteenth centuries, the limited-war mentality established and maintained an uncertain beachhead. And the pressures of wilderness warfare notwithstanding, the attitudes of Americans were not markedly different from those of articulate Englishmen or continental Europeans by the end of the colonial period. To be sure, Englishmen in America became different from those who remained in England, but not regarding attitudes toward war. Where differences appeared, they resembled solutions to local problems rather than unique American thrusts. For example, when hostile feelings arose against the Spanish in the 1720s and the 1730s, colonial newspapers aired anti-Catholic views. But the real concern was New England's penetration of the Spanish markets in Central America.[51] The Louisbourg campaign balanced opposing tendencies in 1745. Massachusetts' Governor William Shirley wanted a conquest to further his personal ambitions. Fishermen and merchants wanted to retaliate for French raids and seizures, and the rank and file went for loot. But when Louisbourg surrendered, it received full honors of war and the tired New Englanders grumbled because the terms of capitulation prohibited looting.[52]

The two kinds of warfare in colonial America produced two parallel traditions. The frightening clashes with the Indians on the frontier were always savage in character, but often restricted in scope. After 1740, colonial warfare lost its predominantly raiding character because frontiersmen from Britain and France were brushing up against each other and increasing in numbers and ambitions. When regulars sailed to reinforce frontier militia, the imperial struggles began to resemble European warfare. The limited-war conventions of the *jus in bello,* which the officers brought with them, reinforced tendencies already running in colonial thought. General Edward Braddock's unfortunate expedition to the Ohio region in 1754 was to recover lost territory and hold the French at arm's length. And the Virginia House of Burgesses agreed with such a policy, much to the dismay of Royal Governor Robert Dinwiddie, who wanted a war of conquest. In Maryland in 1758, Governor Horatio Sharp stated that "defensive war is the utmost any of our Assemblies will think of or provide."[53]

The colonial experience was thus ambiguous. Neither limited nor unlimited views dominated American thinking; for that matter, the same could be said of contemporary Europeans. A similar mélange of conflicting, contradictory, and uncertain hopes, fears, and ambitions existed throughout the western world among those articulating the limited-war mentality. As its proponents well knew, particular viewpoints could produce contrary interpretations on the same conflict.[54] Benjamin Franklin, William Shirley, and Robert Morris, all avid land speculators, viewed the French and Indian War as a life-and-death struggle, but few rank-and-file colonists seem to have accepted such a judgment. Only the prodding and the financial subsidies of William Pitt's ministry transformed this conflict into a war of conquest in North America.[55]

The continuous interaction between the Old World and the New regarding military affairs makes it misleading to distinguish between American and European attitudes toward war. Limited and unlimited tendencies swirled together, reflecting the tension between objectives formulated by political leaders and the commitment required from the members of society to follow through on the plans. A sense of restraint was clear, even though the wilderness setting in America meant that war might touch frontier communities more directly there than in Europe. But by the mid-eighteenth century, when the tide of settlers lapped at the Alleghenies or crept into the interior valleys, towns, plantations, farms, and villages along the coastline were largely secure. Except when regulars landed on the wharves and were supplied for a march to the west, or warships or privateers outfitted in their ports, the citizens of Philadelphia or New York in 1760 found war as remote as did the people in Liverpool or London. They knew that a conflict existed, but few were directly involved.

By the late colonial period, a dual tradition of war existed — frontier skirmishes and raids, and imperial wars of policy. This last suggests the final in the series of major components which constituted the limited-war mentality — the link between state policy and the employment of force. For troops constituted a tool to further the interests of the sovereign, as well as to defend against attack. The basic survival of states was not often threatened, but inheritances, territory, trade concessions, and personal dynastic considerations, along with maintenance of the balance of power,

were the principal reasons why sovereigns marshalled their
troops and fleets. These princes considered themselves equals,
even though they commanded resources that varied vastly in
power. Alliances therefore perpetually formed and dissolved, as
states maneuvered for advantage or defense. Overseas trade and
colonies introduced complicating factors. Colonists discovered
that local ambitions and interests could instigate collisions
involving their metropolitan countries, even as European dynastic clashes could pit unwilling colonials against one another.
This was a reciprocal relationship, not a one-way flow, and it
became increasingly complex as the colonies grew in number,
size, and social and economic sophistication.

Power and the use of force dominated the thought of policy-
makers. Only doctrinaire pacifists challenged the validity of the
use of force, but their peace plans reveal that even they relied upon
the collective might of nations in concert to deter unscrupulous
monarchs from military adventurism.[56] Advanced political
thinkers saw force as an agent of revolution, a view that went far
beyond the accepted canons of the limited-war mentality.[57] The
English colonists in North America also saw war as an instrument
of policy. All the governors and councils acted as *de facto*
sovereigns, able to raise troops to defend the colony, assist
neighbors, or even launch offensive wars.[58] Governors could not,
however, grant letters of marque and reprisal, or risk open war
with a European power. From 1719 to 1749, the governor of Nova
Scotia was to correspond with the governor of Canada to adjust
minor difficulties and maintain the peace. Only a royal decree
permitted reprisals against powers with which the crown was at
peace.[59]

Colonial Americans understood this clearly. The minister
Charles Chauncey, for example, maintained that the magistrates
must provide for the defense of society since they were responsible
for the liberties, lives, and goods of the citizens.[60] New Englanders
frequently went beyond this because they found privateering a
lucrative investment and lobbied the General Court of Massachusetts to issue letters of marque and reprisal whenever they lost
vessels to the French or Spanish, regardless of imperial policy.
The merchants also understood that Britain's wars served mercantile interests anywhere in the empire, even as colonial assemblies
discovered that they could obtain preference for commodities and
cash subsidies for participating in England's conflicts.[61]

Europeans and Americans therefore shared the tenets of the limited-war mentality on the eve of the imperial crises which would lead to the American Revolution. Americans accepted the inevitability of war, loosely applied the rhetoric and criteria of the *jus ad bellum,* attempted to conduct civilized warfare, and saw force as an instrument of policy. The principal difference between European and American attitudes toward war has been attributed to the impact of the frontier, of war in the wilderness by communities of settlers against Indians.[62] Yet this is an oversimplification, a legend, and not a legacy solidly rooted in fact. On the fringes of settlement, whole families and communities did experience war in a way that contemporary Englishmen or Europeans did not. The longer-settled coastal towns, plantations, and farms, on the other hand, were as secure from the Indians in 1760 as towns in Dorset. And although colonial methods of warfare against the Indians differed from those employed against regular European troops, this too varied with circumstances.

As members of western civilization, American colonials carried the limited-war mentality that had developed over the period from first settlement to the end of the French and Indian War. This mentality stood in tension with human impulses unleashed by conflict, but it did not alter appreciably down to 1763. Colonial society and politics changed enormously, but habits of mind about war and peace did not. As the imperial crises evoked a martial response from the more militant colonials in the early 1770s, the limited-war mentality proved to be the framework within which these men made what they considered morally justified decisions about the use of force. Even when they contradictorily asserted that rebellion was a right, and ambitions were rights, they adapted the limited-war mentality to serve new ends — American independence. This mentality provided a set of assumptions about war with which the Revolutionary leaders in particular confronted a civil clash, the struggle for independence, and then the problems of independent nationhood in a hostile international environment. The legend of Americans rejecting European attitudes toward war because of their wilderness experience and their idealistic ambitions is just that, built upon myth rather than reality. The legacy for the Revolutionary generation was the limited-war mentality of western civilization in the mid-eighteenth century.

2

THE LIMITED-WAR MENTALITY
AND THE AMERICAN REVOLUTION

The amalgam of thought that constituted the limited-war mentality had an important role in the American Revolution. Although not a cause of the colonials' break with Great Britain, this set of ideas provided a moral framework for justifying the resort to arms, a set of guidelines for conducting a war, a means of relating force to the objectives sought, and an underlying assumption about the continued likelihood of war in human affairs. But the limited-war mentality usually informed the views of leaders of governments. The *jus ad bellum* especially provided rulers with criteria to determine if the use of force to redress international grievances was morally justified before the laws of God and man. How could colonists think in terms of relating military force to state policy? They could believe war was inevitable or determine that it be conducted in a humane manner. These ideas flowed from broad currents of thought afloat in the eighteenth century. But applying the whole of the limited-war mentality to the American Revolution seems impossible without fracturing it into its components.

This would not be the case if a convincing argument for Romantic nationalism among Americans prior to 1775 could be advanced. But it cannot. Despite many common cultural elements shared by all British colonists (whether in the thirteen colonies that rebelled or those that remained within the Empire), despite increased intercolonial communication through committees of correspondence, and despite a sense of loyalty to America as a place, American nationalism lay in the future. Colonials felt multiple loyalties — to the Empire, to their province, to their locale, and to America. The latent whig-republican ideology, shared manners and customs, a common language, Protestantism, roughly uniform legal institutions and codes, and an intercolonial awareness through the exchange of trade and newspapers or increasing travel by leading colonials, had not overcome provincialism and local interests and horizons. The emotional commitment to America as an idea was lacking. Even the sense of a common cause which emerged by the mid-1770s resulted from acts of the British Parliament and a fear that the king would no longer protect the colonies. The multiple loyalties felt by American colonials were not predestined to conflict, even after the Stamp Act Crisis. Loyalty to England remained strong into 1776, and perhaps twenty percent of the colonists refused to support independence. Even many of the Revolutionary leaders were highly reluctant rebels.[1]

At the same time, Englishmen had a heritage of using organized force to oppose what they considered unjust measures and men. The English Civil War and the Glorious Revolution are the best large-scale examples of this. The tradition was firmly embedded in whig-republican thought and swiftly taken up over the Stamp Act in 1765. And such action occurred not only in America, but also in Ireland and England herself, as the troubles surrounding John Wilkes illustrate. On a local level, this use of organized force could emerge as a mob resisting a press gang or intimidating an unpopular customs officer. Frequently, such action embodied community wishes and had the sanction of local magistrates. It was not simply the eruptions of the tumultuous lower orders, either; the best members of society could be involved.[2]

Those participating in such events cannot be metamorphosed into nationalists. But the heritage from which they drew inspiration can be joined to another piece in an intellectual mosaic to explain how colonists applied the tenets of the limited-war mentality in a revolutionary situation. The strictures of the *jus ad bellum* were not followed slavishly, but interwove with the political and intellectual currents of the Revolution.

The right of revolution flowed from the right of opposition when authority proved unjust and obdurate to the point of threatening tyranny. When resistance arose to the Writs of Assistance, the Stamp Act, and subsequent measures, colonials embarked on a path toward forcible action. Along the way they cited republican ideology, constitutional rights, and the natural-law doctrine in defense of their position. The centrality of these ideas for the emergence of the American Revolution is well-established. Natural law justified resistance to parliamentary, and then royal authority, on the grounds that the social compact had been broken.[3] At the same time, the Revolutionary leaders confused this somewhat by voicing universal principles in their rhetorical attacks on the measures of the ministries, Parliament's refusal to control the ministry, and the king's refusal to control the Parliament. Since ultimate sovereignty lay with the people, when the social compact fractured it was reconstituted on a more limited scale in America. But republicanism, not constitutional monarchy, was the new form.[4] In retrospect, the process, the rhetoric, and the ultimate victory created the illusion of a national movement even as they retroactively justified armed rebellion.

The doctrine of resistance to unjust acts included the use of armed force and revolution as a last resort. This could only come when constituted authority was deaf and immovable before the pleas of the people. As early as March of 1770, George III had displayed his contempt to London petitioners, who carried the hopes of Americans when they entered the royal chambers. After fighting broke out in 1775, colonial claims to local sovereignty gained strength until in 1776, *Common Sense* and the Declaration of Independence effectively transferred the focus of allegiance from the crown to a local institution, the Continental Congress. Congress, the argument ran, now embodied the will of the American people.[5] Once the revolutionaries assumed sovereign status, they could draw upon the limited-war mentality in its entirety. They would not do so procrustean fashion, for their eclectic intellectual and political heritage, as well as their flexible habits of mind, turned them away from precise blueprints, but the four main facets of the limited-war mentality appeared in their thought and actions. It was an integral part of the colonial legacy.

Even as they debated what to do during the imperial crises, colonial spokesmen instinctively betrayed the habits of mind and followed the impulses of conventional eighteenth-century states-men. They had civilized attitudes which came from their English backgrounds, their Enlightenment pretensions, and their social status. Order, reason, and restraint were ideals that colored their world view, whether in draughting legislation, maintaining their plantations and counting houses, or confronting an arbitrary parliament and corrupt royal officials. Despite the dangers of international linkages in a world where power ruled and statesmen were ruthless with enemies and allies alike, some colonials, like Robert Morris, Silas Deane, and Richard Henry Lee, were positively eager for European intervention in the dispute with Great Britain.[6] They sought and eventually gained an alliance with France and thereby injected the would-be United States into the politics of the Atlantic world. When American ministers sailed for the courts of Versailles or Madrid, or to arrange loans with Dutch bankers, they pledged future American revenues and offered what little weight the United States could throw onto the international scales as bait for assistance.

The Revolutionary leaders followed a logical path when they moved to defend first their rights, and then their actions, in response to the British efforts to renovate the Empire following the great victory of 1763. The colonials began with protest, followed this with petition, and employed economic sanctions and further petition before resorting to force of arms. Whig theory, like the *jus ad bellum*, required forbearance and the exhaustion of all measures before taking the most extreme step. The colonials failed to move an apparently corrupt England despite initial success with protest and commercial coercion. Ministerial, parliamentary, and royal stubbornness eroded the ground upon which colonial moderates stood as they pleaded for patience. And whig theory coincided with the *jus ad bellum* in permitting the use of military force if all else failed. War supported revolution. For example, Thomas Mason, writing of the Boston Port Act, urged Americans to "draw your swords in a just cause and rely upon that God who assists the righteous to support your endeavours to preserve the liberty he hath implanted in your hearts, as essential to your nature."[7] Other revolutionary spokesmen such as Thomas Jefferson in a "Summary View of the Rights of the Colonies" and Christopher Gadsden, mounted similar arguments.[8]

When Thomas Gage as military governor of Massachusetts made a bid to forestall rebellion by sending troops out to Lexington and Concord to seize military stores and perhaps some leading rebels into the bargain, he precipitated a war. In an avalanche of letters, statements, and pamphlets, Revolutionary leaders now called for the armed defense of rights and liberties. Benjamin Franklin wrote to a member of Britain's Parliament that "you have begun to burn our towns, and murder our people. Look upon your hands; they are stained with the blood of your relations! You and I were long friends; you are now my enemy."[9] In the same spirit, Congress authorized the seizure of military stores at Ticonderoga and Crown Point, New York. A Fast Day invocation of 1775 called for a redress of grievances and a restoration of invaded rights, all in unstated accord with the tenets of the *jus ad bellum*. And by October, a Hostile Acts Committee of Congress had compiled evidence of continued British perfidy as a testimonial to the resort to arms.[10] Congress justified rebellion against the crown as though it were a just war of defense against an alien invader.

Throughout, the members of Congress assumed the behavior of a sovereign government. The process had begun in subtle ways with the Continental Association's enforcement of nonimportation after the Townshend Acts, but it accelerated with the first and second Continental Congresses. A popular base for this resistance had gathered from town meetings and extra-legal sessions of local assemblies that had endorsed resistance. Now, many of these same men sat in Philadelphia making policy for a would-be country. The *jus ad bellum* provided a moral sanction which admirably suited the American situation, even though the Revolutionary leaders did not cite it directly. And because these men saw themselves acting in self-defense, with the consent and support of the people, an elaborate explanation for the use of war was not initially required. Hugo Grotius, Emmerich de Vattel, and a host of legists and philosophers all agreed that defensive wars needed no justification. They were automatically condoned in the eyes of men, nations, and God.

At the same time, the Revolutionary leaders buttressed their appeal to arms with rhetoric. A general rebellion far exceeded riots directed against press gangs, stamped paper, or tea. It could only come at the end of a long trail of tears. But this point seemed to have been reached as British troops marched and as clashes occurred at Bunker Hill in Boston, and elsewhere. The dynamism of armed conflict now confronted colonists with the issue of allegiance. Congress issued an official statement, the "Declaration on the Causes and Necessity for Taking Up Arms," which was logically linked with the Declaration of Independence and the formation of the Articles of Confederation. In all cases, the justice of defensive war was argued or assumed.[11] Other pamphlets emphasized that the colonial army had not been raised for conquest, and George Washington's manifesto to Canadians in September of 1775 characterized the struggle as a just war in defense of liberty, property, and family.[12]

By the spring of 1776 a majority of Americans active in the revolutionary movement had made their choice for independence. They were abandoning allegiance to the crown and fastening it upon the United States, loosely defined, but nevertheless comprising republican government and independence, as well as older ideals of English liberty. This was a vital step toward an American nationalism. The war had eroded the moderates' ground and confronted all with the issue of legitimate authority. George III rejected the final appeal of the Olive Branch Petition. He was too much a part of the British political structure, too blinded by the glare of rebellion, to exercise other than a partisan perspective in this crisis. Thus armed resistance to Parliament became rebellion against the crown, the war for independence became a civil war, and later it merged with the continuous struggle for power among the major states of the European world in the eighteenth century.

The political philosophy which underlay the thought of the Revolutionary generation legitimized the process of rebellion and the transfer of patriotic allegiance. When the compact of government lay in ruins, power momentarily reverted to the people, according to whig-republican doctrine. Congress advised the states to form their own constitutions, which they promptly did. Reconstitution of the polity took place at both the provincial and continental levels. In each case, the people's representatives assumed *de facto* and *de jure* power. The rebellion and the war for independence were highly decentralized, the existence of the Continental Congress notwithstanding. Congress had more the function of a federation council directing a war effort than the powers of a central government; given that one thrust of the American Revolution came from suspicion of focussed power, this is not surprising. Now embodying the civil authority, both Congress and the state governments sanctioned the war. And once the commitment was made, as Robert Morris noted, those who had so voted must "conquer or die."[13] Great Britain did not take treason lightly. So republican theory combined with the fact of war to thrust the Revolutionary leaders into their historical roles.

In New England, where the rebellion and war had begun, the Congregational church stood foursquare behind the struggle. The clerics raised arguments common in military sermons of the seventeenth and eighteenth centuries to explain the present situation.[14] Piety and patriotism intertwined. Even before 1775, sermons had warned that armed resistance might be required to defend political rights. And the clerics included concepts like human rights, which flowed from nature and God, thus contributing to the universalist rhetoric of the Revolution. After 1775, clerical militancy quickened.[15] Jacob Cushing epitomized this development when he stated in 1778:

> If this war be just and necessary on our part, as past all doubt it is, then we are engaged in the work of the Lord, which obliges us (under God mighty in battle) to use our swords as instruments of righteousness, and calls us to the shocking, but necessary, important duty of shedding human blood; not only in defence of our property, life, and religion, but in obedience to him who hath said, "Curse be he that keepeth back his sword from blood."[16]

These ministers drew from a Christian tradition that had made a major contribution to the development of thought on war. Given their political sympathies, they subjectively interpreted the circumstances of 1775 and the struggle for independence. Armed with social and political self-righteousness, religious imagery, and biblical parables, the ministers created a moral framework for their listeners within which a resort to arms was just. God had called his people to war before, and he did so again now. Beyond that, the ministers accepted the declaration of the Revolutionary leaders that the United States had sovereign status.

Even minor Revolutionary figures mirrored clerical thinking in this regard. For instance, Alexander Hamilton initially justified the war by the laws of nature and the demands of necessity. But later he drew more heavily from the law of nations because he began to understand that the United States sought to become one country among many. The Revolution transformed a series of general tenets about war into a set of specific guidelines. In turning to these arguments to justify their political positions,

Hamilton and others in the Revolutionary generation revealed
how much they stood within the mainstream of eighteenth-
century thought on war and peace.[17]

In retrospect, the speed with which these people began to talk
and behave as conventional eighteenth-century statesmen is
astonishing, creating the illusion of an American nationalism
springing fully matured from colonial ground. In reality, the
Revolutionary generation proceeded by untidy stages from being
English colonials to being American patriots and nationals.

Throughout, the language of the limited-war mentality was
employed. The Virginia Assembly tried to separate the just causes
of civil and international wars. The former defended life, liberty,
and property. The latter protected government and constitution,
for when these were attacked, the "rights of the whole community
in their political capacity are hazarded."[18] George Washington
consistently fell back upon British aggression as the main
justification for taking up arms. The rhetoric of the *jus ad bellum*
appeared again and again, even as the circumstances shifted from
resistance to rebellion to revolution.[19] Another indication of the
progression of thought arose in the Revolutionary generation's
characterization of the loyalists. This was unquestionably a civil
war, but the loyalists were condemned as apostates and traitors by
the Revolutionary generation out of necessity as well as personal
and political differences. But the negative perception of loyalists
reflected nationalistic feelings among Americans accelerated by
the shedding of blood.

The citing of the *jus ad bellum* reveals how bodies of thought
eased the transition from a colonial to an independent perspective
among Americans. It justified the resort to war, paralleled the
whig theory of resistance, and worked from the assumption of
sovereign status. Revolution could only come at the end of a
lengthy trail of abuses along which appeals for redress of
grievances had been spurned. Just wars could only result when
rights were invaded and an aggressor had disdained the claims of
the injured party. In both cases, restraint was the principal
watchword. Revolution was to insure order, not to produce
political and social anarchy. Similarly, a just war was to obtain
rights and peace, not to engage in military excess.

Invocation of the *jus ad bellum* did not mean that crusading
rhetoric was absent. Nor did it mean that popular enthusiasm

should be suppressed. John Adams believed that the war would have positive social value. Setbacks would force Americans to purge themselves of vices and hedonistic habits.[20] Tom Paine trumpeted what he saw as a popular war for popular rights and in 1783 "A Moderate Whig" celebrated the victory: "If the ground be lawful, the call clear, the necessity cogent, the capacity probable, they that have the law of nature, the law of God, and the fundamental laws of the land on their side cannot want authority, although they may be destitute of a king to lead them."[21] Previously, English colonials drew from the *jus ad bellum* to construct apologias for fighting Indians and imperial enemies alike; now that idea provided sanction for a war for independence.

American objectives in this war were limited in an important way. The Revolutionary generation had not engaged in armed rebellion lightly, however inevitable they thought it had become by 1775. Nor, apart from later territorial ambitions, did the objectives of the fighting extend beyond the granting of independence. If the impossible had occurred, and the ministry, Parliament, and King George III had redressed colonial grievances after the skirmishes at Lexington and Concord, moderate opinion would still have had sufficient strength to stop the fighting. But creaky and confused, convinced that the colonists plotted rebellion and treason, and quick to resort to force, the triumvirate of the imperial government pushed on to war. The Howe brothers were crippled by directives to wage war and peace simultaneously, and by the time the Carlisle Commission arrived independence had become a *sine qua non* of peace for the Americans.[22] But British attempts at concession came before they had lost a second army at Yorktown. Because Carlisle's Commission could not grant independence, the fighting continued.

Still the war remained limited. Other great revolutions of modern times, in France and Russia, acquired a crusading fervor from their ideologies that carried their armies beyond their borders. The American situation was different. Though revolutionaries, the leaders were conservative, restrained men. The invasion of Canada in 1775 resulted more from military exigencies than ideological crusading, despite enthusiasm for gaining converts to the cause against Britain. David Ramsay, the Revolution's first major historian, wrote that the expedition had been dispatched to forestall attack. Further, American military leaders

were strategically and tactically conservative — legends about
riflemen, guerrillas, and partisan warfare notwithstanding.[23]
Despite calling upon the people for support, issuing loyalty oaths
for all civil and military officers to sign, and relying by necessity
upon the local militia, Congress issued no call for a leveé en
masse as the French Convention did 23 August 1793. Instead,
Congress requested troops through the newly-established state
governments. And the Commander in Chief worked mightily to
construct a regular eighteenth-century army and command
structure with which to defend the United States.[24]

The division among Americans over this conflict was a
complicating factor. Loyalism notwithstanding, enthusiasm
waxed and waned. As the war ground on, Washington's army
occasionally dwindled to a skeleton force. Recruiting sagged and
the militia frequently proved unreliable. Crusading fervor
sprouted at the local level, but at the level of policy-making,
objectives remained limited. And how far into American society
the commitment to the cause extended remains unclear. Loyalism
accounted for perhaps twenty percent of the population, and not
all British-American colonies had joined the Revolution. But this
does not mean that eighty percent of the population in the
thirteen rebellious colonies stood unflinching in its allegiance to
the cause of independence. Many undoubtedly hoped that the war
would bypass them, that armies would not march through their
villages seeking billets or forage, and that the local committee of
safety would overlook their lack of interest in who prevailed. Over
time, the war probably instilled and confirmed new loyalties to
the local and continental governments.[25] But human motivation
was not simple and the process of conversion was uneven and
sporadic.

Other factors render impossible any simple characterization of
American attitudes toward this war. Congress and the states
disputed political jurisdictions, the states were mutually jealous,
personalities clashed, and personal, local, and even regional
ambitions found themselves in conflict. Holy-war rhetoric appeared alongside calls for restraint; the private correspondence of
the leaders suggests restricted goals, yet sermons, pamphlets, and
congressional tracts for popular consumption suggested a crusade. Assuming that the members of Congress were a kind of
intellectual clearing house for these seemingly contradictory

currents, contrasting perspectives may be explained by varying perceptions of the situation. The Revolutionary leaders had limited goals, but needed to arouse popular enthusiasm to achieve them. At a local level, a popular sense of enthusiasm would be most apparent. And here too the fighting could take on a narrowly personal quality as men defended their homes and families or sought to settle old political and personal scores. Patriotism could slide into the background in such an atmosphere, smothered by revenge.[26] And the limited nature of the war could become lost. Practical attitudes toward such problems are evident in the suppression of a historical anti-Catholicism to woo France. Even the annual antipapal tirade at Harvard was quietly discontinued to avoid offending the new ally.[27]

The Revolutionary leaders further reflected the tenets of the limited-war mentality by seeking to mitigate the human and social misery consonant with combat. Benjamin Franklin and John Adams urged that all farmers, fishermen, and merchants be left free to go about their business. War was a political affair between governments, not a clash of societies, in their view. If powers at war were permitted all liberties, the American ministers in France wrote to the Comte de Vergennes, the French foreign minister, then "all the horrors of the barbarous ages may be introduced and justified." The Revolutionary generation also believed that private property should remain inviolate during wartime. Alexander Hamilton was appalled by random seizures of civilian goods. After all, those protesting the Writs of Assistance and parliamentary taxation measures cited the sanctity of private property as one of their major arguments. When Congress issued letters of marque and reprisal to permit colonial privateers to seize British shipping, it wanted all international conventions observed and any property that did not qualify for seizure left alone. Only articles directly applicable to warfare qualified as contraband. Americans championed the doctrine of free ships, free goods, a goal of eighteenth-century idealists, but also of men who believed in the sanctity of private property, the existence of war notwithstanding.[28]

On land, George Washington tried to adhere to the same spirit. He forbade looting and insisted that enemy prisoners be well treated. But it was not possible to control troops on the march, much to Washington's chagrin, and he ruefully observed that

American soldiers took more from their own people than the enemy did. The treatment of prisoners was more closely regulated. Only armed Britons were considered enemies, and Washington and Congress strove for a general cartel for the proper exchange of prisoners. The British balked at this, because such agreements were made between equals, and Britain fought to deny the United States sovereign status. Even so, exchanges periodically occurred on an *ad hoc* basis.[29]

The evidence is clear that prisoners on both sides were generally well treated. Instances of mistreatment were isolated, even though charges and indignant denials sporadically flew back and forth.[30] Thomas Gage refuted American accusations with a remark that epitomized the limited-war mentality: "To the glory of civilized Nations, humanity and war have become compatible, and compassion to the subdued is become almost a general system." Jefferson, in like manner, observed to Patrick Henry that such advances benefitted all, "friends, foes and neutrals."[31]

This benevolent attitude toward national enemies did not invariably prevail. When he was governor of Virginia, Jefferson had British Major Henry Hamilton thrown into irons on the basis of Hamilton's frontier reputation as a "scalp-buyer." More to the point as far as Governor Jefferson was concerned was Hamilton's employment of Indians as allies. Their reputation in the treatment of enemies, prisoners, women, and children alike, made Hamilton a savage by association. But the Virginia Council ordered Hamilton released after a flurry of correspondence with Jefferson, noting that wreaking vengeance on captives would not affect the outcome of the war. James Madison, on the other hand, thought that men fighting for their country needed the protection of a doctrine of retaliation to deter enemy barbarity. In 1781 he chaired a congressional committee on reprisal. The final report noted that to tolerate further British atrocities would be inconsistent with American dignity and expectations, and "with the respect due to the benevolent rules by which Civilized nations have tempered the severities & evils of war."[32] But the attitude of restraint, rather than that of vengeance or retaliation, characterized the broad American conduct of the War for Independence.

Despite squabbles, the Revolutionary leaders drew from the guidelines of the *jus in bello*. Congress never adopted retaliation as a policy. Even major André, Benedict Arnold's accomplice,

was well treated after capture on the express orders of George
Washington himself. Many observers contrasted the gentlemanly
bearing of André with the perfidy and skulking treason of Arnold,
for whom anything seemed justified, so that when Arnold led the
British invasion of Virginia in 1780-81, Jefferson, still governor,
dallied with a scheme to kidnap the turncoat so that he could be
tried and hanged. Arnold's treason apparently excused such
thoughts.[33]

American restraint was also apparent in the treatment of
pacifists. Apart from Quakers in Pennsylvania, pacifism existed
only among scattered and isolated sects in the American colonies.
Although all adult males were theoretically liable for militia duty
during the colonial period, pacifists had usually been able to
escape service through small fines or providing substitutes to
serve in their stead. The pressures of war altered pacifists'
circumstances, but not drastically. Jefferson thought that the
Quakers' religion led them to give first loyalty to England instead
of their own country, which was untrue. Pennsylvania authorities
left doctrinaire Quakers alone for the most part, and the same was
true for sects in other states, like North Carolina. At worst,
pacifists acquired a taint of loyalism and were occasionally
compelled to pay special taxes.[34] Pressures for wartime conformity notwithstanding, the limited-war attitudes of the Revolutionary generation helped to stem a slide toward anarchy. Freedom of
conscience remained, in this case at least.

Many civilians found that they were able to carry on business as
usual. Some profiteers did grow fat on the war, but there were not
so many as army grumbling implied. A fear did arise that the
republican dedication required to render the Revolution a moral
success was distinctly lacking among Americans. Especially in
the bleak years of 1780 and 1781, before the Yorktown victory,
committed patriots doubted that Americans were worthy of their
own independence. Profiteering figured in such thinking, but in
eighteenth-century wars rulers commonly continued trade with
an enemy if it proved advantageous. For one thing, exorbitant
special fees could be charged, producing revenue at a time of
heavy demands on the treasury. And for their part, colonial
American merchants had rarely permitted war to interfere with
their pursuit of profits. One factor behind imperial renovation
after 1763 had been admiralty reports about the great number of

colonial vessels in Louisbourg's harbor when it was captured. Torn between pocketbook and duty to the crown, Americans had often chosen the former. After the Declaration of Independence, they frequently made a similar choice. To the embarrassment of Congress, specie from the French loans even went to pay for forbidden but still highly prized British imports.[35]

The tenets of the *jus in bello* emerged in other respects as well. Clerics admonished that revenge had no place in war. Captives must be well treated. John Carmichael stated in 1775 that although a just war was a legal action, he could not condone illegal acts. Armies had been raised to defend the rights of the people. Once this was accomplished, the sword must be put aside and friendship restored with the former enemy. Those noted for strident anti-British tirades shared such a view. And some even attempted to defend loyalist refugees in New York from vengeance.[36]

Americans applied European laws of war. When General John Burgoyne surrendered to Horatio Gates at Saratoga, he received munificent terms. In part this stemmed from Gates's concern that Sir Henry Clinton might appear and rescue Burgoyne if the arrangements were not concluded swiftly, but such largesse to a surrendered army was common in eighteenth-century wars. And finally, although by the laws of war anyone bearing arms inside a fortress taken by storm could be executed, the American troops who carried Stoney Point by bayonet spared all who surrendered.[37]

The Revolutionary leaders also insisted that they waged no campaigns of conquest. To some extent, this belied expansionist designs and one cannot take at face value the statement of the Comte de Vergennes in 1779 that "conquest & ambition were not the objects of this alliance, nor of any of the allies." Colonial expansionism had been thwarted by the Proclamation of 1763, and during the War for Independence it sallied forth again.[38] But in general, the Revolutionary leaders were sincere when they denied that conquest was their objective.

Tendencies toward a spirit of vengeance occasionally poked through the blanket of restraint so often professed. In 1776, Gouverneur Morris of New York wrote a "Burning Report" for a congressional committee. Since Parliament had defended naval raids along the American coasts, Congress should authorize the torching of London and other British towns and then announce that Americans were prepared to meet their enemies in whatever kind of war they chose to wage. Congress balked at this, but later, John Mathews moved for retaliatory burning of British towns "for the wanton acts of cruelty committed by the enemy and as a duty we owe to our constituents."[39]

Frontier warfare and the loyalist-patriot clashes provided many examples of excess in the American Revolution. The ambivalence of the colonial heritage remained. On a local level, simmering hatreds erupted into vicious fights. A British army chaplain in New York ventured that the war had transmogrified Americans into "monsters, implacable, ravenous; party rage had kindled the spirit of hatred between them, they attack and rob each other by turns." In New Jersey, fiery Congregationalists urged that Anglican churches be razed. The beautiful Wyoming Valley was reduced to a charred stubble by raids and counterraids.[40] In the southern colonies, the partisan war generated similar abuses. In South Carolina Thomas Sumter collected so-called patriots less to fight for the Revolution than to exact vengeance on local loyalists. The Battle of King's Mountain, fought entirely between loyalists and patriot militia units, was a savage clash where surrender did not guarantee quarter. The number of wanton executions was nonetheless few, probably because most of the loyalists, including many who had been taken prisoner, escaped.[41] The furies of war could easily smother civilized pretensions of restraint. Civilian loyalists could also feel the cutting edge of persecution. This exceeded a legitimate concern that they constituted a potential fifth column in the patriot midst. Maryland taxed loyalists at treble the regular rate. Delaware and Rhode Island declared them enemies, and Massachusetts banned their return. In Virginia, the assembly declared that because loyalists had sided with tyranny, they had lost their social rights.[42]

Once again, such actions suggest a dichotomy between popular enthusiasms and the restraint of the Revolutionary leaders. For example, John Adams noted to his wife that

> In a time of Warr, and especially a War like this, one may see the Necessity and Utility of the divine prohibitions of Revenge, and the Injunctions of forgiveness of Injuries and love of Enemies, which we find in the Christian Religion. Unrestrained, in some degree by these benevolent Laws, Men would be Devils, at such a time as this.[43]

Adams understood the anarchic and brutal impulses of war. Only moral inhibitions could contain them. Others agreed, despite having been in the forefront of protest during the early phases of the Revolution. They had worked to contain violence and now hoped that there would be no spirit of vengeance that would survive the war.

A measure of growing patriotism among the Revolutionary leaders can be taken from their concern about their new country's honor. National reputation had inherent value. For example, as best they could American ministers overseas assisted captive patriot sailors in escaping from prison hulks in British ports. But at one point it seemed that a general cartel to cover such prisoners would be established. Accordingly, the diplomats issued a circular stating that continued aid under the new circumstances would compromise American honor. A word of bond given to the enemy would perforce be kept. Prudence and even policy could lie behind such views, but Alexander Hamilton believed that any breach of faith in prisoner exchange would only work against American interests in all respects. Washington was especially sensitive on such points. When a British ship and crew were captured while under a flag of truce, he ordered them released to "remove from our Army every, the smallest Imputation of an Infringement on the sacred dignity of a Flag." If reports of firing on other British flags of truce proved true, he wanted a proper apology issued to General Howe and steps taken to insure that such incidents did not recur. American officers violating their paroles were to be forced to return home, where they had been waiting for exchange, because "we have pledged ourselves to the enemy."[44] The Revolutionary leaders did not believe that ends justified means. They were convinced that humane ideals and moral restraint could control violence.

Even as the guidelines of the *jus ad bellum* had surfaced in explanations of the resort to arms, so did facets of the *jus in bello* appear in American attitudes toward the conduct of the War for Independence. The Revolution became a vehicle into which the Revolutionary leaders loaded those eighteenth-century doctrines which suited their temperaments, ideology, and circumstances, and this vehicle propelled a collection of attitudes into the future of independence when the United States would be a sovereign equal with the other powers of the western world. The Revolution transformed the limited-war mentality from an amalgam of attitudes toward war and peace into a national outlook.

This process is confirmed with the consideration of the third major component of the limited-war mentality, the belief that force was an instrument of state policy. During the colonial period, this existed only in rudimentary form among the settlers. But the altered circumstances created by the quest for independence rendered it of great significance. States embody societies, and Americans believed that war should be used in defense of community values, as the "Declaration on Taking Up Arms" had revealed. This attitude flowed naturally from the thrust of the *jus ad bellum* in combination with republican ideology. Even the colonial experience of relative isolation from the metropolitan center of Great Britain had encouraged an independent cast of mind within which such ideas could find a comfortable resting place.

Once the steps toward sovereign status had been taken and the Revolutionary leaders articulated national objectives of independence and future security, the link between force and policy was obvious. These men recognized clearly that self-interest, not philanthropy or a sharing of ideals, united countries as allies.[45] Washington was pleased when in 1778 France became an ally of the United States, but he knew that for the French this was a marriage of convenience.[46] The Revolutionary leaders were anything but innocents, despite their lofty ambitions and their lack of experience as independent statesmen beyond the provincial level.

More to the point was the notion of territorial expansion during the War for Independence. Universalist rhetoric makes the leaders appear hypocritical in this regard, but they were operating on different levels when championing the liberties of man, on the one hand, and obtaining satisfactory boundaries, on the other. In 1777, for example, the Committee on Foreign Affairs declared that Americans fought for human rights and for the establishment of a refuge from persecution and tyranny. This was one of the legends of the Revolution, since the same group prepared a plan for the invasion of Canada a year later. But in their minds conquest would add to the refuge, as well as serve more strictly military ends. The expedition never developed, scotched in part by the French, who did not want the emergence of too-large a United

States, which might threaten long-range French plans in North America.[47] Even though Washington's strategy revolved around defending the United States against occupying and invading British armies, some revolutionaries viewed dragging Europeans into the contest as a sure means of expansion. As George Mason suggested to fellow Virginian Richard Henry Lee, "war is the present interest of these United States; the union is yet incomplete, & will be so until the inhabitants of all the territory from Cape Breton to the Mississippi are included in it."[48] Defensive-mindedness did not preclude larger ambitions, and it reveals a link between force and policy in the minds of the Revolutionary leaders which again places them in the mainstream of eighteenth-century thought on war.

Revolutionaries occasionally differed among themselves about which specific objectives constituted proper national policy. For New Englanders, the fisheries and trading rights loomed large. For Southerners, whose people were already moving into the valleys west of the Allegheny Mountains, navigation of the river systems draining into the Gulf of Mexico was important. Middle-state men wanted a western frontier pushed as far west as possible to remove the British to arm's length and maintain a hold on the still-valuable fur trade. Benjamin Franklin epitomized the men embracing several goals simultaneously, any or all of which could be achieved through the application of force. Thoroughly committed to independence, he voiced the universalist rhetoric common to the Revolutionary leaders. He was self-righteous toward the British, convinced that their cause was unjust. He piously hoped that commerce would replace power politics as a guideline in the international world, but all the while his territorial ambition remained clear.[49]

In the limited-war mentality, force was a sovereign instrument, and therefore the Continental Congress strove continuously to assert its authority. Although the Articles of Confederation vested Congress with war and peace powers, that document lay unratified from the time it was drawn up in 1777 until March of 1781. Localism and provincialism remained strong, despite the development of intercolonial cooperation prior to independence and the existence of Congress thereafter. Even so, as early as 1776, Governor Nicholas Cooke of Rhode Island thought that all ideas of individual defense should be abandoned, since the common interest could only be protected by collective power wielded by central authority. For Cooke and others, Congress must have the war power.[50] Whatever the conflicting tensions in the United States — local, provincial, regional — when delegates to Congress experienced firsthand the frustrations of central direction of the war effort, they usually came to the same conclusion. War was a policy of the State, but not of the states.

The leaders who urged the Constitution of 1787 were more aware of this than most. If the war power were not firmly vested with the central authority, George Washington believed, then even independence could become an impossibility. He and other officers constantly witnessed the paralytic impact of divided and hamstrung authority. After an initial flush of cooperative enthusiasm, the states reverted to their colonial individualism and obduracy. When James Madison first came to Congress as a delegate from Virginia, he was shocked to discover that the states had been flaunting their defiance of congressional prerogatives. In 1782, for example, Pennsylvania had seized goods bound for British prisoners under a congressional passport. Congress launched a blistering protest, but the nature of the Confederation rendered it impotent, apart from rhetorical harangues and persuasion, to enforce its ostensibly constitutional authority. These problems led in the early 1780s to a movement to strengthen the powers of Congress, but this collapsed as Americans relaxed after Lord Cornwallis's surrender at Yorktown.[51]

The Revolutionary leaders, because of their experience with the war at the center of affairs, came to appreciate that force was an instrument of state policy. Among eighteenth-century statesmen and monarchs this approach had led to cynical diplomacy. But the Revolutionary leaders believed that their society embraced more humane and honorable principles than did monarchy. Their structure was liberal, democratic, and republican, in its institutions, social attitudes, and political goals. As the people's representatives, the leaders came easily to the view that they were best suited to define and pursue national policy objectives. And they assumed that in a democratic-republican state, war as an instrument of policy could not be abused.

The objectives of the young republic emerged in foreign policy formation, the first goals of which were survival and security. Given that society was under siege, war was the only instrument for achieving those goals. Once obtained, independence would be secured by the policy of neutrality or non-alignment. If this failed, however, the Revolutionary leaders understood clearly that force would be needed.[52] The moral problems involved were not lost on them either. Robert Morris, for one, regretted dragging other powers into war to serve American ends, and inquired if morality and policy were not related. Then he answered himself by writing: "Perhaps it may not be good policy to investigate the Question at this time." And once the goal of independence seemed assured, other specific interests surfaced and sought to shape national policy in their favor through the success of the war.[53] These blended with the practical goals of survival and security, the economic interests that sought the protection and expansion of trade, and the territorial ambitions of nationalists and speculators — not to mention the dreams of the idealists.

The American Revolutionary leaders thus embraced the three principal tenets of the limited-war mentality, using them to understand and attempt to solve the problems of their country. The dynamics of revolution made doctrines used by nation-states in the eighteenth century applicable. The leaders defended their struggle for independence as a just war using the terms of the classical *jus ad bellum*. They sought to apply the civilized canons of their time to warfare, drawing upon the guidelines of the *jus in bello*. They understood that force was an instrument of national policy. And if the fighting was frequently savage, or if crusading rhetoric and holy-war tendencies emerged, they can be traced to the brutal dynamics of all wars, the ideological thrust of the Revolution, and the fact that it was a civil war. Even so, the presence of conflicting tendencies did not overturn the limited character of the American War of Independence.

The fundamental view of the limited-war mentality — that military conflict was inevitable — acquired a republican cast in the minds of the Revolutionary generation, since that generation tended to accept the eighteenth-century republican myth that monarchs lay at the root of all wars. Tom Paine asserted, for example, that it was "the pride of kings which throws mankind into confusion," and John Witherspoon, speaking on the Articles of Confederation, noted the historical pacifism of republics.[54] The foundations of an American self-delusion about republican pacifism flowed from eighteenth-century thought into a developing American doctrine about the origins of war.

At the same time, other perspectives emerged. Alexander Hamilton found the passions of man "abundant sources of contention and hostility" among nations. The United States had emerged into a predatory universe, where states were arrayed in perpetual antagonism. John Jay believed "that nations should make war against nations is less surprising than their living in uninterrupted peace and harmony."[55] The Revolutionary generation was not entirely self-deluded. It realized that flawed human nature was a cause of strife.

Benjamin Franklin's ideas on war embraced many strands of thought. Commerce could propel nations toward either war or peace, since man's affairs interacted with his nature. As Franklin wrote to Edmund Burke in 1781 when the War for Independence was winding down, "since the foolish part of mankind will make wars from time to time with each other, not having sense enough otherwise to settle their differences, it certainly becomes the wiser part, who cannot prevent those wars, to alleviate as much as possible the calamities attending them." This was the Enlightenment speaking: wars are inevitable; since they cannot be eradicated, we must temper their worst abuses. Men, Franklin remarked to Joseph Priestly, were too easily provoked, too deceitful, too proud, and too bellicose. Franklin's pessimism led him to doubt the efficacy of blueprints for peace. He had some confidence that the United States, because its people had so much land and because they were removed from Europe, might avoid wars. But were this not the case, he implied, Americans might tend to become conquerors for their own profit like all other peoples had in the past.[56]

John Adams had a similarly complex view. He saw the struggle against tyranny as central in human history. Adams believed that as a consequence of the pattern of historical evolution, the whole world was liable for the calamities of military conflict. Warfare also flowed from human passions and found frequent expression in the jealousies of states. Adams cited Athens and Great Britain as the respective instigators of the Peloponnesian and Revolutionary wars as examples supporting his theses. Human nature did not love war, but men still fought for "frivolous purposes of avarice, ambition, vanity, resentment, and revenge." Princes had more than their share of these attributes, but Adams sidled toward the delusion that because she had republican institutions, America would be able to avoid all save defensive wars.[57] This conviction would grow in the minds of the Revolutionary generation to acquire the stature of a national myth. At the moment, it was one perspective among several on the origins of war and the future relationship of the United States to international affairs.

The views of American clerics had not altered since the colonial era. They still believed that human sin accounted for war. As long as evil stalked a degenerate world, men would prey upon one another. Local sin combined with British depravity in the case of the Revolution to bring condign punishment down upon American heads. To Quaker Anthony Benezet, sin and war were reciprocal partners that propelled man in a circle of misery. But at times, clerics too fell prey to the myth that monarchs caused war and its corollary that republicanism was the path to peace.[58]

The beliefs that monarchs were bellicose, that nation-states were naturally predatory, that commerce generated conflicts, and that human nature inclined toward aggression, all combined to convince the Revolutionary generation that future wars were inevitable. Thus these men used facets of the limited-war mentality to understand the relationship between conflict and the world around them. This was not an interpretation of all strands of violence, although some of the same themes could apply. Rather, it was a means of understanding the origins, nature, and purposes of war.

The inevitability of war suggested the need for preparedness. George Washington, in collaboration with Alexander Hamilton, draughted a design for the peacetime military establishment of the United States. Weakness invited aggression and potential predators lurked everywhere. Even conflict in remote Europe could evolve into a vortex that would suck America down to destruction. Hamilton, Madison, Oliver Ellsworth, James Wilson, and Samuel Holton presented a report to Congress on Washington's proposals. Because future wars were certain, a deterrent force had to be both comprehensive and controlled by Congress. Regular troops, engineers, uniform militia regulations, and frontier and coastal fortifications should be complemented by arms manufactories.[59] This was a plea for military autarky, not a call for a nation in arms. Even so, these impulses toward preparedness collided with an entrenched antimilitarism in

American thought, a flaccid congress, and an empty treasury. Only by exploiting a series of diplomatic and frontier crises in the 1780s and 1790s were the Federalists able, first, to establish a stronger central government more suited to national defense, and second, to construct a small but comprehensive peacetime military structure for keeping frontier and domestic order and defending the coasts and sealanes. But fears persisted, and quarrels over the army and navy constituted one thread in the developing tapestry of partisan politics in the young republic from 1789 to 1815.

The danger of entanglement in foreign wars led many to argue for a detached neutrality as a principal buttress to preparedness. This would restrict the need for standing forces and thus prove fiscally sound as well as ideologically acceptable to a majority of congressmen. Some feared that the Franco-American treaties of 1778 would involve the United States in future French wars — no idle fancy, as the events of the 1790s would reveal. Apart from that, unexpected predators were ever likely. Peace would not come of its own. John Jay noted that virtue and knowledge were essential for liberty and union, but these could not flourish unless enemies were deterred from aggression. Other Revolutionary leaders accepted this general thesis, their commitment to neutrality notwithstanding. For example, John Adams admonished his son John Quincy to study diligently and prepare himself for the future councils, negotiations, and wars of his country. These would be inevitable, Adams noted, because the world had not yet reached that idyllic state where nations could disband their armies and live unmolested.[60]

Thus both the legacies and legends of the eighteenth century became part of the American national outlook on war and peace by the close of the struggle for independence. The Revolution had been the mechanism whereby its leaders had appropriated a set of general attitudes and transformed them into a perspective to explain their own circumstances and future needs. The circumstances of the revolutionary war itself, along with those of the wilderness, had placed special demands on the Revolutionary generation. So had the fact that the Revolution had been a civil struggle, a part of the international competition for power in the eighteenth century, and a fight for independence. Frontier communities had experienced the impact of the fighting more severely than those in other regions of the colonies. Yet the war wandered. Now coastal towns burned because of naval bombardment. Then valleys and villages felt the weight of occupying or struggling armies. On the whole, few escaped some direct experience with the war. If British and American troops did not clash in a region, loyalist-patriot raids and counterraids could be anticipated. In the latter cases, the civilized trappings suggested by the *jus in bello* were often discarded in favor of more primitive drives for revenge.

Finally, there is little doubt but that the Revolutionary leaders absorbed and intended to apply the principle of force in pursuit of their objectives. Thomas Jefferson revealed that at an unexpected moment. He sent some classical statuettes to Abigail Adams, who was in London with her husband, John, the new American minister at the Court of St. James. Jefferson had selected a Minerva, Diana, and Apollo, as requested, and explained a fourth, free choice thus:

> At length a fine Mars was offered, calm, bold, his faulchion not drawn, but ready to be drawn. This will do, thinks I, for the table of the American Minister in London, where those whom it may concern may look and learn that though Wisdom is our guide, and the Song and the Chase our supreme delight, yet we offer adulation to that tutelar god also who rocked the cradle of our birth, who has accepted our infant offerings, and has shewn himself the patron of our rights and the avenger of our wrongs.[61]

The Revolutionary generation proved to be in the mainstream of its time when it came to thought on war and peace. The American version of the limited-war mentality was an amalgam from republican theory, classical politics and philosophy, Christian theology, historical experience, and the diverse probings and reflections of the most civilized, humane, and intelligent minds of the seventeenth and eighteenth centuries. This generation had a balanced view of human nature. Reason competed with passion for control of human behavior, and thus optimism and pessimism intertwined in American expectations about peace and war, so that philosophically American leaders could avoid despair.[62] The Revolutionaries would proceed to apply many of the precepts of the limited-war mentality to their political institutions and to their foreign and military policies. These precepts in turn would respond to new forces — internally the continued development of nationalism and the rise of political parties, and externally the French Revolution. That revolution would wreak enormous changes on war in Europe, but the United States remained on the fringes of its reverberations, still guided in foreign and military policy by the tenets of the limited-war mentality.

3

CONFEDERATION PROBLEMS
AND THE CONSTITUTIONAL SOLUTION

The Revolution had led Americans to adopt the limited-war mentality as part of their national outlook. After 1783 the way in which American leaders interpreted problems and devised solutions suggested how firmly the tenets of the limited-war mentality had become embedded in their thought. In the Constitution of 1787, for example, Americans institutionalized the republican myth concerning the origins of war. Believing, as most republicans did in the eighteenth century, that monarchs were the dominant source of war, the architects of the Constitution reasoned that popular control of the war power would contribute to a pacific future. True, other nations might commit acts of aggression, but America would commit none of her own. In 1776 it had been clear that the Americans had rejected monarchism in favor of republicanism. Quite apart from the reaction to the personal inadequacies of George III, Americans concluded that monarchism as a system of government would not meet their libertarian political and social requirements. So it was inevitable when America's political structure was more closely defined in the summer of 1787 in Philadelphia that war and peace powers would rest with the people's representatives, rather than with the executive branch of government; it was one line of continuity between the Articles of Confederation and the Constitution.

But the Constitution of 1787 evolved from a complex historical background. The Revolution created fresh issues and failed to resolve old problems, with ramifications that extended far beyond the exchange of ratifications of the Treaty of Paris in 1784, which

which brought the War for Independence to a close. The relative impotence of the United States in the international world exacerbated diverse emotional, financial, and political legacies. Territorial and economic ambitions generated additional frustrations because of old-world powers that retained colonial possessions on America's borders and because of the way Great Britain, Spain, and even France proved reluctant to broaden commercial links with the aspiring Yankee merchants and diplomats preaching free trade. The colonial inheritance of disputed and vague boundaries, complicated by the migration of aggressive settlers and the presence of restive and resentful Indians, simply continued. In this respect, ironically enough, the Confederation government confronted the same frontier problems that had perplexed the British imperial government at the close of the war in 1763. And the treaties with France, which constituted a defensive alliance with American guarantees for French possessions in the Caribbean, did not evaporate with the coming of peace either. Thus, a combination of revolutionary legacies, national weakness, international and local circumstances, and ambitions all propelled the United States into the perilous atmosphere of late-eighteenth-century European politics.

As American leaders confronted problems in foreign affairs, the main tenets of the limited-war mentality shaped their perceptions and responses. They drew upon this amalgam of thought to negotiate boundaries, react to the depredations of the Barbary pirates, deal with Indian wars, and reform their government. Britain and Spain proved a menace through their covert policy of containing American territorial advancement while attempting to avoid a clash. The Barbary pirates found American merchantmen poking into the Mediterranean vulnerable, stripped now of the passes they had flourished when still part of the British Empire and thus under the protection of the Royal Navy. On the western frontier, over-eager settlers shouldered their way onto Indian lands in defiance of the natives' sensibilities and negotiated treaties alike. The foreign debt collected interest with no reduction in principal because Congress had no taxing power, which constituted another danger because, as many pointed out, nations often unleashed warships to pry payments from recalcitrant debtors. The individual American states also violated the terms of the treaty with Britain in response to local pressures. And however justified British protests were, Congress could no more control the conduct of New York or Georgia than those states could control the actions of their own citizens on the frontier. All these problems interwove with political and economic concerns to culminate in the constitutional solution of 1787.[1]

The importance of the limited-war mentality as a national doctrine emerged in many ways. To begin with, Americans had no retrospective doubts about the justice of the War for Independence. Countless July 4 orations affirmed the choice of a resort to arms with the rhetoric of the *jus ad bellum*. The appeal by arms to God's judgment had come only at the end of a long trail of forbearance, and success was the sign of God's favor. And besides, "the love of liberty out-weighed the horrors of war," as W. C. Jackson put it in 1786.[2] The Revolutionary generation continued, therefore, to deny that the loyalists had taken a legally, politically, or morally legitimate stand, and insisted that Great Britain was a separate and hostile power by 1775. A national perspective began to characterize historical judgments. Any reluctance surrounding the decision for independence began to slip from American memories. Calls for moderation toward the loyalists went largely unheeded and those loyalists inclined to attempt a return to their former homes met with anger, resentment, intolerance, and little redress through the courts for property losses. Those in exile could only turn to the British crown for compensation.[3]

If a sense of moderation toward the loyalists did not survive the early phases of the revolutionary movement, the sense of restraint associated with the *jus in bello* remained alive in the minds of the leaders. The war being over, American leaders were eager to gain foreign recognition and acceptance through treaties of amity and commerce, both for prestige and for the advantages and opportunities necessary to a country whose economic life had been severely disrupted and left largely prostrate. The Model Treaty of 1776 provided the principal guidelines for American ministers overseas. In several ways, its clauses reflected the *jus in bello*; the rights and immunities of noncombatants must not be violated in wartime, for example, and merchants should have leisure to settle their affairs and depart peacefully if war should arise between the contracting parties. Merchants should also be exempt from seizure, even when blockades were established, if "rendering the necessaries, conveniences and comforts of human life more easy to obtain." Such ideas appealed to representatives of a bourgeois society that promoted free trade and hoped to prosper from neutrality. These ideals became part of the formal guidelines adopted on the same day that John Jay from New York became the secretary for foreign affairs in the Confederation government.[4]

John Jay's conservatism, combined with international realities, diluted most of these noble ambitions, but such guidelines indicated two realities about the influence of the limited-war mentality on American thought on foreign policy. First, the Revolutionary leaders conformed to the prevailing practices of their time, which stressed the contractual obligations established by treaties rather than the more ethereal goals of international law as the cardinal means of regulating the relationship of states. Second, the leaders sought to institutionalize the enlightened eighteenth-century view that wars were between governments, and not peoples. Like contemporary monarchs, the leaders attempted to shield society from the impact of war.

Thomas Jefferson, as minister plenipotentiary to France replacing Benjamin Franklin, epitomizes the limited-war mentality in action. Jefferson was exceptionally widely read, even for the Revolutionary leadership, and when he examined Congress's Model Treaty, he set to work improving it. He wanted to eliminate the concept of contraband during wartime altogether, and he specified the noncombatants who were to be protected — women, children, and scholars.[5] If paper results are any indication, both Jefferson and the Americans enjoyed success in their endeavors to institutionalize such aspects of the *jus in bello*. A grace clause for merchants in the event of war between the signatories had appeared in the treaties concluded with France in 1778 and with the Netherlands in 1780. When the American Commissioners in Europe opened discussions with the envoys from the King of Prussia in 1784, they advanced these clauses again. The age had witnessed progress in other spheres, why not in war? It was "for the interest of humanity in general, that the occasions of war, and the inducements to it should be diminished." If plundering were prohibited, it would discourage war and promote peace. Evidently, such arguments were persuasive, or advisers considered the clauses harmless, because they subsequently appeared in the final Prussian-American treaty ratified by Congress in March 1786.[6]

During the Confederation period other Americans worked to humanize, if not to abolish, war. Franklin argued that nations should be shown that any advantage acquired by war could be more cheaply purchased with cash. But reason had to prevail in human affairs first. Richard Henry Lee urged upon Sam Adams that if men maintained a "philosophic" temper they could avoid the anger that drove so many nations at one another's throats. John Jay noted that mankind had become more civilized about war, and cited the abandonment of the practice of unilaterally erasing lawful debts when fighting broke out to illustrate his point. War must not affect legal contracts, in Jay's mind, for law had a moral binding force transcending national differences and disputes. And for all his experience with conflict, George Washington wrote to his old ally and comrade-in-arms, the Comte de Rochambeau, that the "rage of conquest" had abated in this enlightened age, and perhaps even more liberal policies and systems would emerge in the future.[7] The Revolutionary generation sustained the optimism which was central to civilized thought in the eighteenth century and a principal thrust of the limited-war mentality. And Americans retained a balance between optimism and pessimism because evidence and logic told them that human behavior seldom lived up to men's best hopes.

American pessimism most clearly emerged in the belief that future wars were inevitable. As Washington wrote to Sir Edward Newenham, "but what shall we say of Wars and the appearances of Wars in the rest of the World? Mankind are not yet ripe for the Millennial State."[8] Men must accept what they could not change, such as flawed human nature or the selfish norms and daily betrayals of international politics. Impartial benevolence signified little. John Jay prophesied in 1783 that "while there are knaves and fools in the world, there will be wars in it; and that nations should make war against nations is less surprising than their living in uninterrupted peace and harmony."[9]

Power as an instrument of policy emerged in John Adams's tour at the Court of St. James. Adams was the first American representative to the former mother country and he read in Congress's instructions that passions and interest moved nations as much as men. Adams knew this better than most Americans, but he went on to read that since neither passions nor interests were sufficiently understood or applied, none could know which might prevail with the councils of a foreign country at any given moment. Adams, in short, must be prepared to translate a cypher with a constantly shifting key. Nations had no courts in which to settle violations of their rights. They could always resort to force, and were frequently inclined to do so. For his part, Adams feared that the more prosaic elements of commercial difficulties, especially discriminatory tariff barriers, could "excite passions on both sides which may break out into a military war." British policy-makers did not intend to provoke another clash with the United States, but American fears are understandable. And as if to underscore the truth of Congress's reminders and Adams's belief, James Madison, enraged by British obstinacy over trade discrimination, asked of James Monroe if America should not try to extort redress for its grievances.[10] Madison was no warmonger here, for he meant only retaliation on a commercial level, but he illustrated how frustration could by turns become anger and then action. By the 1790s, he would call for embargoes to force British compliance with American demands.

The republican orthodoxy that monarchs lay at the heart of war mingled with an accelerating American nationalism that portrayed the United States as superior in virtue, if not power, to the nations of Európe. To the American mind darker forces of human nature seemed especially hard at work among European princes. The myth of the pacifism of popular rule had begun to take a firm hold on the imagination of the Revolutionary generation. And if some of the heat with which Americans denounced monarchs on this score subsided after 1783, the basic assumption remained. In addition, Americans believed, as they had during the Revolution, that Europeans were still wallowing in a pit of luxury, vice, and corruption, where violent, capricious, and depraved behavior was normal.

American superiority could be sustained or even enhanced by insulation from the European virus. One essayist in the *American Museum* wrote that "the causes, which create war among European powers, do not here exist." Richard Henry Lee wanted all republics to isolate themselves from rampaging monarchies, and John Jay feared for the Dutch, a republican raft afloat on a monarchical sea.[11] This linked with an important thread in American as well as republican thought: there were institutional solutions to human problems. If the form of government were properly constructed, then human behavior would adapt accordingly. This structural behavioralism would not produce overnight miracles. But confident of republican superiority, hopeful for a future of liberty, virtue, and independence, and hewing a path of neutrality, Americans expected that their country would enjoy a more peaceful existence than most of its contemporaries.[12]

In France, Jefferson developed the same view. Every time princes rattled their sabres, he braced himself for a holocaust. For example, he was certain in November 1784 that battle was imminent between the Dutch and the Austrians over free navigation of the Scheldt River; he wrote home theatrically, "the lamp of war is kindled here, not to be extinguished but by torrents of blood." Fortunately, the torrents of blood did not flow on this occasion, nor on many others. If Europeans were cynical in their statecraft, they were professional, vigorous, and assiduous in its practice. In time, Jefferson came to see these qualities and he ceased to cry havoc when Europeans began to quarrel. But he never doubted that monarchs were tempted into wars for personal, frivolous reasons, and could squander their subjects' lives and resources because of their monopoly of political power.[13] Jefferson did not think much more of Louis XVI of France than he did of George III of England, despite the rather different roles those monarchs had played in the struggle for American independence. Jefferson also feared that the French treaties of 1778 would snag the United States into European wars in which the Americans would have no direct interest. Although he realized it was an impractical dream, Jefferson, in company with other Revolutionary leaders, wished that his country could be utterly isolated from world affairs.[14] But Jefferson and his generation also hoped that their country would profit by being neutral carriers and suppliers when the Europeans fell into perennial conflicts. The Americans betrayed their own brand of cynicism by expressing a willingness to fatten on Europeans hard-pressed by war.[15]

Subtle forces were at work to undermine American hopes for a peaceful future. The overseas commerce and domestic wealth of the United States could expose the country to insults abroad and tempt potential aggressors. Trade and prosperity had their drawbacks; Jefferson and Adams both knew that Americans would no more abandon trade than they would forsake independence. Both the mercantile elements of the seaboard regions and the producing farmers with surpluses for export relied on this commerce for their prosperity. The New Hampshire delegates noted to Mesech Weare, the president of their state, that the central government needed powers over trade if for no other reason than to protect it. This thread wound into the movement that culminated in the Constitution of 1787. James Monroe foreshadowed attitudes not yet mature when he noted that while Americans must work to avoid war, they must also preserve the honor and dignity of their country.[16]

Monroe's comment reflected a natural subjectivity of judgment which contradicted the impulse toward republican pacifism, although the Revolutionary generation did not understand this. Some men choose to be insulted easily, and some nationalists are overly sensitive about slaps at their country's honor. Despite the experience of the Revolution, most Americans remained unaware that national wars are always just to patriots because the enemy invariably becomes an aggressor. And if dissenters disagree, the forces of conformity arising from the sense of the homeland in danger brand them as traitors. For the United States to fight an unjust war seemed impossible for increasingly patriotic republican Americans.

This issue of national preparedness arose directly from the leaders' conviction that wars were inevitable and from the specific dangers the United States confronted. John Adams warned that the British would remain stubborn until impressed with American power. And John Jay, as secretary of foreign affairs of the Confederation, warned that if Americans proved hesitant to assert their rights by arms, "your secretary thinks that no Nation can, consistent with the experience of all ages, expect to enjoy peace and security any longer than they may continue prepared for war."[17] Others knew that a failure to reduce the foreign debt held over from the Revolution would sully America's reputation to the point where she would be unable to locate future allies or credit in an emergency. Thus she would become doubly vulnerable.[18] Throughout the Confederation period, Americans, whether at home or abroad, knew that their country could neither use force to sustain diplomacy, nor support a war. They believed that this rendered the United States an international joke as a consequence, and these convictions led them to argue for constitutional revision as a first step toward remedying this problem.

The ideology of republicanism and the structure of the confederation government provide the principal explanations for these problems. Congress was destitute, even worse, deeply in debt to the American people and foreign bankers alike. It lacked energy because of the disinterest of the states and it wanted proper fiscal and executive authority. And when Washington and others urged a modest military establishment at the close of the War for Independence, they ran into widespread hostility to such a plan. Fear of standing armies under central authority arose from the seventeenth century. Oliver Cromwell and his military dictatorship loomed large in American thought, for the Revolutionary generation could not escape from its English heritage, despite separation from the British Empire. And the regulars and mercenaries of the Revolution itself made a military establishment seem an odious copy of European practices. The alleged Newburgh Conspiracy and the mutinies in the Continental Line warned that even in a republic, the military could be dangerous. Finally, Americans feared centralized authority in any form. The Federalists discovered that adequate defenses for the United States could be constructed only in piecemeal fashion, and by exploiting military crises as they arose. The Revolutionary leaders appreciated the vital link between force and diplomacy, but for the moment they were powerless to provide for future defense needs, and even fearful of the consequences if they succeeded.

Upon close analysis, American antimilitarism appears ill-founded and logically inconsistent. But such internal flaws did not deter the rhetorical potency of such anti-army congressmen as Elbridge Gerry of Massachusetts.[19] Besides, many Americans placed great faith in the republican myth of pacifism and distance from Europe to protect them from war. Consequently, the United States was largely helpless if faced with a military alarm on either land or sea.

One problem of the Confederation period which illustrated this inconsistency graphically was the first encounter of independent Americans with the Barbary pirates. The Barbary states — Algiers, Morocco, Tripoli, and Tunis — huddled against the Mediterranean and Middle-Atlantic coasts of Africa. They enjoyed the dubious protection of the Sultan of Turkey as nominal sovereign and the defender of Islam. Raiding the sea lanes off their shores was their principal economic activity. Only those nations with powerful navies or full treasuries for tribute could expect that their merchantmen would be left alone as they plied the waters of the Straits of Gibraltar and the Mediterranean Sea. Before the Revolution, British passes and men-of-war protected American traders. This shield evaporated in 1776, but the consequences did not come home to the Americans until after 1783, when Yankee ships began to establish commercial contacts with the Levant.

When the first American ship was captured, word filtered initially to American consuls and ministers in Europe. Jefferson argued immediately for a policy of war. The European practice of tribute seemed disgraceful. "We ought to begin a naval power," he ventured to James Monroe, and "can we begin it on a more honourable occasion or with a weaker foe?" Back in the United States, John Jay agreed, and he hoped that this insult might overcome congressional lethargy in foreign affairs. He reported to Congress in October of 1785 that Algiers had declared war on the United States and urged action to protect trade and defy the pirates. He wrote to John Paul Jones, the Revolutionary naval hero, that it would not "become us either to return an unprovoked declaration of war by overtures of peace or offers of tribute."[20] Jones predictably argued for action, as did William Carmichael, the American representative in Madrid. All thought that the application of force would enhance America's reputation abroad.[21]

But others disagreed. Some believed that the United States could not carry on any military action, no matter how justified. Others argued that war would further expose America's defenseless commerce and ultimately cost far more than tribute. John Adams so believed, for example, and told Jay that although a war would be heroic, it would also be imprudent. Benjamin Franklin sensibly noted that since the pirates had no commerce of their own, naval retaliation would be difficult.[22] In Congress, some doubted that sufficient funds could be added to the original allocation of $80,000 to purchase a peace. Others simply trembled at the thought of the expense. The issue of force and policy did not even cross their minds. All they could see was an empty treasury, debt, and no prospect of revenue. Tribute seemed the cheapest solution to the Barbary problem.[23]

When the advocates of war saw that a policy of force was unlikely, they changed their tack. Jefferson thought that a league of the smaller powers suffering from Barbary depredations might be formed to coerce the pirates collectively. This idea probably originated with Franklin, but Jefferson championed it and Jay argued its merits in his reports to Congress. Richard Henry Lee was impressed, and in July of 1787, a motion emerged to have Jefferson form such a confederacy with the European powers then at war with Algiers, Tunis, and Tripoli. Morocco was left out because the Americans had recently ratified a treaty of amity and commerce with her. The whole proposal then went to John Jay for his comment as the secretary for foreign affairs.[24]

Meanwhile, Jefferson was hard at work in France. He probed for potential allies. Would France, the American commissioners asked the Comte de Vergennes, still the French foreign minister, consider a war against Algiers when her current treaty expired? If so, would France consider a joint operation with the United States? To John Adams in London, Jefferson suggested that since Portugal was currently at war with Algiers, perhaps a potential ally existed there also. But by the following summer, Jefferson's thought marched beyond bilateral alliances. Portugal, Naples, and even Russia, because of her running dispute with Turkey, might combine forces with the United States, who could furnish a "couple of frigates," establish a convention, and cruise against the Algerian coast. Two or three nations might begin such a campaign in collective security, and others could join later.[25]

In 1786 Jefferson marshalled his ideas and his friends behind a formal proposal. The Marquis de Lafayette and the Comte D'Estaing, who had fought with Americans during the War for Independence, proved ardent converts. Jefferson argued for a confederation to force a peace. The ambassadors of the cooperating powers at the Court of Versailles would constitute a directing council. Jefferson knew that John Adams did not entirely approve of the proposal, so he had Lafayette present the scheme to Congress to avoid offending his friend and colleague.[26]

But the whole thing collapsed both at home and abroad. John Jay reported as directed. He told Congress that it would "always be more for the Honor and Interest of the United States to prefer War to Tribute." The country possessed the resources to participate in a joint operation of this kind, but it lacked the financial base and the executive efficiency to act effectively. Thus the secretary for foreign affairs recommended against American association with other powers in a war on Algiers. Jay echoed what others also believed. A few months earlier, George Washington had told Lafayette that the United States had neither the money to bribe nor the arms to punish Algiers, even though he personally favored a policy of war. And congressional supporters of the collective proposal came to the same conclusion. It was better to suffer humiliation in silence than disgrace the country by making commitments that could not be honored.[27]

The scheme fared little better in Europe, where national self-interest ruled international politics. Vergennes instructed Lafayette to disengage himself from the venture. France and Spain formally declined to participate, and although many of the smaller powers — Portugal, Venice, and Sweden — expressed interest, they would do nothing without French accession, which was not forthcoming. John Paul Jones tried to resuscitate the idea by suggesting a bilateral alliance with Russia, but this attempt failed, and the proposal for joint action slid into diplomatic storage to gather dust.[28] A league to enforce peace, even against so contemptuous a nuisance as the Barbary pirates, was an idea whose time had not yet come; it lacked both persuasive power as a liberal measure in a reactionary age, and the force to override the individual interests of entrenched national policies.

This episode nevertheless illustrates several points about how the limited-war mentality had emerged as an adopted American doctrine since the Revolution. First, most of those who considered the Algerian problem clearly understood that war was an instrument of state policy. They only disputed whether it was a better policy than tribute under the circumstances. Second, if force were to be used, it would be in a limited war of policy. Third, and concomitantly, there was no hint of a crusading impulse in the minds of those urging the policy of war. Fourth, by implication, Americans accepted that their country lived in a world of predators, where a *casus belli*, such as the Algerian seizures, could occur at any time. Therefore, some standing forces were necessary for deterrence and retaliation. But they also realized that antimilitarism, an empty treasury, and a feeble government contradicted even minimal preparedness. The Barbary crisis was thus one issue steering Americans toward governmental reform as an initial step on the road to international security and respectability. Given a powerful, albeit circumscribed, central government, the United States would seem openly capable of waging effective war, even away from its own shores. Potential predators would therefore pause before casually inflicting injuries on the country.

The Barbary crisis gave Americans no reason to alter their view that wars originated from external causes. This reinforced the republican myth. The Revolutionary generation assumed that their country was free of blame throughout this period when military confrontations threatened. The Algerian action seemed especially immoral, and the United States would certainly have been justified in responding with war. None questioned that. Finally, and linked with the belief in republican pacifism, was the belief that there were institutional solutions to human problems. The league to dictate and enforce a peace against the Algerian pirates was thus an external manifestation of the thought behind the Constitution of 1787. And it would be resurrected by the Wilsonian internationalists in the twentieth century.

The Revolutionary generation still balanced optimism and pessimism. It thought in terms of limiting war's worst abuses, rather than in terms of eliminating it outright. War remained a necessary instrument of survival and a means of redressing grievances in the absence of higher international authority. Americans had adopted righteous attitudes during wartime, yet they did not have a crusading view of conflict among states. They adopted a legal perspective, buttressed by moral arguments drawn from the *jus ad bellum*, to determine when military force could be employed. To be sure, as heirs to the limited-war mentality, and by overlooking the emotional power of rising Romantic nationalism and the call to arms, by sustaining restraint, the leaders failed to appreciate one development of their own struggle for independence. They thus approached the war of the French Revolution with an essential innocence which left them handicapped. Total or unlimited war was beyond their ken. The Revolutionary generation remained within the eighteenth-century mainstream when it adopted the limited-war mentality as a national doctrine. In the near future, Americans would become one of its few practitioners.

The threat of war from the Barbary pirates had come from one of America's frontiers — the ocean. But another frontier also raised

the specter of conflict — the western wilderness. British territory
to the north and west, and Spanish holdings to the south and west,
bracketed the American borders. Indian tribes lay sprinkled
through the interior valleys, justly disturbed by, but nevertheless a
murderous menace to, the settlers who usurped their lands and
hunting grounds. This westward migration was beginning to
grip the American imagination. A western imperial vision had
stirred Benjamin Franklin and other frontier speculators in the
pre-Revolutionary period. Now, the Revolutionary generation
sketched the outlines of continental expansion and the Manifest
Destiny movement of the mid-nineteenth century.[29]

During the 1780s the issue was not new land so much as proper
control over that which Americans believed was already theirs. As
settlers pushed west, they encountered British and Spanish
agents, who encouraged the Indians to erect barriers against
American expansion. Both these European colonial powers used
natives as proxies to resist American migration, fortified by a
conviction that the rickety United States could not last long. But
the Treaty of Paris of 1783 gave Americans a strong sense of justice
in their claims to these western lands. In their minds, political
possession approached the status of a mandate from nature.[30]

Wilderness security was a major problem. In 1784 a congressional committee reported on frontier posts and suggested that the
Indian tribes should be politically divided as much as possible to
reduce the danger if trouble erupted. The committee members
feared the expense of war, but became steadily more impressed
with what they regarded as justified American claims, national
interests, and national pride. It would be good policy, a report on
southern Indian affairs noted, for example, to balance concessions with demands, provided this did not compromise the
national interest, and did not risk a war, which could cost more
than the value of the lands sought.[31] Once again, this was the
limited-war mentality finding expression. The report balanced
the costs of force with the costs of the object in view. When the
former exceeded the latter, the use of force fell into doubt.

Despite official caution, several factors combined to drive
various Indian tribes into sporadic and deadly warfare with the
United States. Some Americans unfairly blamed the British. The
Revolution had pushed loyalists out to the frontier in the

northwest, and these people harbored an intense bitterness toward
the United States, even though British ministries wanted to avoid
provocation. In addition, Henry Knox doubted that Indians and
whites could ever be good neighbors, and referred to the "wicked
and bloodthirsty dispositions" of the Wabash as an example. The
old colonial distinction between native and European enemies
seemed alive and well. And Indian commissioners often adopted a
haughty demeanor, as though the tribes were already conquered
because of their link with the British during the War for
Independence. For example, congressional agents dictated the
so-called treaties of Fort Stanwix in 1784 and Fort McIntosh in
1785.[32]

The settlers themselves created most of the problem. The
frontiersmen were aggressive, often violent, and drew no distinctions between friendly and hostile Indians. Neither Congress nor
the states could control them. Their numbers and links with the
east gave them a local political power that undercut Congress's
occasional efforts to deal justly with the Indians. As early as 1784,
it was clear to some that war was inevitable unless the settlers
could be barred from Indian lands. Henry Knox admitted freely
that injustices occurred on both sides.[33] And the dreary pattern of
raid, retaliation, and a descent into savagery established through
the colonial era simply continued. The central government
controlled war and peace according to the Articles of Confederation, but it found that it could not exert its authority. War on the
frontier was less a policy of the people than the result of local
ambitions and truculence. This situation contradicted both a
cardinal tenet of the limited-war mentality and a dictate of
common sense.

Congress found that it could not prevent itself from being
propelled into Indian wars that it did not want and that it would
have great difficulty winning. Arthur St. Clair, who later led an
ill-fated expedition against tribes in the northwest, noted in
September of 1786 that Virginia had mustered troops against the
Indians, in direct violation of the national faith as pledged by
treaty, "which would probably involve the United States in a
general and unjust war." A year later, a congressional committee
reported that an apparently imminent war with Indians northwest of the Ohio River would not be just. And John Jay went
further by observing that Indian affairs had been bungled, whites

had murdered Indians without punishment, and who could wonder that war seemed so likely?[34]

The Indian crisis highlights the problems the Confederation government had in functioning as a national body. These frontier difficulties had plagued successive British ministries during the late colonial period. The Indians were not nations like France or Prussia; for one thing, they lived on territory within America's political boundaries, and for another, their social and political structures were markedly different from European countries. Arthur St. Clair argued in a spirit of equity that Indian treaties should nevertheless be honored like any other. Congress asserted that it should conduct all Indian affairs and apply the criteria of the *jus ad bellum* before resorting to force. The contradictions and problems seemed manifest, but solutions remained hidden. Henry Knox pointed out, for example, that although Georgia had control over its western lands, it had no jurisdiction over the Indians living on it. Yet Georgia was going ahead anyway and preparing for a private Indian war. Congress vainly insisted that there must be a "manifest violation" of a treaty, followed by a rejected demand for redress and then a proper declaration before a policy of war could be adopted. Knox ordered Josiah Harmar to distinguish carefully between regular tribes and what he termed "banditti" when retaliating for Indian attacks. And the Northwest Ordinance of 1787, which in some respects was America's colonial policy, stated expressly that Indians would have rights and guarantees by treaty that could not be taken from them except in "just and lawful wars authorized by Congress."[35]

But if Congress had war powers according to Articles VI and IX of the Articles of Confederation, it lacked the necessary concomitants of taxing authority, direction over military power, and legal control over the states. As a result, Congress's policy of appeasement from 1786 forward could not prevent a slide toward Indian wars in several places on the frontier.[36] Under the Articles of Confederation, the country's leaders simply could not apply the tenets of the *jus ad bellum* as they thought they should. In this way too, the limited-war mentality contributed to the forces gathering behind constitutional reform at Philadelphia in the summer of 1787.

Clashes with the Indians provided only one possible source of frontier war. Another lay in the presence of British and Spanish power. Washington feared that western settlers might be wooed away from American allegiance once they moved toward British or Spanish influence, and he foresaw the dangers of separatism and war as a consequence. Anglo-American relations remained frosty because of American suspicion of the British and the bitter hostility of the wilderness loyalists. But Spain, especially because of Mississippi navigation, was an equal problem. In both cases, regular diplomacy could not always move quickly enough to ease tensions generated by the incipient violence of the frontier.[37]

In the northwest, the British retained nine posts on American soil, contrary to the terms of the Treaty of 1783. They alleged American violations of the treaty as an excuse, and did not intend to remain for long, but only to hold a bargaining token and temporarily control the fur trade. To some Americans the British presence on the now national soil was an affront to honor. Patriotic subjectivity produced a belligerent mood, and even John Jay asserted that Americans must defend their rights or expect further insults. A policy of bluster would do little good with the British since behind it would lie only pusillanimity, and this could lead to further encroachments and conflict.[38] But war with Britain could prove a disaster and destroy what some Americans already considered a floundering United States.[39]

The southwest looked no more promising. Congressman Samuel Hardy wrote to Patrick Henry of Virginia that although current circumstances forbade a policy of war, Americans must still actively resent any Spanish insults. If something were not done, the country would be in jeopardy. The 50,000 settlers already in the lower Ohio and Tennessee and upper Mississippi river basins constituted an increasingly powerful lobby for action. The cement of nationalism had yet to harden in the 1780s. George Washington's fears of separatism were well-founded. James Madison believed that Spain would see the wisdom of yielding to the inevitable and would not bar American navigation of the Mississippi River. But he added that if Spain depended "on the pacific temper of republics, unjust irritations on her part will soon teach her that Republics have like passions with other Govern[men]ts." Unconsciously, Madison contradicted the republican myth about war. But he was correct in thinking that events in the wilderness might seize policy-makers by the forelock, as local retaliation at Vincennes for Spanish seizure of American property in Natchez implied. At the same time, he knew that the country was incapable of war.[40]

American impotence was also clear during the John Jay-Don Diego de Gardoqui discussions, which occurred in May 1785, to deal with the problem of navigation on the Mississippi River. Jay found that while Gardoqui was charming, he was singularly unimpressed with either the legality of American claims or with the power of the United States to enforce national interests. Another decade would elapse before even a transitory settlement temporarily removed the specter of a Spanish-American war. For his part, Jay used these negotiations to prod Congress. Georgia must stop her people from molesting the Spanish, he stated. Congress must understand that even if the American claim were "expressly declared in Holy Writ, we should be able to provide for the enjoyment of it no otherwise than by being in a capacity to repel force with force." If the negotiations with Gardoqui ended unsatisfactorily, the United States would have to choose among accommodation, war, or disgrace, and in Jay's view, the first was the only sensible alternative.[41] Jay's practical argument exposed the link between force and policy in American thought. The issue became urgent after independence because the members of Congress began to identify and pursue national interests.

The delegates in Congress writhed over insoluble problems given the structure and fragmentation of the United States under the Articles of Confederation. Although the Americans accomplished notable achievements under this government, in foreign affairs its inadequacies seemed especially apparent and dangerous. The members disagreed over the ramifications of a future war with Spain, but tended to agree that given the state of the union, a policy of force was impossible.[42] The Jay-Gardoqui discussions, the Northwest posts, frontier Indian problems, and the Barbary crisis all pointed to the same solution — a reformed national government. The imperatives of the limited-war mentality reinforced the more fundamental concerns of ideology and economics, as well as a growing nationalism among the leadership of the Revolutionary generation, to produce the Constitution of 1787.

Many Americans believed that the United States would not survive unless constitutional reform was forthcoming. Congressmen felt the sting of foreign insults as the United States seemed helpless before Indians, pirates, Spanish, and English alike. And as Shays' Rebellion suggested, no power existed to control domestic disturbances. Because American leaders believed firmly in the justice of their country's rights and claims, they blushed over their inability to marshal military force to sustain national policies. Conflict seemed perpetually likely, republican pacifism notwithstanding, since local feuds could catapult the country into full-scale war. Greater unity would generate power, and from that would flow increased security. A stronger central government would encourage both foreign and domestic peace. To be sure, the adoption of the Constitution would not dissolve all these difficulties. But it would give the central government greater powers and authority in its search for solutions.

Few seem to have entertained any doubts that the national government must determine policy on war. James Madison and Arthur St. Clair noted in 1785 that individual states could no more have their own powers to make war than they could have commercial autonomy. If complaints arose about the conduct of other nations, then these must come before Congress for processing according to civilized international practice and treaties in force, in Madison's view. James Monroe wrote to Jefferson that the Confederation was little more than an offensive and defensive alliance, and if Congress lacked the power to raise troops, then it was only defensive. In March 1786, Charles Pinckney told the New Jersey assembly that the central government had to possess all the powers of nations, including exclusive rights in peace and war. In April 1787, Congress itself resolved that it must have autonomy in foreign affairs since perpetual war would ensue if individual states had the ability to abrogate treaties at will. Others looked inward and came to a similar conclusion. Civil war might erupt if some better form of central government were not adopted.[43]

These Revolutionary leaders, whom we can now term Federalists, exploited all these fears and exerted their formidable intellectual and political talents in reforming the Articles of Confederation into the Constitution of 1787. Like the mentality that guided their thinking on war and peace, the Constitution was the product of seventeenth- and eighteenth-century political philosophy. The war clauses of the Constitution turned out to be straightforward. Congress received the express power to declare war, grant letters of marque and reprisal, regulate the confiscation and capture of property during wartime, raise armies and a navy, and raise funds for their support. It could also regulate and summon the state militias in national service against domestic enemies or foreign invaders. The states could only defend against what they saw as an invasion or an imminent danger of attack. Consistent with republican doctrine, the war power lay with the people's representatives. The president as chief executive officer was commander-in-chief of the armed forces, and of any militia in national service. He waged war and was the country's principal diplomat.[44] Taken together, these powers meant that the president could muster America's military strength to sustain national policies as defined by Congress, which embodied the will of the people and the states through the House of Representatives and the Senate. The Federalists balanced republican faith in the pacifism of their system with the need to relate force and diplomacy in a single executive officer.

The limited-war mentality informed these clauses of the Constitution, even as they were a response also to specific American needs during the 1780s. The Constitution institutionalized the concept of force and policy, implying the perpetual likelihood of war, and implying also that the people would determine when the resort to arms was justified. Subsequent events have tugged at the intentions of the Federalists, usually in the direction of greater executive authority in times of crisis. But contemporary critics still return to the original statements of the framers of the Constitution to judge the actions of succeeding presidents.[45]

These war clauses evoked little discussion in Philadelphia, suggesting a tacit consensus, given the extended debate over so many other points. The war powers went from the stage of proposal to finished product with scant comment. In his propositions of 29 May, Charles Pinckney of South Carolina made the Senate the primary policy-making body regarding war and diplomacy. Alexander Hamilton suggested on 18 June that the Senate should declare war, and in his extended speech of the same day, James Madison concurred.[46] Those who spoke opposed any executive control, and given the predilection for popular supervision of the war power, the Committee on Detail presented all these points with no evidence of prior discussion or subsequent dissent.[47]

On 6 August the system of distribution of powers which formed the Constitution came before the delegates for consideration. On 17 August the framers dealt with the war powers, which now rested with the legislature in general, rather than the Senate in particular. Charles Pinckney ventured that proceedings in the House might prove too slow if an emergency arose. Pierce Butler thought that the president could have the war power, since he would never exercise it without national support, but this was ignored. Madison, and Elbridge Gerry of Massachusetts, moved to substitute "declare" for "make" in the phrasing, and this passed after a brief discussion.[48]

Subsequently, only minor aspects of the war powers arose. Gerry thought that letters of marque required specific allocation, since he did not believe that the general clauses covered this form of limited retaliation. Madison, arguing for federal control of exports, mentioned parenthetically that an embargo might some-day prove necessary to sustain national policy, but James McHenry of Maryland believed that this could flow from powers already established. Eventually, the Committee of Eleven presented further refinements on 5 September. A marque and reprisal clause, but nothing on embargoes, had been added. A brief discussion arose two days later over whether regular treaties should be separated from treaties of peace for the purposes of ratification, but nothing came of this. Now the Constitution provided for limited wars of policy as a method of arbitration, and there seems little doubt that the Federalists distinguished between what were referred to in contemporary phraseology as "perfect," or fully declared, and "imperfect," or limited wars.[49]

The Revolutionary generation did not identify sharp dividing lines between war and peace. International law, as codified in the works of Vattel and others, argued for stages of protest, diplomacy, remonstrance, ultimatums, private reprisal, and limited action with public forces before proceeding to full-scale war. Subsequent American diplomacy would follow such steps, and the war clauses of the Constitution created the institutional framework within which such action could occur.

Once the Constitution had emerged from the Philadelphia convention, the Federalists bent their energies and talents to ratification by the states. Although many clauses encountered opposition or skepticism, the war powers went undisputed. Most

Americans accepted the judgment that the country was in imminent peril if forceful measures for greater security were not forthcoming.[50] Elbridge Gerry and Patrick Henry feared that the president might acquire too much power, but this was a general concern about the office, and not about the role as commander-in-chief. In all state conventions, Federalists emphasized America's weakness. Oliver Ellsworth and John Randolph, opening the debates in Connecticut and Virginia, respectively, sketched a United States being swept away by foreign predators if a greater capacity for self-defense were not established. In New York, Robert Livingston argued that the mere existence of monarchism in Europe raised the specter of aggression. Thomas McKean of Pennsylvania defended the military clauses of the Constitution on the grounds that wars were inevitable and the United States could not stand defenseless. When critics suggested that republican pacifism would stave off conflicts, such doubters were told, as John Marshall put it in Virginia to Patrick Henry: "Look at history [and] human nature. They will tell you that a defenseless country cannot be secure. The nature of man forbids us to conclude that we are in no danger from war."[51] Throughout, the Federalists refused to budge from their view that the United States would rest secure under the Constitution.

The Federalists promoted their vision of a stronger United States in public statements and private correspondence. George Washington believed that the Constitution would help to keep the country out of foreign wars. If individual states were permitted to drift, they might tend to fall into alliances with Europeans out of self-interest. They would also quarrel among themselves and threaten anarchy in North America. James Wilson even argued that the United States would henceforth be invulnerable, although few could have taken such hyperbole seriously.[52]

The Federalists overstated the case, but they were engaged in advocacy, not dispassionate historical analysis. Their beliefs and their ambitions for their country intertwined in such a way, however, that separating the two is impossible. At the very least, the Federalists believed that the United States was vulnerable under the Articles of Confederation, that potential enemies existed, and that preparedness constituted deterrence. They knew that the Constitution would not institute national security by a wave of the legislative wand, but it would create the framework within which problems could be dealt with effectively.

And these Federalists did not fear that central control of the war powers would subvert their proposed government or prove a cause of conflict. Although they did not place reliance on this control alone, the republican myth of pacifism influenced their thought. The mere division of authority would deter adventurism on the part of the executive. John Dawson of Virginia, although generally skeptical about the Constitution, believed that the bane of the British system had been exorcised because Congress possessed the power to declare war and raise armies and the president only waged the conflict and negotiated peace. Others felt equally secure in this regard.[53] And from France, despite minor misgivings, Jefferson wrote that the Americans had created "one effectual check to the Dog of War by transferring the power of letting him loose from the Executive to the Legislative body, from those who are to spend to those who are to pay."[54]

A final word should come from the *Federalist Papers,* still the most coherent, comprehensive, sophisticated, and systematic presentation of the thought behind the Constitution. The war clauses received little specific attention, yet the American limited-war mentality poked through the analysis at several points. To begin with, the *Federalist* authors saw war as an inevitable aspect of the human condition. Men had a powerful impulse to quarrel, James Madison argued in Number Ten. John Jay believed that nations would wage war for real or imagined causes whenever they sniffed profit. For the cynical Hamilton, the "fiery and destructive passions of war reign in the human breast with much more powerful sway than the mild and beneficent sentiments of peace." Human emotions would override rational and moral considerations, even in republics, since they too were ruled by men. And only good faith, a frail reed, sustained treaties. Americans might themselves be moderate or unambitious, Hamilton concluded, but they could not count upon others to be the same.[55] Madison feared that Europe would prove a source of aggressors. If war erupted there, and "all the unruly passions attending it be let loose on the ocean, our escape from insults and depredations, not only on that element, but every part of the other bordering on it, will be truly miraculous."[56] This was prophecy arising from sound historical and political analysis. Precisely this would happen during the Napoleonic struggles, and Madison then, as president, would face the issue of war directly.

These statements suggest that the *Federalist* authors derived their definition of just wars partly from their republican ideology. Whenever the subject of war arose, these papers implied that aggression would come from without. Conflict erupted because of the ambitions and passions of others, and not because those forces were at work among Americans. Only Hamilton, with his dark pessimism about human nature, balanced this republican optimism and subjectivity. But he also noted that once nations went to war, pride and resentment could carry men to extremes to parry disgrace or avenge insults. The hope of restraint was there, but qualified by the *Federalist* authors' appreciation of human nature.[57]

Finally, the *Federalist Papers* discussed the topic of force and policy. Hamilton was emphatic on the point. Nations needed force to sustain their interests, and he went on to argue that the United States would be able to carve a niche for itself in the political corner of the Atlantic world by the judicious use of its slight strength. And he warned that countries must define their interests carefully and withstand popular pressures, which had even pushed monarchs into wars, "contrary to their inclination, and sometimes to the real interests of the state."[58] John Jay and James Madison both agreed that war was a necessary instrument for defense, and a defensive mentality did not contradict the notion of force and policy.

Madison launched a flight of rhetorical fancy in another direction. He foreshadowed a pamphlet he would write during the turbulent political partisanship of the early 1790s. If such a federal system as the Constitution embodied were adopted world-wide, he argued, it could lead to the "universal peace of mankind."[59] Madison combined the noble, even ethereal, hopes of the Enlightenment with his advocacy of the Constitution. He provided an example of how the Revolutionary generation mixed universalism and particularism in its political thought.

The Federalists thus expected that the Constitution would prove to be a catch-all solution to the problems of the Confederation period. The influence of the limited-war mentality shone through in the clauses concerning war and peace, and in the debates that preceded the implementation of the Constitution.

Now this mentality was truly part of the national doctrine, embedded in the fundamental institutional framework of the country. And the Constitution meant more than structure. It expressed the political and social ideology of the Revolutionary leaders. The republican myth on war led directly to the implication that all future American wars would be just because outsiders invariably would be the aggressors. There was no hint of the crusade in this attitude. Although this view had been present during the Revolution, it arose from the dynamism of war itself, with its pressures for conformity, and it arose too from the elemental passions which combat arouses among men. Withal, the limited-war mentality seems to have been an assumption, a near consensus among Revolutionary leaders. Given that the issue of foreign affairs played a role in the adoption of the Constitution, and given the close connection between foreign policy and the limited-war mentality, thought on war can be linked with the process of constitutional adoption, as well as formation.[60] It now remained to be seen what the Federalists would make of the Constitution, and how the limited-war mentality would shape their policies as they planned their country's future.

4

FEDERALISM, FORCE, AND POLICY

The Constitution centralized war powers in order to create a national monopoly of military force as an adjunct to diplomacy and domestic order. If policy-makers deemed it necessary, troops could be mobilized and funds voted to sustain a martial effort. The Revolutionary generation trusted to constitutional counterbalances to guard against executive adventurism. The limited-war mentality had now advanced from being a broad outlook to being a part of the organizational structure of the United States. And the concept of force and policy in particular came to dominate American foreign affairs in the 1790s, intertwining with the burgeoning nationalism of the Revolutionary generation and with the unforeseen and unsettling development of partisan politics in the first congresses. In the international world, the fury of the French Revolution compelled the Americans to look to all forms of defense as they struggled to maintain independence and national pride, even as they pursued neutrality and overseas economic interests.

As the Federalists and Jeffersonian-Republicans separated into opposing camps, they tended to form their own interpretation of the components of the limited-war mentality and how these should be applied in specific circumstances. The Federalist Party leaders proved more cynical about both human nature and world affairs than the Jeffersonian-Republicans. They were more conservative men, elitist in outlook, and thus they concentrated more heavily than the Jeffersonian-Republicans on the need for power and force to maintain domestic order and pursue foreign policy objectives. They became more quickly disillusioned with the idealistic liberal hopes of this age, especially when confronted with the excesses of the French Revolution. In reality, the Federalists and the Republicans walked two sides of the same street; viewing each other across common ground, they nevertheless had different perspectives, which caused them to lose sight of their shared reservoir of ideas. Gradually, each became convinced that the other conspired to drag the fragile United States into potentially disastrous alliances. Thus their mutual faith in the pacifism of republics waned because each side became convinced that it reflected true republicanism, which the other had betrayed.[1]

The French Revolution was the principal external propellant behind these partisan perspectives, apart from temperament and intellectual convictions. As the French transmogrified their constitutional revolution by turns into a brutal factional struggle for power, a vicious civil war, and a crusade against the monarchies of Europe, they confronted an alarmed and powerful Great Britain. When the two military giants of the age locked in combat, they generated waves of international pressure that threatened the United States. And the French Revolution wiped away the frail restraints of the limited-war mentality in Europe, producing conflicts on a scale and of a nature not seen since the Religious Wars of the sixteenth and seventeenth centuries. Intellectually, the Revolutionary generation stood outside this shift, uncertain and frightened that even partial involvement would suck its country in to destruction. This volatile situation continued for over twenty years, producing a series of crises — the Nootka Sound Affair of 1790, Edmond Genet's adventurism in 1793, an Anglo-American tension which ebbed and flooded from 1793 to 1815, and the Quasi-War with France from 1797-1801.[2] Europe and her politics, in short, remained a theater of war that perpetually placed national security and prosperity at hazard in the minds of all Americans, Federalists or Republicans.

The limited-war mentality led Americans to expect periodic conflicts, but not on such a scale, not of such intensity, and not of such duration. The dissenting Protestant tradition emphasized mankind's flawed nature, and this remained an important theme in American thought.[3] John Jay, for example, could only advance moral evil as an explanation for war-ravaged Europe.[4]

For James Madison, on the other hand, there were two sources of war — the will of governments and the will of societies. Believing in the pacifism of republics, Madison argued that a universal republican revolution would at least eliminate the will of governments. But for the will of society he had no solution, and concluded that a perpetual peace was a hopeless vision. And as Franco-American tensions degenerated into the Quasi-War in 1797, Thomas Jefferson wrote:

> In truth, I do not recollect in all the animal kingdom a single species but man which is eternally & systematically engaged in the destruction of its own species. What is called civilization seems to have no other effect on him than to teach him to pursue the principle of *bellum omnium in omnia* on a larger scale, & in place of the little contests of tribe against tribe, to engage all the quarters of the earth in the same work of destruction.[5]

Other Americans believed that national ambition would be a principal source of war. George Washington thought that countries would never cease meddling in one another's affairs. Representatives in Congress stated similar convictions on several occasions. Chauncey Goodrich of Connecticut observed that wars arose from the passions and animosities of nations, rather than from the maneuvering of foreign ministers, as critics of America's tiny diplomatic establishment had charged.[6]

In general, Americans expected that Europe would continue to be the principal source of war. "Sad realms of desolation," Timothy Dwight remarked, and John Jay wondered if providence had not deliberately made America an asylum for Europe's weary and war-ravaged population. John Adams concluded that any peace treaties made among Europeans could never be lasting,[7] and this conviction led many others in Congress to argue for a stronger defense establishment as a deterrent.[8] For the more cautious and conservative-minded, usually to be found in Federalist ranks, the belief in republican pacifism was all very well, and a policy of neutrality seemed most prudent, but the real protection would come from the reputation of military capacity.

Thus the Revolutionary generation became isolationists, but only if that term is defined as a commitment to neutrality in Europe's squabbles. Jefferson privately endorsed the wars of republican France against the monarchs of Europe, but wanted his own country to stay clear. So did Albert Gallatin, the Genevan who settled in America and who became Jefferson's economic adviser, House leader, and ultimately, secretary of the treasury after 1800.[9] At the same time, American politicians, whether they had mercantile constituencies or not, realized that overseas sales and the carrying trade would expand whenever Europeans fought. As during the colonial period, idealism and ideology, reinforced now by nationalism among the country's leaders, pushed in one direction; the profits that greased American economic wheels pulled in another.

Some Americans feared that this trade by itself would propel the country into war. Robert Goodloe Harper, an acid-tongued orator from South Carolina, noted that since Europe would spend from sixty to eighty percent of every decade at war, Americans must expect continuous pillaging of their commerce. The more conservative Federalists, especially those from maritime regions, argued for a navy to protect America's commerce. Republicans, on the other hand, were convinced that this would guarantee clashes with other powers. If an American naval vessel ever sought to defend Yankee merchantmen against an attack, Republicans believed that a descent into open war would be unstoppable.[10] But the Republicans discovered, often to their dismay, that the United States was an inevitable part of the international economic system and whatever vicissitudes political turmoil threw into its machinery. And the national pride spreading among Americans began to offset the fear of war. In the end, nationalism would prove the most potent acid for dissolving the objectivity of the limited-war mentality in American thought.

The interior frontier continued to provide specific potential sources of war. The Indians in the northwest seemed to menace until Anthony Wayne's victory broke their power in the Battle of Fallen Timbers in 1794. It remained an article of faith among Americans that the British and Spanish simultaneously pursued North American ambitions and exercised their hostility to the United States by using the Indians as proxies to contain American expansion. Further, Spanish control of the mouth of the Mississippi River at New Orleans rendered exports from the Ohio Valley uncertain. And the British held the Northwest Posts, most of which stood on New York's soil. As Federalist Indian and foreign policy unfolded in the early 1790s, partisanship became a complication. None disputed that the Indians, British, and Spanish constituted a danger, but there was disagreement over whether Federalist policies made war less, rather than more, certain.[11]

The alleged pro-British and pro-French leanings of the Federalists and Republicans heightened partisan suspicions. To be sure, adherence, or even deference, to either Britain or France in the atmosphere of the 1790s made enmity with the other nearly certain. Republicans became convinced that the Federalist submissiveness to Great Britain would evoke French retaliation. The Federalists, fearful of the emotional enthusiasm aroused by republican revolution in France, believed that even open sympathy with that country would arouse British antagonism. That would lead to assaults on American trade and pressure for an alliance with the French Jacobins, who fostered anarchy, obliterated private property and religion, and sought world domination. Both sides argued for neutrality, both sides had distorted perceptions, but because of rising partisanship both sides could not agree, despite their common ground.

Alexander Hamilton believed, for example, that during the Anglo-American tensions of 1793-94 over impressment and impounded vessels, the Republicans led by James Madison really wanted war with England. In 1799, on the other hand, Jefferson believed that the "Anglomen" and "monocrats" sought to maneuver John Adams into a war with France in order to loot the treasury through defense contracts and to subvert the Constitution. William Smith of South Carolina contradictorily opposed Madison's resolutions for commercial retaliation against the British in 1794 and supported measures against the French a few years later on the grounds that the opposition's policies would lead to war, whereas those enjoying his approbation would mean peace. John Adams observed in 1799, after suffering the factional ambitions and divisions of his own party, that politicians promoted peace or war simply to gain votes. Justice had little to do with the matter.[12] His bitterness was understandable, but he tended to confuse partisanship with cynicism. Throughout, both sides drew from the limited-war mentality, but came to opposite conclusions because men can honestly differ, and because partisan distinctions dictated opposing the adversary's point of view.

The possibility of civil war in the United States hovered in the background, seldom openly dangerous, but often in the minds of Americans, as a final source of conflict during the period of

Federalist dominance. The burgeoning western settlements became a ground for competition, even as the westerners themselves looked to the east for national policies to meet their specific needs. Rumors of separatist plots swirled in the politics of the early republic. Only the successful diplomacy of the Jefferson years defused frontier alarm over Spain's control of the Mississippi River and Spanish and British sponsorship of Indians in the wilderness.[13] In the latter case, the War of 1812 would insure American control over the frontier and its natives. In the end force and policy not only secured western territories, but also laid the foundations for further expansion to the Pacific Ocean.

The partisanship of the 1790s obscured the shared views of Federalists and Republicans on the origins of war as the decade passed. The Revolutionary generation persistently feared conspiracies by willful men bent on subverting government to their own purposes. Even the checks and balances of the Constitution did not lay such anxiety to rest. George Washington's integrity and incomparable national stature stemmed many doubts. But Jefferson came to believe that Hamilton was fundamentally a monarchist who exerted an unwholesome influence in the cabinet. This linked with a development in executive-congressional relations that has continued to modern times. Charles Pinckney, for example, argued that the Constitution clearly intended to disperse the war power to prevent corrupt individuals from commiting the country to conflict. Madison stressed the same idea in his "Helvidius" papers in 1793 and wrote to Jefferson during the Quasi-War that if the president were able to convince Congress that war was necessary, then a major safeguard of the Constitution had been erased.[14] Both Federalists and Republicans had similar views on this matter, but partisanship hid their common ground.

If the Revolutionary generation shared a view of the origins of war that partisanship obscured, the same can be said for the *jus ad bellum*. At times, Federalists and Republicans disagreed over the expediency of a resort to arms, but usually they denied that their opponents' arguments had any validity at all. This seems paradoxical since both drew arguments from the *jus ad bellum* to buttress their positions. But partisanship, and different perspectives on such concepts as national pride, rendered objective judgments impossible in the atmosphere of the 1790s.

The Indians Wars are a case in point. The status of the tribes was unclear because in one sense Americans approached the Indians as nations, but in other ways they did not. Members of Washington's administration believed that frontiersmen were just as much to blame for clashes in Indian-white relations as the Indians themselves, and Henry Knox, now Washington's secretary of war and responsible for dealing with the tribes, was preoccupied at times with his country's historical image. He believed that the United States had special obligations to be patient and fair with the natives because it was a more civilized power. Jefferson stated flatly that coercing the settlers would be "more just & less expensive" than subduing the Indians, mixing the *jus ad bellum* with fiscal prudence. Ultimately, the Federal government could not control the frontiersmen, whose views were reflected by such men as Andrew Jackson. Why should Congress negotiate with savages, Jackson inquired, since they honored neither treaties nor the law of nations? If Indians slaughtered settlers and refused to surrender those accused on demand, then the tribe should be punished. All became guilty of the original offense. For Jackson, as for most frontiersmen, to quibble about the justice of war against the Indians was absurd.[15]

The course of Indian relations reflected Jackson's view rather than the restraint of the *jus ad bellum*. American negotiators assumed that the Indians were a conquered people, since they had sided with the British during the War for Independence. For Indians, such a perspective seemed fantastic, and their views on land use and ownership rarely penetrated the minds of the whites who wrote up treaties and purchased territorial rights. When hostilities erupted on the northwestern frontier, Washington's administration adopted a subjective, national view and moved to a policy of limited military coercion. Forbearance had failed, and war was just. But the expeditions under Josiah Harmar and Arthur St. Clair came to grief. Now, wounded national pride reinforced frontier interests and converted coercion into conquest. Perhaps predictably, the embryo opposition in 1791 questioned this policy of war as unjust and wasteful. Besides, that policy threatened the future of republicanism by auguring a standing army and a national debt.[16]

Although Washington's administration faced opposition over its war policy, Jefferson argued that the United States could never accept the Ohio River as the country's western boundary. Negotiations had collapsed, and now that the people could see the futility of discussion, war could follow. Congressmen gasped when Henry Knox asserted that Americans here resembled the Spanish in their conquests of Central and South America. Congress passed bills for funds and troops, generally supporting Washington's policy of war. Ultimately, Anthony Wayne's careful preparations, rigid discipline, and military energies and ability vindicated this approach with a battlefield triumph. And Wayne not only defeated the Indians; he went on to thunder defiance at British Major William Campbell and his garrison in Fort Miami, one of the Northwest Posts still controlled by England. After Wayne's victory, calls arose for the immediate reduction of the military, but Federalists resisted, arguing that to return to a posture of weakness would only invite future aggression. Preparedness, on the other hand, would deter both the Indians and outsiders from attacking Americans and their interests.[17] In retrospect, politicians and most Americans accepted that the Indians' repudiation of American claims justified war, even as victory sanctioned conquest. Few questioned the dynamics of the situation. Territorial ambitions, nationalism among the country's leaders, and frontier incidents that cast the Indians in the role of aggressors had rendered the *jus ad bellum* a dead letter except as a rhetorical device.

This was not the case with the international crises which arose as a result of the French Revolution. Because of France's republicanism, Americans at first did not doubt the justice of her cause. But in time the Revolution changed. As the war in Europe expanded, Americans found themselves subjected to ever greater pressure on their commerce and growing sense of national pride. Seizures of ships, cargoes, and sailors were insults as well as financial losses. Both Federalists and Republicans were firmly committed to American independence and neutrality. But the Federalists, because of their greater conservatism, were quicker to become disillusioned over the fanatical enthusiasm that infected the French drive for republicanism. Their Republican counterparts retained faith in the essential benevolence of the French revolutionary leaders. Thus for them, France's cause seemed just, whereas for the Federalists it swiftly became unjust.

Foreign affairs thus contributed enormously to the growing partisan debate of the 1790s and both foreign and internal pressures combined to play upon the tenets of the limited-war mentality. Rational discussion dissolved into advocacy and suspicion, with both sides invoking the pieties of the *jus ad bellum* to fortify their arguments. The Constitution, which had been designed to assist policy-makers, proved of scant aid in these circumstances. To rely upon the will of the people seemed suitably republican, but since each side suspected the other of subversive intent, the people became objects of political competition instead of independent jurists.

A review of the principal foreign policy crises of the 1790s suggests how this process evolved in practice. The first jolt to American neutrality came with the Nootka Sound Affair in the spring and summer of 1790. Spanish officials had seized English traders attempting to penetrate the Pacific Northwest of America. England demanded restitution, reparation, and rights for trade, brandishing her fleets as a coercive buttress to her forceful diplomacy. Spain hesitated, but found that she was alone because France was convulsed by the Revolution. Distance separated Americans from rapid changes in the diplomatic situation, and Washington's cabinet gathered to debate contingencies, since the affair offered both opportunity and danger to the United States.

Reduced to its essentials, the crisis suggested the following. If France were to support Spain against England, the Franco-American treaties of 1778 might confront the American administration with the unpleasant prospect of either fighting the British or ignoring its treaty obligations, and thus risking moral opprobrium and possible French retaliation. On the other hand, Americans might use this incident to pry free navigation of the Mississippi River out of Spain as the price of American neutrality. Further, additional territory might be acquired, since the Spanish might sooner sell it to the United States than lose it by war to Great Britain. Finally, and to Washington's cabinet the most frightening possibility, the British, in the event of war, might march troops through American territory and conquer Spanish holdings in Louisiana. This raised the specter of British encirclement of the United States.[18]

The cabinet did not know that the Nootka Sound Affair would be blown away by diplomacy. But until this became clear, the arguments of the *jus ad bellum* wove in and out of the discussions. Jefferson was secretary of state by now, and he thought that it was only a matter of time before western settlers went to war to gain free navigation on the Mississippi River. When that happened, the United States could either agree to support such a fight as just, or risk western secession. At the same time, Jefferson would vote for war to prevent British encirclement, even if it meant entanglement in the European holocaust. In theory, Hamilton stood close to Jefferson, even though the two would disagree vehemently in debate. If England did march her troops across American lands without permission, then Hamilton argued for calling the legislature, seeking foreign alliances, and waging war against the British if they refused to accede to American demands to desist. Vice-president John Adams stood in the middle. He preferred negotiation regardless of what the British did.[19]

The cabinet was united in its commitment to American national security. Individually, all these men drew from the limited-war mentality. Jefferson and Hamilton had remarkably similar perspectives, despite their surface disputes, but they differed drastically in their views of England. Where Jefferson feared the British, Hamilton was merely inclined to be cautious. In the end, Spain capitulated to British demands. The danger of encirclement had been real, although the British would have assaulted Louisiana through a naval expedition to the Gulf of Mexico rather than mounting a risky overland trek. But even the latter would have been a "just" cause of war only if the Washington administration chose to view it that way. Subjectivity and partisan perspectives, as well as personal viewpoints and temperament, drew different conclusions from the same facts and selected different arguments from the same body of thought, the limited-war mentality. Despite this, the common themes of the *jus ad bellum* and the link between force and policy underlay the advocacy on both sides.

The same trends appeared in 1793 with the onset of full-scale war in Europe as the masters of the French Revolution used foreign conquest to employ armies and solve their financial and political problems. American leaders once again agreed on the policy of neutrality, but angrily debated specifics. This advocacy contributed to the rise of the first party system in the United States and once again both sides drew arguments from the limited-war mentality. And the views of government leaders were vastly complicated by popular enthusiasm in the country for France's cause. The gloss on the republican revolution in the former ally did not dull for most Americans until after the Quasi-War of 1797-1801.[20]

France's cause seemed justified almost by definition at first. Here was a blooming sister republic, jettisoning the shackles of monarchy and developing a written constitution. But when radicalism surged and the wrath of mass delusion seemed to turn against property, order, and religion, not to mention ostensibly innocent foreign nations, the Federalists drew back, appalled. And they feared that deluded popular ardor at home might plant the Jacobin weed in American soil. George Washington's initial sympathies for the French faded as he read the reports of the brilliant but biased Gouverneur Morris. And Robert Goodloe Harper summarized the view of many Federalists when he later commented that as long as the French had fought for their national independence, "every heart was with them." But when they embarked on an unjust war of aggression and conquest, true Americans abandoned them.[21] Harper did not speak for the Jeffersonian-Republicans, but he was right in the sense that no true American wanted to risk national security and independence for the sake of ideological solidarity with a European power.

The more trusting Republicans, both in the emerging congressional opposition and in the country at large, at first excused French excesses. James Madison thought that an "Anglican" party had arisen which sought to divert the United States from its proper links with France and liberty into the arms of Great Britain and monarchism. Popular presses, dominantly Republican, exploded into American politics along with a number of Republican societies in 1793. Their rhetoric threatened to overwhelm any rational judgment that might emerge from the tendencies of the limited-war mentality, which had arisen in response to the excesses of the Religious Wars, but could not stand against the power of crusading fanaticism.[22] This made the application of neutrality, upon which the Revolutionary generation agreed, doubly difficult, for few appreciated how different the wars of the French Revolution had become from America's own fight for independence.

Differences of opinion, betraying how the limited-war mentality could be subverted by subjectivity, emerged in Washington's cabinet. Privately, Jefferson hailed the French, but he argued that America must remain neutral. Washington's private views coincided closely with his neutrality, and he eventually concluded that France was an aggressor because she fought an offensive rather than a defensive war. Washington drew directly from the *jus ad bellum* for his reasoning. He agreed with Hamilton that France had broken the law of nations by encouraging insurrections in other countries and fraudulently claiming foreign territory. If the United States were too partial to France, this would give England a just cause of war. But Hamilton would have gone even further. If France ever violated American neutrality, the United States must demand reparations and could legally and morally resort to arms if they were refused.[23] Hamilton's conception of American neutrality favored benevolence toward Great Britain and coolness toward the former ally. Jefferson's view was directly opposite.

Regardless of perspective, all drew rhetoric and arguments from the *jus ad bellum*. In 1793, when Edmond Genet's scheming threatened American neutrality, Richard Henry Lee insisted that countries could only enter war for real injuries, and not out of a desire to help friends. John Jay made the same point in more formal legal language, but the Chittenden County Democratic-Republican Society in Vermont insisted that Britain had "wantonly plunged herself into a war in direct opposition to the cause of humanity." James Madison dismissed Hamilton's argument about distinguishing between offensive and defensive war as a foundation for legal and moral judgments. Who fired the first shot was the question, for on this ground, the cause for France was clearly just.[24] Ideological preferences strained at the leash of impartiality which the limited-war mentality had sought to attach to policy decisions. Each side tended to interpret the insistence of the other on legalism and prudence as partisan cant.

As events in Europe unfolded, and the Anglo-French clash spread into new-world theaters, tension that threatened open war developed between Britain and America in 1793 and 1794. The issue ceased to be academic, or a matter of personal preferences. Broadly speaking, memories of the Revolution, British retention of the Northwest Posts, a wide belief that the British incited the

Indians to attack American frontier settlers, and British seizures of American merchantmen, vessels, cargoes, and sailors in the West Indies combined to produce in the minds of most Americans the conviction that Great Britain was unremittingly hostile to the United States. The British seemingly assaulted liberty and republicanism on two fronts, and threatened America's national independence into the bargain. But would firmness produce war or peace? None could say with certainty. The limited-war mentality counselled restraint in the face of provocation and even attack. National pride, however, made many Americans impatient with restrained policies, and advocates in both partisan camps asserted that their schemes would avoid war.

As British pressure mounted, the members of the House of Representatives saw themselves at the center of responsibility because republican ideology vested war and peace powers in Congress. Federalists feared provoking Britain, and as a result opposed reprisals of any kind. But such Republicans as the fiery William Branch Giles of Virginia argued that the United States could retaliate if sufficiently injured. Richard Henry Lee, alarmed at the prospect of a second Anglo-American war, argued in terms reminiscent of the *jus ad bellum* as interpreted by Vattel and the other legists: "And if such proofs are produced of injury offered other Nations as a good & wise man would think deserved national vengeance, firm and Decent remonstrances accompanied by such proofs, if they failed of success, would put such offenders so palpably in the wrong as to justify the strongest measures on our part in the Judgment of Mankind."[25] This was the course most Americans wanted to follow. But emotional pressures of various kinds and intensities pushed them away from reasoned and restrained judgments.

Popular clamor and their own indignation notwithstanding, most Congressmen balked at direct action. The moral issue was not in doubt, even for Federalists. What did seem at stake was the country's very future. The logic of the *jus ad bellum* had to be linked with national self-interest. Most Americans feared that once they embarked on the path of reprisals, however limited, there would be no escape. A process of escalation would lead to open war.[26] America was still too weak, and any action would shatter neutrality, and perhaps the country's independent status. Even the leaders were not confident that violence could be restrained, once unleashed.

The limited-war mentality did provide maneuvering room, and the government and its advisers sought to exploit this. John Jay, for example, pointed out that Congress could consider many intermediate steps between peace and open war — remonstrance, demands for reparations, limited reprisals. If all this proved unavailing, the mere process would contribute to greater American unity once the government was forced to resort to arms. Hamilton's thought ran in a similar pattern, but he wanted military preparations to buttress diplomacy. A true practitioner of the limited-war mentality, Hamilton understood that the object of international traditions and conventions was to avoid war. The law of nations therefore required restraint.[27] In any event, diplomacy failed to gain much from Britain, but it did avert war. The price seemed high, because George Washington hesitated to approve the treaty John Jay sent back from England, fearful that the Senate would reject it. Although ominously divided, the Senate did pass Jay's Treaty. Jay himself, despite misgivings over what he had accomplished, had preserved peace and also had made a modest contribution to the progress so beloved of limited-war champions. He and the British established a mixed commission that functioned satisfactorily to arbitrate claims. This was positive evidence of the application of reason to international affairs, even if the accomplishment did become buried by the ensuing partisan avalanche.

Controversy over the justice of armed action occurred again when John Adams called for defense against French depredations in 1796 and 1797. Support for Adams's requests came not simply from rabid Federalists, but from many in Congress convinced that France had inflicted serious injuries on the United States. Partisanship notwithstanding, many congressmen combined neutrality and national pride, taking both seriously.[28] Some Republicans, however, saw French depredations as a just response to the offensive Jay Treaty and Adams's retaliatory measures as evidence of a conspiracy for war as Britain's ally. Adams, for his part, believed that the country had been both moderate and pacific. He wanted to settle Franco-American differences, but, as he said to Henry Knox, "old as I am, war is ... less dreadful than iniquity or deserved disgrace." Adams was a patriot for whom national self-interest included a difficult to measure, but nevertheless substantial, sense of national pride. As chief executive, Adams believed that he embodied this and could speak for the country. At the same time, he resisted those Federalists who sought open war with France, just as he opposed Republicans who tried to block or discredit any firm measures of defense. Thus Adams was closer to the impartiality recommended by the limited-war mentality than either the militant Federalists on the one hand or the Republicans on the other. He knew, as Jefferson so cogently expressed, that "the insults & injuries committed on us by both the belligerent parties, from the beginning of 1793 to this day, cannot now be wiped off by engaging in war with one of them."[29]

Jefferson raised, as Adams had in his own mind, the question of what precise difference war would make if it were not strictly limited to the objective of defense. Adams's message to Congress requesting defensive measures sketched an aggressive, truculent, and unrepentant France. And when the XYZ Affair became public, the militant Federalists pressed harder for open war, gleeful over Republican discomfort. Even the excuses manufactured by the Republican presses could not quiet popular indignation over the French request for a douceur. But moderate Federalists were content with limited action, consistent with the limited-war mentality. And Adams subsequently received a flood of petitions supporting his policy. The pulpit also expressed approval, shocked over ostensible French atheism. Jefferson mistook popular clamor as a cry for open war, but the public was generally satisfied to await developments from Adams's combination of diplomacy and defense.[30]

Republican partisanship had mingled with the forces of republican ideology, nationalism, and specific interests in national survival and the expansion of American trade during Washington's two administrations. Throughout, the American version of the limited-war mentality intertwined with the Revolutionary generation's attempt to define and pursue national self-interest. In Europe, restraint lay in tatters, shredded by the fury of the French Revolution and its military expression. Yet in America, because of the outlook of the Revolutionary generation and its dominance of policy from the struggle for independence down to the period immediately following the War of 1812, the limited-war mentality survived and remained influential. The American Revolution had put Americans and Europeans on

separate historical tracks, but the Revolutionary generation retained an essentially eighteenth-century outlook as it grappled
with the problems of national independence. The concept of force
as an instrument of state policy further underscores this argument.

The Federalists of the 1790s had a generally more conservative,
even pessimistic view of human nature and the affairs of states
than their Republican counterparts. Alexander Hamilton's perspective was typical, although notably incisive. The optimism of
republican ideology did not touch the Federalists as deeply as it
did the Jeffersonian-Republicans, and Federalists also became
more quickly disillusioned when faced with popular enthusiasms.[31] Federalists and Republicans never disputed whether force
could be used as an instrument of state policy. They debated
whether the circumstances of the moment warranted a resort to
arms. Thus the third major pillar of the limited-war mentality fell
prey to partisan perspectives also. And while Americans had
institutionalized facets of republican ideology and the limited-
war mentality in the Constitution of 1787, the president possessed
a powerful combination of military and diplomatic prerogatives
which gave him great initiative and wide discretion in foreign
affairs. The Constitution, as a compact ratified by the people, also
created circumstances whereby the people's representatives could
authorize a war for state policy on behalf of their constituents. But
as nationalism muddied the waters of the *jus ad bellum,* so
partisanship muddied the waters of congressional deliberations.
The use of force as an instrument of policy was less the product of
popular consensus than of legislative majorities. The Federalists,
elitist and conservative, had a plebiscitarian concept of democracy, and remained undisturbed about the corrupting influences
of power. Republicans, on the other hand, took a directly
opposite view since they were on the other side of the political
street and out of power as well.

The Revolutionary leaders agreed in theory that war was
perpetually likely, recognized specific threats, and shared a view
that some preparations for defense were needed, even during
peacetime. George Washington had long counselled military
autarky, arguing to Congress in 1793 that the United States
deserved a rank among nations which it would lose if it acquired a
reputation for weakness.[32] John Adams made the same point

when he became president. And Federalists in Congress promoted preparedness. Even though no one believed that the country should stand defenseless, these proposals ran afoul of the more pristine republican ideology of the Republican partisans. The differences were in emphasis and perspective, but this did not make them any the less real.[33] And it was only by exploiting a series of military and diplomatic crises that the Federalists were able to erect even a modest defense establishment.

The concept of force and policy linked these debates over specific problems as much as republican ideology and partisan rancor. Washington argued for war, tribute, or negotiation to pacify the Indians. Some doubted that bribery would prove effective, even though they opposed war on fiscal and ideological grounds. The same alternatives emerged in discussions about the Barbary states, still troublesome despite treaties and yearly tribute. As in the 1780s, congressmen and others debated the relative merits of throwing good money after bad or embarking on a policy of war. Although some believed that extensive commercial links would ultimately lead to peace, early American diplomacy usually tried to keep commercial and political affairs in separate compartments to avoid becoming entangled in European affairs. Lacking a navy, the United States could not do much about Algerian piracy and extortion, and what few ships existed, authorized to defend Mediterranean commerce during Washington's administration, were diverted by the demands of the Quasi-War. Jefferson still favored a policy of force, as did a Senate committee which probed the problem. American consuls in European and North African stations sent a stream of pleas to the State Department for naval vessels to coerce the pirates. When American frigates and supporting ships did venture into the Mediterranean as the Quasi-War died away, their commanders only echoed these entreaties.[34] Force was an instrument of policy to protect trading interests and uphold the national honor.

Attitudes toward Britain were similar, but different policies emerged because of Britain's immense power. During the Nootka Sound Affair, Hamilton's analysis of the issues confronting the United States constituted an extended essay wherein he cited Enlightenment writers at length to support his arguments. If the British violated American territory, then the United States could only choose between war or humiliation, and Hamilton saw the

84

former as the lesser evil. Jefferson agreed. If the British seemed about to seize Louisiana, the United States should fight to prevent it.[35] The national objectives here were territorial integrity and forestalling a British cordon around America's frontiers. Both Hamilton and Jefferson thought that national interests would warrant the use of force, if the country seemed pressed.

The point emerged again in the discussions over neutrality in 1793. Jefferson, Hamilton, and all agreed that it was necessary to keep out of the European political mire. War was not anyone's preferred policy. But this commitment to neutrality annoyed the French, whose government viewed the presidential proclamation of 22 April 1793 as a violation of the Treaty of 1778. Some French partisans in the United States believed that neutrality would assist France more than open collaboration, whereas others celebrated the Franco-American tie, condemned Washington's policy, and called for a republican crusade.[36]

This policy of restraint and prudence almost ran aground with the arrival of Edmond Genet, the misguided romantic who, as representative of the Girondist regime in France, exceeded his instructions and threatened to drag the Americans into conflict with both Spain and England. He commissioned privateers and concocted plans to launch frontier invasions of Spanish territory adjacent to the United States. He received such adulation from the American people that he made direct popular appeals instead of working through Washington's administration. He overplayed his cards so preposterously that even Jefferson and Madison abandoned him as a menace to Republicanism. Popular enthusiasm notwithstanding, no sane political leader saw profit for his country in a republican crusade. At the same time, the Americans discovered that to declare neutrality is not to guarantee it. Eventually, force must be used to remain at peace if belligerents in a world at war press a nation beyond physical and emotional endurance.[37]

The Genet episode suggests the growing national perspective engendered by independent republicanism in the United States. James Monroe, a vehement French partisan, wrote in retrospect that, although all Republicans wished France well, they never thought of fighting with her, despite Monroe's own biased behavior while in France.[38] The Republicans, like the Federalists, feared internal political anarchy, not to mention debt and a

loss of independence, as a part of the bill for participation in an
international republican war. When Americans tried to enlist on
French privateers or in Genet's expeditions, the administration
moved to stop them. Congress, not individual citizens, determined national policy on war. Popular opposition frequently
frustrated the efforts of the administration, but ultimately this did
not compromise Washington's policy of neutrality. In time, his
firmness, the good sense of his cabinet, a reaction to the mounting
excesses of the French Revolution, and the way such enthusiasms
have of running their course combined to render American
neutrality the most stringently defined and applied in history to
that time.[39] Americans remained true to the application of reason
and law to produce restraint, a policy founded on national
interests, and this reflected the underlying thrust of the limited-
war mentality.

In the Anglo-American crises of 1793 and 1794, Republicans
advocated a policy of force and Federalists sought to brake a
threatened slide toward war. Jefferson capsuled the broad national feeling when he stated that he wanted peace with honor.[40]
Unlike the Nootka Sound Affair, which never became more than
an alarming rumor, and the Genet Affair, which was handled
primarily by executive authority, the Anglo-American crisis was
protracted to the point where Congress became involved. As the
losses to the British mounted, Republicans called for retaliatory
embargoes, which most Federalists opposed as short-sighted and
perilously provocative. Some Federalists, on the other extreme,
stated that proposed economic measures were too feeble because
war already stared America in the face.[41] In truth, few understood
either the probable effects or the implications of the policies they
advocated or opposed.

Fearful of a clash, Congress moved toward a consensus for one
final diplomatic effort before confronting the unpalatable prospect of forceful retaliation. But few could decide whether firmness
would produce peace or war.[42] Given the uncertainties of human
behavior in stressful international situations, such questions are
always moot. But inflamed by partisanship and national indignation, many spoke as though they were ready to march to war,
even as they conceded that this could cost the United States more
than it would gain. And when they finally agreed on a policy of
further diplomacy, these men clearly understood that prepared-

ness, reprisals, and perhaps even a final petition still stood between themselves and open war, if John Jay's London mission failed.[43] When Jay's Treaty came, Washington's reservations yielded to his conviction that it at least sustained national self-respect.[44]

Partisanship blinded most Republicans to Jay's difficulties and accomplishments. Even after the treaty had been ratified, they still sounded as though they preferred war to peace, but this bluster was for the sake of party identification with the treaty, and not an expression of policy preference. In the midst of this storm, Washington's advice in his Farewell Address seemed a still small voice. If Americans avoided factionalism and maintained an efficient government, he stated, they would be able to defend their neutrality and "choose peace or war, as our interest, guided by justice, shall counsel." Washington presented here an enlightened eighteenth-century view. The practical interests of state and the idealism of impartial justice were to stand in balance when rulers chose peace or war. And in this statement, Washington spoke for the Revolutionary generation, partisan divisions notwithstanding. Despite his British inclinations, for example, Hamilton argued for preparedness in 1793 and 1794 and there is little reason to doubt that he would have supported a second Anglo-American war if in his judgment republicanism, national honor, and national security were imperilled.[45]

As the British crisis eased, American leaders slipped into a confrontation with France. The Directory, fighting for its political life and that of the French Revolution, embarked on a policy of pressure to force the United States into a more favorable neutrality without producing open war. In part because of sharp disagreement in Congress, John Adams responded cautiously at first, but eventually recommended and prosecuted a limited war of policy to defend American interests and honor. He stated the alternatives clearly to Elbridge Gerry, one of a new diplomatic team bound for France:

> If possible we shall certainly avoid war, but would a war with England be more comfortable to us than a war with France? If a war with France cannot be avoided but by an unjust and unnecessary war with England what would you say then? I would engage in a war with either or both together rather than prostrate our honour or surrender our Independence.[46]

Adams emphasized American interests — independence and national honor. Unfortunately, both were prey to subjective and even partisan interpretations.

The forces of restraint competed with those of escalation as the Quasi-War with France unfolded. The war faction of the Federalists exploited fears of a possible French invasion. Rumors swirled of French plans to liberate Canada from British rule and acquire Louisiana to resurrect a new-world empire. In 1797 the British seized arms bound for Vermont, ostensibly to equip the local militia, but apparently to be used in a scheme to republicanize Canada. The scheme was scotched, and John Adams believed that there was no chance of seeing a French army in America. The French had gone to Egypt and India, but Horatio Nelson's destruction of their fleet at Aboukir Bay in 1798, along with the collapse of the Egyptian adventure, rendered President Adams's judgment sounder than Timothy Pickering's nightmares. Adams chose a policy of limited war. A majority of moderates, including the war faction, voted the measures Adams recommended.[47] In any event, those who argued that firmness would compel France to see reason were correct. Limited war prevented open war. It was a middle policy between full-scale conflict and passive humiliation and loss.

Republicans heartened themselves with assurances that the American people did not want war. But the trend of events alarmed them, especially the Federalist willingness to grant President Adams a free hand. Jefferson feared that this would undermine the Constitution. He wanted Congress to adjourn so that, true to republicanism, representatives could take the pulse of their constituencies. Jefferson also knew that delay could bring a solution to the problem by shifts in European politics.[48] Some Republicans spied ideological bogeymen. Henry Tazewell, Senator from Virginia, wrote to Andrew Jackson that he would support a war to defend commerce were it not for those who would use it to "assist the triumph of Kings over France" and thus defeat republicanism everywhere. But President Adams stood between the militant Federalists on the one hand and such Republican opposition on the other. And he retained close control over the war by sustaining diplomatic probes through agents in Europe. The war atmosphere was real in the United States, and the militant Federalists were able to have the Alien and

Sedition Acts passed to root out disloyalty and the opposition.[49]
But they were unable to proceed further than this.

Adams followed closely both the spirit and the letter of the
limited-war mentality as the Revolutionary generation understood it. This meant that he also conformed closely to the tenets of
the Constitution. Internal politics in France, the French war with
England, the ambitions of Talleyrand and Napoleon, and the
likelihood of an Anglo-American alliance if the Quasi-War
escalated combined to convince the French to settle with the
United States.[50] The limited war of policy had been a success from
the American standpoint, and a failure from that of France.

Throughout the 1790s, American thought in this respect
remained consistent. Against Spain, for example, political leaders
linked force and policy to frustrate what they thought were
Spanish schemes to contain the United States. John Adams knew
of Spanish efforts to harass American surveyors, and his advisers,
Timothy Pickering and Rufus King, were certain that Louisiana
would be part of a new French empire in America. Pickering even
dabbled with the idea of an understanding with the British to
block French ambitions and seize the territory. And he thought
that if an open Franco-American war arose, or even if not, Spain's
link with France might justify seizure of Louisiana and West
Florida for the sake of American security. This dovetailed neatly
with Hamilton's caesarism and the dreams of such other American expansionists as King, the artist Jonathan Trumbull, and
those who assisted Francisco de Miranda's plots for a crusade of
republican liberty in Latin America.[51] Territorial ambitions
constituted a policy for some, and they were prepared to consider
war to achieve their dreams.

Even as the Quasi-War spluttered, there was still support for
military preparedness. Predictably, this support came from the
Federalists, and was opposed by Republicans, who argued from
the standpoint of fiscal restraint and ideology. Members of
Congress, not wanting to dismantle the American military and
naval apparatus utterly while peace with France remained
uncertain, pointed out that America needed some deterrent force
against future wars. Harrison Gray Otis, representing the maritime regions of Massachusetts, argued that overseas turmoil could
again threaten American interests. But the coming of peace and
the Republican electoral triumph of 1800 insured military

retrenchment. Throughout these debates, and partisanship not-withstanding, politicians clearly accepted that force was an instrument of American policy. As John Quincy Adams told Williams Vans Murray, who had been central in orchestrating peace with France, force was necessary in human affairs, and "whoever in this world does not choose to fight for his freedom, must turn Quaker or look out for a master."[52] The events of the 1790s had demonstrated that regardless of partisan persuasion, Americans would do neither.

The fourth pillar of the limited-war mentality, the *jus in bello*, permeated American thought during the Federalist decade as well. Control of war remained the objective, and Americans continued to include such clauses in treaties as the grace period for merchants if war erupted between the contracting parties, which reflected the thrust of enlightened bourgeois opinion. Some optimism existed that men would exercise greater control in the future. The Reverend John Kirkland noted in 1795, as war raged in Europe and threatened the United States, that Christianity had reduced the terrors of conflict. Madison, though arguing that universal peace might come from widespread republican revolutions, doubted the immediate prospects of either. And Jefferson observed that the age had made great progress toward a liberalized law of nations in recent times.[53] Here was American optimism taking heart from the urgings of the limited-war mentality.

The Revolutionary generation also believed in the morality of coercion and limited retaliation. Restricted reprisals did not constitute war in their view. Samuel Sewell, when introducing the Alien Enemies Act during the height of the Quasi-War, argued that seizure of enemy property was a form of "just retaliation" for losses.[54] This might seem sophistical under the circumstances, but Republicans argued that economic coercion would be an intervening step between war and peace. Madison and his supporters wanted commercial retaliation against Britain in 1793 and 1794. Both Washington and Adams utilized temporary embargoes. Many, including Republicans, defended Adams's selective embargo against the French as a proper buttress to naval action.[55] Throughout the Revolutionary generation, there was support for this variation on the theme of force as an instrument of policy. But on the whole, Republicans embraced the idea of economic coercion with more fervor than Federalists, who concluded that embargoes would do more damage than good.[56]

Throughout the 1790s, Americans were uncertain where restrained coercion would lead, despite their agreement that it could be applied. Self-interest can receive wildly distorted definitions during times of national stress. The sense of wounded pride can ignore rationalism. When Washington's policy of limited coercion against the Indians failed, for example, the persistence of the problem, the wasted funds, and a sense of pride combined to transform a punitive expedition into a war of conquest. On embargoes, Alexander Hamilton opposed commercial warfare on the grounds of self-interest, and out of fear that it would escalate into a military clash. When Madison wanted to sequester British debts as a form of retaliation, Hamilton retorted that "to begin with reprisals is to meet on the ground of war and puts the other party in a condition not to be able to recede without humiliation." Partisan differences notwithstanding, the point was well-taken. In 1798, John Quincy Adams did not know whether or not a full-scale war would develop out of the limited conflict with France. In all cases, adversaries argued back and forth whether more or less coercion would produce greater or lesser tendencies toward peace. William Giles of Virginia, who supported retaliation against Great Britain in 1794 as the surest road to peace and security, argued the reverse during the Quasi-War. Federalist Robert Goodloe Harper disagreed. "While we persist in this wise policy, of keeping the sword unsheathed in one hand and presenting the olive branch with the other, we shall be in no danger."[57] Harper overstated the case, but in the Quasi-War, his perception was accurate.

Americans struggled in the 1790s to maintain national independence when they lacked broad experience in foreign affairs. Republican ideology provided them with several guidelines, as did the limited-war mentality and what experience the Revolutionary leaders had acquired. But for the rest, it was a case of meeting crises as they arose, arguing policies, and probing for the desired results. In fairness, the whole issue of escalation of limited war is still very much open to question.

At the same time, Americans cherished restraint for its own sake. The settlement of 1800 with France was termed a convention to maintain the polite fiction that the peace had never really been broken. More than that, in 1798 Congress had rejected William Giles's contention that neutrality and war were the only available alternatives. John Rutledge of South Carolina distinguished between offensive and defensive war. And Harrison Gray Otis supported exempting Santo Domingo from the general embargo applied against France. "It is very possible," he stated, "to be at war with a nation, and yet at peace with a certain portion of its territory."[58] This judgment represented the practical advice of the limited-war mentality.

Insofar as such perspectives can be referred to a high judiciary, the Supreme Court agreed. In *Bas* v. *Tingy* of 1800, a prize case, it declared that war consisted of all authorized military action between two nations. But Chief Justice Samuel Chase also distinguished sharply between a declared, general conflict, which would fall under accepted international rules, and "*partial* war" which could be closely controlled by domestic legislation. Congress had never declared war on France "in general terms," although it had sanctioned hostilities on the high seas. And Justice Bushrod Washington thought that national conflict could be "limited as to places, persons, and things, and this is more properly termed imperfect war."[59]

The limited-war mentality, American policy objectives and ideology, the Anglo-American legal tradition, and the circumstances of the 1790s meshed more comfortably than the internal partisan rancor over foreign affairs suggests. Proper definitions of war were integral to the Revolutionary generation's understanding of the *jus ad bellum* and the link between coercion and state policy. On the whole, Americans believed that only sovereign authority — Congress as the embodiment of the people's will — could declare formal, open war. But the executive could use limited force with congressional approval. Throughout, Americans recoiled from the kind of war where wanton destruction of property, the slaughter of innocents, and political obliteration of the enemy were commonplace. Here American republican attitudes stood in sharp contrast to those of republican France. In Europe, republican ideologues were responsible for the death of the limited-war mentality; in America, they sustained it.

One example of this contrast lay in the Quasi-War. The Americans treated their prisoners well, working for formal exchanges. Naval captains in the West Indies tried to establish cartels with French authorities. But Thomas Truxtun of the United States frigate *Constellation* found the French dissembling and untrustworthy. The Americans were also scrupulous about insisting that only French armed vessels could be captured, even though the French had displayed no such restraint. Vessels ferrying French émigrés sailed under flags of truce, and all American commanders received strict injunctions that for the sake of national honor, no flag of truce must be violated.[60] The pulpit, a source of crusading rhetoric during the Revolution, endorsed John Adams's limited war. And Adams's own calls for days of "solemn humiliation, fasting, and prayer," reflected the Puritan strain in both Adams's and America's thought. It was a device to emphasize discipline and repentance, not a call for a crusade. Only small, isolated voices argued the contrary.[61]

By the same token, some Americans saw the war in Europe as new and unnatural. John Jay thought that it was "as unlike common wars as the great plague in London was unlike common sickness." The difference was not simply one of scale. Hamilton recoiled from what he saw as the French renunciation of Christianity and a relapse into barbarism. Timothy Pickering condemned France because she sought universal dominion and Robert Goodloe Harper saw the French seeking empire and pillaging and oppressing the countries they conquered under the banners of liberation. Republican Henry Tazewell saw a clash of ideologies where war would not cease until either monarchism or republicanism had been expunged from Europe.[62] Americans set themselves apart physically and intellectually from this Arma- geddon and kept their own dogs of war on a close leash. By their reactions, the Revolutionary generation suggested how much it remained within the limited-war mentality of the eighteenth century.

The Revolutionary generation had adopted the limited-war mentality as a national doctrine and applied it both consciously and unconsciously during the decade of Federalist dominance following ratification of the Constitution. At the same time, political leaders discovered new forces at work. Nationalism built upon common values, religion, language, institutions, and republicanism to introduce greater subjectivity into the applica- tion of the limited-war mentality to domestic or international crises.[63] Although partisanship dissolved the rough consensus on foreign policy and distorted interpretations of events, it could not destroy the consensus that the primary national interests were survival of the state, protection of commerce and territory, maintenance of national pride if faced with foreign insults, and neutrality in European affairs. A common commitment to the republic underlay sharp disagreement about specific policies.

The Constitution had not been a panacea for America's national problems in peace and war, nor in other matters. But the dedication, energy, and skill of the Federalists at least insured a stronger country, in reality and potential, than had existed at the close of the struggle for independence. And something of a special Federalist perspective emerged in their tendency to emphasize coercion as a fundamental instrument of state policy. No less committed to republicanism than their partisan opponents, the Federalists nevertheless were uneasy with democracy and did not fear that the use of power would lead automatically to corruption. They viewed themselves as the best men in society, and drawing from the eighteenth-century Anglo-American tradition of deferential politics, assumed that their policies would seem responsible and correct to the electorate, especially in foreign affairs. They advocated military preparedness more strenuously than Republicans and were likewise more willing to delegate power to the president to wield force and diplomacy in pursuit of national objectives. For them, constitutional checks and balances were sufficient safeguards against abuse. And they were confident that the use of force, the firm stand against threats or aggression, would deter future encroachments, although their arguments were often advocacy tailored to circumstances. The Federalists used both the rhetoric and the arguments of the limited-war mentality to pursue national objectives. But their Republican opponents thought the Federalists unwise, and even malevolent.

The Republicans consciously placed themselves on the opposite side of the street. They developed a different outlook which led them to argue for different applications of the tenets of the limited-war mentality. They were more willing to trust the masses and less willing to trust men in power. They did not fear popular enthusiasm and did not become disillusioned by witnessing the French Revolution. They feared rather that standing armies and navies would be too expensive for America's limited resources and a political danger because they would be under the control of an executive. But they also believed that passion and reason existed in man's makeup. They were nationalists if that is defined as a commitment to the United States, its values, its survival, and its prosperity. Republicans did not fear being firm in the face of national insults or losses any more than the Federalists did. They too advocated coercion. But they had greater confidence in economic retaliation as a step before resorting to armed force. The boycotts prior to the Revolution had damaged British merchants and even created pressure for removal of the parliamentary measures which had aroused colonial fears and ire. A humane instrument, economic coercion attacked pocketbooks. Reason would lead its victims to see that self-interest dictated moderation. Coupled with a willingness, but not eagerness, to use force, it therefore had become an important element in the evolving American attitude toward war.

Whether this tendency would develop along a track separate from, or merely intertwined with, other strands remained to be seen. In short, despite genuine distinctions between Federalists and Republicans, it may be misleading to insist on Federalist or Republican perspectives in considering the significance and ramifications of the limited-war mentality for Americans. The test must come from an examination of the Republicans in power. They discovered, for example, that there are important differences between reacting to and criticizing policies, and formulating them in response to external and internal crises. And there are differences between formal responsibility and leadership and merely giving voice to a loyal opposition from the corridors, rather than the council chambers of power.

The Republicans also confronted many of the same problems that had frustrated Federalists — territorial ambitions and economic interests; political partisanship; national pride; restive Indians; turbulent frontiersmen; sullen and hostile neighbors; and most important, a world at war. When the lull of the Peace of Amiens settled onto Europe, American difficulties eased. But Napoleon's relentless ambition soon propelled him back to the battlefields, creating an international environment even more treacherous than that which had existed in the 1790s. The Republican response to the resultant crises would expose whether there really were Federalist and Republican perspectives, or rather a complex web of American attitudes toward war from which any party in power could draw to understand and cope with national problems.

5

REPUBLICAN ALTERNATIVES
AND HALF-WAY PACIFISM

The two principal leaders of the Republican party were practical statesmen with strong ideological inclinations. Through the later 1790s, they had maintained that Republicans had a better grasp of American national interests and principles than the Federalists. When the Republicans came to power in 1800, they had the opportunity to demonstrate their understanding of national interests by operating from positions of authority and responsibility, instead of as partisan critics. Thomas Jefferson saw his election as a revolution to equal that of 1776, and in a sense he was correct. But continuity underlay the ostensibly radical shifts of office. The Federalists had defined goals of national independence in the international world through a policy of neutrality. The Republicans continued along the same path. The Federalists had sought to protect and expand American trade. So would the Republicans. The Federalists had defended national honor and occasionally had cast covetous eyes toward Spanish and British dominions in North America. The Republicans would do them one better in this regard. And the pressures of the Napoleonic Wars, which began in 1804, paralleled those of the European conflicts from 1793 to 1800.[1]

Although the Republican platform had criticized many Federalist policies and institutions, in time Republicans came to appreciate the wisdom and even the necessity of a national bank, increased taxation, and an augmented regular army and navy. Partisan rhetoric was one thing; national needs proved to be another. The broad outlines of republican ideology and the limited-war mentality remained common reservoirs from which both Federalists and Republicans drew. And the newer Federalist politicians adopted Republican techniques to overcome the liabilities of the narrow base of elitism and outmoded deference politics that had defeated their party in 1800 and which still characterized the outlook of the older leaders.[2]

Vestiges of the foreign orientation of the partisan camps, which had been a subject of vehement debate, remained. The Federalists viewed Great Britain as a bulwark against French tyranny, as fighting the battles of freedom. They also continued to urge that a close Anglo-American accord was vital for future American security and prosperity. But the Republicans no longer placed any faith in France as a counterweight to Britain, except in terms of the European balance of power. Jefferson and Madison understood Napoleon for what he was, an unscrupulous imperialist, a supreme egotist, and a ruthlessly ambitious tyrant. Despite Federalist accusations down to 1815, there is no evidence of an American subservience to French policies, although there is ample and convincing testimony of Republican suspicion, even hatred of Great Britain. Anglophobia, if not Francophilia, characterized the Republican attitude toward foreign policy.

Though a staunch partisan, Jefferson emphasized unity. He worked to establish Republican influence in the judiciary and neutralize the Federalist dominance of America's small civil service. He pursued frugality and reduced military expenditures by nearly two-thirds from 1800 to 1803. But this would have come even under continued Federalist rule with the demise of the Quasi-War. At the same time, the Republicans authorized the establishment of West Point military academy and maintained a core of regular troops and frigates, even while stressing the militia and gunboats as properly republican bastions of defense.[3] And Jefferson reflected the Republican view, as distinct from the Federalist, when he stated that "sound principles" would not justify taxing Americans to accumulate a war chest which might in itself constitute a temptation to fight. Besides, part of his personal philosophy emphasized that each generation should pay for its own wars, and not mortgage the future.[4]

The Federalists and Republicans shared a common view on the inevitability of war that did not shift noticeably in American thought throughout the era of the Revolutionary generation. As the fiercely Republican editor of the Philadelphia *Aurora,* William Duane, wrote in 1809: "It is vain that human wisdom exclaims against ambition, and that religion raises her bland and benevolent ethic, to stay the sword of rapacious avarice. The existence of the passions which produce war, leave no choice to the virtuous between passive subjection to every usurper or invader, and the resolution to resist them."[5] Faced with a trespass on national pride, Republicans would respond as Americans, not partisans. Others expressed similar views. When Colonel Jonathan Williams addressed the Military Philosophical Society, which had a prominent bipartisan patronage, he noted that preparedness would guard against other nations trying to plunder America's wealth. Members of Congress agreed. Without a reputation for strength and determination, Americans would be more frequently called to demonstrate their country's fitness to survive.[6]

Anglophobia was a prominent Republican theme. Jefferson, Madison, and others believed that Britain waited to avenge her humiliation of 1783, using Indian proxies to contain American frontier expansion in the meantime. Few appreciated that Indian hostility was natural, even inevitable, given local land hunger and arrogance toward the natives. Andrew Jackson, to take a militant but representative example, was certain that British agents stirred Creek resentment into open warfare, and he wanted this English incubus removed and the Creeks crushed. When he was secretary of state, James Madison sought official disavowals from the British government over frontier raids. Ministerial protestations of innocence were genuine, although old loyalists and new British officers stepped beyond their government's policies in supporting Indians in the northwest.[7] As a result of this contradiction, Americans would not be persuaded of British good will, and isolated clashes constantly threatened to erupt into international crises. The issue of free navigation on the Mississippi River and the troublesome Barbary pirates raised the same possibilities. In each of these instances the British seemed implicated. Many Americans believed that it was tacit British policy to persuade the pirates to plunder England's commercial rivals in the Mediterranean. And Anglo-Spanish connections seemed to represent another link in the chain of British hostility.

The Republicans held to eighteenth-century attitudes in their ideology and outlook toward European politics in general. This view contributed to a widening gulf between European and American attitudes toward war, as toward much else. When Napoleon chased his imperial dreams across Europe, Jefferson wanted the United States to remain an impartial observer. He and other Republicans did not entirely appreciate how the French Revolution, not to mention Napoleon himself, had transformed the nature of war in Europe. Warfare was once again a brutal, fundamental clash of peoples and nations, no longer a method of arbitrating restricted differences between governments or maintaining a delicate balance of political power. The Republicans consequently overestimated their ability to remain neutral, reassured by their ideology, their own liberal impartiality, and their reliance upon reason and the rule of law as engines of historical progress. When Madison excoriated Britain for relying upon power to enforce her arbitrary Rule of War of 1756, for example, he at once grasped the dynamics of Atlantic politics, yet exposed his naïvete by expecting the British ministry to rely upon courts and axioms rather than fleets and cannon to fend off Napoleon. Samuel Smith, a Baltimore merchant and a leading opponent of Madison's policies, observed with greater penetration that "the law of nations is with us, the law of power is against us."[8] Smith realized that legalism and moralism are straw houses in the hurricane of unlimited war and appreciated too that the United States could be exempt neither from historical forces nor from contemporary affairs.

The territorial ambitions of Americans, both Federalists and Republicans, complicated the issue of neutrality. The Republicans in power proved ardent for additional lands, even though this augured clashes with the nations that claimed them. When Jefferson secured Louisiana from France in the winter of 1803, he immediately turned his attention to the Floridas, still held by Spain. Madison proclaimed administration policy when he wrote that West Florida, from the Mississippi to the Perdido Rivers, was essential and East Florida, from the Perdido to the Atlantic Ocean, was important to American interests. The Republicans sought to acquire territory on the southern and western borders, fearing that in the turbulence of the European war these might pass to hostile powers, such as Britain or France. There was a strategic and ideological logic to this Republican ambition, but it was aggressive nevertheless. Jefferson and Madison inflated Louisiana's borders, dusted off old spoliation claims from the Quasi-War, insisted that Spain control the Indians within her territory, and talked vaguely about national boundaries in a manner Louis XIV would have appreciated. When the Spanish harassed American surveyors, Jefferson informed Congress, noting that although war was neither necessary nor probable, some use of force might be required if the Spanish did not desist.[9]

A liberal, humane spirit and a republican ideology did not prevent the Republican leadership from falling into the trap of national ambition and belligerence. In addition, the Americans had a heritage of anti-Spanish feeling which drew initially from the "Black Legend" of Spain's brutality in Central America and gained force with the imperial wars of the eighteenth century, America's prevailing Protestantism, and republicanism's contempt for monarchies. At the close of the Quasi-War, a few Federalists had schemed to liberate the Spanish-American dominions, but had not ventured beyond the talking stage. In 1800, Daniel Webster argued that America could seize Florida by force of arms, if necessary, to defend her interests (which he failed to spell out with any precision). Later, Aaron Burr's plot, while intertwined with Burr's own murky ambitions, attracted a scattering of recruits willing to follow a military adventurer against the tyranny of the Dons. Andrew Jackson told W. C. C. Claiborne of Louisiana that he hated the Spanish and "would delight to see Mexico reduced," although he refused to subscribe to treasonous conspiracies. Burr's expedition collapsed, but in 1806, a contingent of American volunteers sailed from New York to aid that indefatigable Venezuelan visionary, Francisco de Miranda. Jefferson's administration held Miranda at arm's length, but private citizens risked life, liberty, and health for his cause and the prospects of booty and adventure. Most of them wound up in Spanish prisons.[10]

This Republican belligerence was not Manifest Destiny. Jeffersonian expansionism arose largely from a concern for secure boundaries, and did not draw from Romantic nationalism and its mystical sense of future greatness. The practicality of the Republicans tempered their ideological convictions. Jefferson relied principally on diplomacy and exploiting European difficulties, but Madison pursued these territorial ambitions more vigorously. In 1810, arguing that he had no wish to provoke a clash, he averred that the United States could justly seize West Florida to prevent other powers from taking it. A mini-revolt by the sprinkling of American settlers there occurred with at least Madison's knowledge, and the president swiftly instigated a military occupation to safeguard national rights and interests.[11] When congressional Federalists protested that he had trampled on legislative prerogatives by so using his powers as to generate a possible war without the consent of Congress, Henry Clay dismissed such protests as inconsequential. Republican majorities swept aside Federalist arguments in a rush to pass sustaining legislation in secret session.[12] During the War of 1812, Madison made an unsuccessful bid for East Florida. The United States had to await the Transcontinental Treaty and 1821 before completing its control of territory around the eastern Gulf of Mexico.

The Republicans therefore encountered sources of danger and opportunity for their country similar to those the Federalists had confronted in the 1790s. And in some cases they responded more aggressively. Their attitude toward military preparedness was nevertheless markedly different. Heirs to English Whig republican thought, Jefferson and his party maintained an intense suspicion of standing forces. They relied instead for defense upon the ideologically and politically acceptable militia. The Republicans made only minimal additions to America's military establishment. Jefferson professed to Congress that he would suggest expansion if this seemed necessary, but combined army and navy expeditures went from $2 million in 1803 to only $4.75 million in 1808, even when many argued for military action if the embargo of 1807 failed to produce results. By 1811, on the eve of war with Britain, this spending totalled only $7.75 million.[13] The resentment of a minority of militants in the Republican party, the scare following the attack of HMS *Leopard* on the USS *Chesapeake,* and the incessant pressure from both Britain and France, could not shake the conservative Republicans out of their military lethargy. And they remained perpetually concerned about a political reaction to extra spending by Congress.

Thus when Republicans talked about preparedness, they said one thing and did another. Their ideological heritage and political qualms undermined both defense and foreign policy as a result. They tried the dangerous expedient of negotiating without military backing, became truculent and presented demands, still without making military preparations, and then wandered into an unsuccessful war. Only after 1815 would James Monroe's administration give serious attention to proper standing defenses, and even then, he would have to prod a balky Congress.[14] The Republicans believed that war was an instrument of national policy, but they differed from the Federalists in their reluctance to prepare for and execute it. This contradiction between assertion and action convinced both the British and the Federalists that the Republican administrations were not serious about going to war over impressment and the Orders in Council, even in 1811 and 1812.

Here was a genuine difference between Republicans and Federalists. Although they both understood the limited-war mentality in the same way, they did not apply its tenets identically. The Federalists feared neither standing armies nor debts, and while their arguments in Congress sprang from political motives, they reflected a different perspective of the relationship and application of force and national policy. If a standing military were not maintained, Harrison Gray Otis warned in 1800, the country would "incur the contempt of other nations," which would ignore treaty obligations "in the full confidence of impunity." In 1803, the Federalists tried to goad the administration into precipitate action over the Spanish closure of the Mississippi River the previous year. The Republicans rightly rejected these arguments as warmongering for political gain, but Gouverneur Morris presented the Federalist interpretation of force and policy. Power would produce both peace and security. Without the means of defense, the country might be conquered by the first enemy that came along. Morris was occasionally given to hyperbole, and that was partly the case here, along with partisanship. The Spanish threatened no conquest, but the point was clear. Congress authorized Jefferson to call upon the state governors for militia if the president thought that he needed armed force.[15]

The Republican attitude toward preparedness reveals a confused and even contradictory interpretation and application of the limited-war mentality. Interests, personal and partisan viewpoints, and fear of power and standing armies all intermingled with ideology. Although they defined America's interests in terms of their own ideological inclinations, the Republicans confronted the force of power in international politics, which limited their ability to obtain their policy objectives. In theory, Republicans agreed that they were protected against war if they were prepared to confront it, but they relied upon the militia and a full, or at least a balanced national bank account to provide deterrence. Since republicanism made them believe that their country would only fight defensive wars, these precautions seemed sufficient. For a time, the gap between their ideological expectations and the realities of international politics was not evident. But in a world at war, merely having the president's initiative balanced by congressional control over declaring war actually handicapped policy. The alternative was an overpowerful executive, which the Revolutionary generation had rejected in 1776 and banned in the Constitution. But Congress was too amorphous and fractious, even with strong executive leadership and party majorities. Although ideology helped the Republicans define national interests, it also crippled their abilities to apply force and policy to achieve them.[16] It was an insoluble dilemma; only a series of shocks could shake men with such a mind-set from a paralysis of their own design.

The issue of preparedness became more insistent after the *Chesapeake-Leopard* affair in June of 1807. This was one shock which created some militants in Congress. Jefferson's administration did not want to fight, and neither did the country at large, but the strident and unified response to this act of wanton arrogance brought the United States to the brink of open conflict. Jefferson embarked on a campaign of diplomacy and economic coercion that muted militancy because of public confidence in his leadership. At the same time, representatives from coastal regions scurried to complete fortifications, and by the time Congress assembled in the fall, the war fever had broken. Even a burgeoning militant faction, which shortly urged more forceful measures against Britain, was momentarily content to await the results of Jefferson's efforts. Republicans thought that economic coercion was a significant weapon. But it could fail, so some concluded that there should be simultaneous military preparations.[17] The absence of further British aggression calmed American fears. The *Leopard*'s commander had acted on his own, and

no. on orders from Adm. Berkeley

although squadrons of British warships hovered off American ports, they mounted no further assaults. Finally, Americans at large and Republicans in particular understood that both Britain and France sought to coerce the United States into at least a tacit alliance against their enemy. And for many Republicans, merely making military preparations could be a provocative act leading to more British belligerence, and from there to uncontrollable open war.[18] The shock of the attack on the *Chesapeake* was not sufficient by itself to shake Republicans into more active preparedness for applying force to national policy.

To some extent, the Republicans appeared to be pacifists because of their ideology. Assuming that monarchs were the primary source of war, and that if the people ruled, they would never fight except in self-defense, Republicans concluded that their political system would deter conflicts. This was not pacifism in the philosophic sense — an utter rejection of the use of force in any circumstances. Rather, it was a half-way pacifism, that overemphasized the moral distinctions between offensive and defensive war. It also feared the impact of war on republican societies. George Clinton of New York warned in 1803 that if the United States launched a premature attack on Spain over free navigation of the Mississippi River, it would bloat executive power, threaten republicanism, and transform America into an international brigand. James Jackson of Georgia voiced his conviction that "peace is the interest of all Republics and war their destruction." When a bill came before Congress in 1803 to grant Jefferson funds to purchase the land around New Orleans, the preamble stated that America's government was unique. Princes fought for glory, contrary to their subject's interests. In America, the people ruled, and the country went to war only for self-defense.[19]

Eventually, this view became part of the American war myth. It was only one interpretation, but it represented the majority party, and members of the administration believed in it. As republicanism and nationalism increasingly interwove in American thought, Americans automatically viewed their conflicts as justified because of their ideological persuasions. In addition, the core of the *jus ad bellum* was a definition of the unjust war, which was always aggressive. Just wars, on the other hand, were invariably fought in self-defense. America's republican ideology caused Americans to take an element of the limited-war mentality and establish it as national doctrine.

Congressional comments confirm this point. Republican Thomas Worthington of Ohio stated that although force could be used for self-defense, peace was "the soul of our Government." Philip Key, a leading Maryland Federalist, argued that standing forces, if used in offensive war, would doom republicanism.[20] Once again, Federalists and Republicans surveyed each other across shared ground, drawing from a common reservoir of thought, but placing diverging interpretations upon policies and actions because of their partisan differences. The mainstream Republicans had no monopoly on republican rhetoric. Federalists, insurgents such as John Randolph and his Quids, independents such as Matthew Lyon of Kentucky or Joseph Varnum of Massachusetts, as well as Jefferson and Madison themselves evoked republican half-way pacifism in their arguments.

The limited-war mentality of the Revolutionary generation comprised a set of cultural and moral inhibitions about the resort to force. Events prior to the War of 1812, a combination of politics and nationalism, weakened these intellectual and ideological barricades so that some would find war imperative for the future of republicanism, instead of a danger to its survival. The sense of wounded national honor touched deep wellsprings in the American consciousness, thereby broadening the impact of the militant faction. Even so, Federalists and many conservative Republicans opposed the war, convinced that it was aggressive — and hence immoral and unjust — and unnecessary.

Despite their half-way pacifism, the Republicans used force as an instrument of policy. In 1801, Jefferson decided to accept a challenge from Tripoli and wage war rather than pay additional tribute. He had long advocated action against the Barbary pirates, and as president had the power and resources to follow through. Critics protested that the cost of the war would exceed the value of the Mediterranean trade, but John Rutledge, Jr., voicing majority views, believed that the commerce of all citizens must be protected, regardless of the cost, for the national government to maintain respectability before its own people. National pride was at stake. Federalists used the same argument to urge action against the Spanish. Over the Spanish closing of the Mississippi in 1802, James Ross of Pennsylvania argued that Americans could use force to obtain redress "by the law of nature and nations," because this navigation was essential to the national existence.[21] And as the negotiations over the Louisiana Purchase revealed, Jefferson and Madison were willing to use force, but only after all other avenues had been closed to them.

Against the British, Republicans coupled force and policy in unmistakable terms. James Monroe, for example, thought peace was certainly desirable, but not if it sacrificed national honor. Even the pacific James Madison would only refrain from war until it compromised national pride. Fiery Andrew Jackson, on the other hand, exhorted his Tennessee militia commanders to be ready to "die in the last ditch" defending national rights and liberties.[22] Jackson had a flair for extravagant language, but the sober Senate resolved in 1806 that British actions were an "unprovoked aggression upon the property of the citizens of these United States, a violation of their neutral rights, and an encroachment upon their national independence." By the tenets of the *jus ad bellum,* all warranted a military response. Nationalism was bipartisan by the Jeffersonian era, and it had eroded Enlightenment objectivity about the use of force. Diverse elements, such as the "invisibles," led by Michael Leib and Samuel Smith in the Senate, and a young Vermont Federalist, James Elliot, all preferred war to national disgrace.[23]

When partisanship and hyperbole are boiled away from such statements, an irreducible residue of national pride and a willingness to choose war over humiliation remain. Increasingly, Republican policy sought to sustain national pride against foreign assault. In time this maintenance of pride outweighed protecting commerce for its own sake. The human side of impressment was never lost on the Republicans, but the sailors forced to work on British men-of-war constituted a symbol of violated national sovereignty that the nationalistic Republicans could not ignore. Party labels were torn off during the *Chesapeake-Leopard* affair. Militancy seized the frontier and seacoast from Maine to Georgia. Anti-British riots flared in Norfolk, the *Chesapeake*'s home port, and newspapers and public meetings alike breathed defiance. Jefferson commented that he had not witnessed such unity since the Battle of Lexington, and his policy sought redemption for the insult to national honor as well as assurances for the future. When diplomacy failed, the administration mustered economic forces behind its assertions, and many congressmen saw the embargo as a means to redeem national pride.[24]

Republican congressmen explained the embargo to their constituents. John Rhea of Tennessee thought that an immediate conflict would be an immense burden for Americans. If war did erupt, it must be made clear that the United States had been the injured party. Many of those who supported war in 1812 argued now for a firm stand while supporting the embargo as a defensive measure. Wilson Cary Nicholas, a close confidant of Jefferson's and a supporter of economic coercion, believed that if the embargo brought not redress but hardships for Americans, then the country would have to appeal to arms.[25]

As the sands of 1808 ran out, it became clear that the embargo would not work, and a faction of Republicans favoring the limited use of force coalesced. At this point, it seemed that war with one belligerent meant submission to the edicts of the other, even though Kentucky militant Richard M. Johnson saw only the British as enemies. In December 1808, Congress resolved that America could not submit to British or French edicts without surrendering national honor. In early 1809, during the debates over what was to become the Non-Intercourse Act, angry western and southern representatives combined with Senate "invisibles" to produce a powerful minority arguing for action. David R. Williams, a militant who remained so in 1812, capsuled their views. It would be better "to die in defence of the country than to live in bondage."[26]

Here was indignant, bruised patriotism seeking relief in a resort to arms, a clear example of why Republicans were at best half-way pacifists. Submission or a weak response to British aggression constituted disgrace. And some of these men saw the future of the Republican party, as well as republican America, tied up with what happened next. Representative John G. Jackson of Virginia, James Madison's brother-in-law and close political supporter, wrote that submitting would spark further outrages until the national spirit crumbled. Then Americans would turn to a Bonaparte or a Burr for rescue. In 1809 Wilson Cary Nicholas, who would later resign from Congress in frustration over continued reliance on economic coercion, wrote that the Republican party and national union were inextricably linked with the fate of the Madison administration.[27] So these nationalists rallied behind nonintercourse once their resolution to arm merchant vessels and issue letters of marque and reprisal failed. The militants of 1809 had pushed as far as they could. Jefferson remarked as he left the presidency that the embargo had been removed because it was costing far more than war. This suggested more forceful action to come, but Jefferson headed into retirement. His successor and close friend Madison played variations on the theme of economic coercion.[28] The militant Republican nationalists had some frustrating years ahead before sufficient pressure mounted to generate a policy of war to redress grievances against Britain.

The decision to wield force in support of American policy was slow in coming. Even during 1811-12, many Republicans were obviously reluctant belligerents. The vote favoring war was substantial, but far from overwhelming, and in the Senate, it was narrow indeed. This glacial advance to war has often puzzled historians, in part, because as the Federalists asked, what was so new in 1812? Impressment, illegal seizures, paper blockades, British and French arrogance, all had been gnawing at American dignity for some time. The war in Europe raged more furiously than ever, and Americans wanted entanglement in such a storm in 1812 no more than they had in 1793. This hesitance suggests that while real, indignant national honor had a high boiling point. But many factors combined to produce war in 1812 rather than in 1809, and Republicans tried many alternatives first. Even the militants of 1809 had asked for carefully defined and controlled employment of force in a manner reminiscent of John Adams's limited war of policy against France.

The nature of early nineteenth-century diplomacy and America's physical location provide one explanation for delay. A round trip between Washington and London could consume from six to ten weeks. Given the need for consultation between diplomats and their governments, despite the wide discretion customarily granted in instructions, further protraction was inevitable. Specifically, six months passed while Jefferson applied diplomacy following the *Chesapeake* attack and before Congress met to apply the embargo. Another fifteen months evaporated while Americans waited to see what results economic coercion would produce. Then, nonintercourse proved the only step acceptable to a congressional majority, and more time passed before the effects of this shift in tactics could be tallied. The false alarms of the Erskine Agreement of April 1809 and the fraudulent Cadore letter of 1810 occasioned still further delay.[29]

The Republican approach to diplomacy contributed to this delay. Actually, the Federalists would have adopted similar diplomatic strategies, if their behavior in the Anglo-American crisis of 1793 and 1794 provides any foundation for judgment. The Revolutionary generation shared the view that reason and law must replace violence as instruments of international affairs if human progress were to be furthered. The limited-war mentality from which both Federalists and Republicans drew offered many alternatives to open war that had to be exhausted before a government could justly resort to arms.[30] Jefferson and Madison also hoped that shifting political currents in Europe might halt the world war that had created their difficulties in the first place. And they knew that their country was unprepared and Congress unwilling to vote funds for military expansion that did not seem immediately necessary. If war came, the militia would provide a defense against initial assaults, and the army could be constructed to carry the conflict to the enemy in a second campaign. Such a strategy surrendered the initiative, but remained within Republican ideological guidelines. This was the fundamental Republican dilemma: Republicans would support a war if it came, but not until it came. Thus Jefferson and then Madison awaited the development of a rough congressional consensus, or at least majority, before urging particular actions.

The place of war in Republican ideology, indeed in American thought, has received little attention in the historiography. Jefferson and Madison believed that any decision to resort to arms should come from the people, up through their representatives, rather than flowing down from the executive. For a president to urge war too freely in the absence of a groundswell for action would be a capitulation to monarchical practices. The Republicans had opposed John Adams's policies on this ground and thus remained consistent with their ideology. Even though Jefferson was planning an embargo after the attack on the *Chesapeake*, he made it clear that Congress would decide what to do next. And Madison was equally scrupulous about treading on congressional prerogatives. He underscored this in much of his private correspondence. At the same time, he was willing to use force, but Congress must express a preference to employ it.[31] This was Republican half-way pacifism combined with the restraint of the limited-war mentality. It was to block, not accelerate, decisions to resort to force. And to some extent, this ideological reticence worked, although it naïvely assumed that others would accept American definitions of reason and self-interest.

The frustrations caused by all the delay without a settlement contributed to the eventual growth of a majority favoring war by the spring of 1812. The very Republican approach to war may, therefore, have helped to generate the popular support republican ideology deemed mandatory when the government considered resorting to arms. But in the short run, as James Monroe wrote in June 1812:

> the misfortune is that we have been so long dealing in the small way of embargoes, non-intercourse, and non-importation, with menaces of war, &C, that the British government has not believed us. Thus the argument of war . . . has not had its due weight. . . . We must actually get to war before the intention to make it will be credited either here or abroad.[32]

Still, the Republicans undercut the essential factor in linking force and state policy. The antagonist, to be deterred, must be convinced that the country will actually do what it says. The gap between executive assertions and congressional activity therefore eroded the effectiveness of both Jefferson's and Madison's diplomacy.

The *jus ad bellum* certainly played its part in delaying the advent of war. The just appeal to arms must be to redress profound injuries so that a government can take a moral stance and claim popular support. John Breckinridge of frontier Kentucky cited Emmerich de Vattel and urged adherence to the steps outlined by the law of nations before resorting to war over the Spanish closure of the Mississippi River, for example. Others echoed this view, for American faith in the law of nations was genuine. Both Noah Webster and James Madison wrote extended treatises rebutting England's adherence to the Rule of War of 1756, stressing how reason and humanity had softened the cruel impact of war on societies.[33] When congressmen moved toward the resort to arms in 1811 and 1812, they drew from a body of international law and from American thought to show that the

British had committed serious injuries, refused redress, and continued their arrogance and aggression. The Republicans used the *jus ad bellum* to place the decision for war in 1812 on solid and acceptable moral foundations. The very factors that explain the delay in the resort to arms explain also why Americans resorted to them at all. A long train of abuses permitted them to reconcile two ostensible opposites — violence and morality — in their attitudes toward the conduct of international affairs.

This reconciliation illustrates that Americans had absorbed a significant facet of the limited-war mentality. War and peace were on opposite ends of a continuum. Between these extremes, nations could employ various instruments of coercion to obtain their ambitions, redress their injuries, or defend their interests. Economic restrictions, sequestering of debts, private armed reprisals, limited reprisals by public vessels or troops, and limited offensive action were all permissible and coequal with diplomacy as methods of avoiding full-scale conflict. Some doubted that policies of force would deter further aggression, fearing rather that they might elicit retaliation.[34] There were no certainties, so men disagreed, usually along partisan lines. But the Republicans did not believe that such passive coercion as the embargo would provoke the British. The embargo was therefore an alternative to armed reprisals, but not an end in itself. And since the prescribed steps of diplomacy and petition had been followed to no avail, the resort to peaceful force had legal, moral, and ideological sanction.

Most scholars have viewed the embargo as Jefferson's personal weapon, although they usually make it clear that Madison was equally responsible for its adoption and implementation in 1807. And behind the Republican leaders lay the corpus of republican ideology. After the *Chesapeake* attack, Jefferson wanted to let Congress determine whether war or his form of peaceful coercion would better gain redress for national grievances. The embargo was not a terrapin policy except in Federalist cartoons, but was in fact one step along the continuum toward war. If it succeeded, then America could return to peace, but if it failed, then other methods would perforce be tried. In March of 1808, Jefferson agreed that war was widely preferred to continuous embargo. In May he reiterated this argument. By June war seemed close, but he would not release American vessels to face seizure without a policy permitting reprisal. In January of 1809 Madison thought that he detected a groundswell for war. He still hoped for a peaceful settlement, but an extra session of Congress would meet in May to adopt a policy of war if there was no change in America's foreign relations. Gallatin urged military prepara- tions, and as early as December of 1807 told Jefferson that he preferred war to permanent embargo. By February 1809, ex- hausted from trying to enforce the unenforceable on the American people, Gallatin reluctantly supported nonintercourse as the next step along the continuum to war. At least, he believed, the administration retained diplomatic flexibility.[35]

Although the embargo was a failure, some Republicans clung to it. Jefferson thought that republican patriotism would gener- ate the unity, discipline, self-sacrifice, and determination to transform the embargo into a successful instrument of policy, perhaps even a substitute for war with future applicability. Other nationalists agreed, and they, along with Jefferson and many Republicans, were bitterly disappointed when evasion, opposi- tion, and disunity proved the principal harvest from the long cultivation of self-abnegation. Perhaps most important, Jefferson provided little leadership during his last year in office, at a time when it was most needed. As 1808 wore on, revolt threatened Republican party unity. Henry Adams later sneered at Jefferson's so-called cowardice — by which Adams was unfair and ahistorical — but in retrospect Adams provided a perspective with which nationalistic Republicans would have agreed:

> If war made men brutal, at least it made them strong; it called out the qualities best fitted to survive in the struggle for existence. To risk life for one's country was no mean act. . . . War, with all its horrors, could purify as well as debase; it dealt with high motives and vast interests; taught courage, discipline, and stern sense of duty.[36]

Thus when war came in 1812, nationalistic Republicans would see a double purpose. Not only would war redress past injuries, but it would purge the humiliation of repeated failure.

Many Republicans agreed that the United States had received ample just cause of war, although opinions varied, at first. Willis Alston, for example, noted that nations could not consider every foreign outrage an act of war unless aggressors refused redress for injuries. On the other hand, Quid Richard Stanford wished the British driven out of North America. In his mind defense was an excuse for offensive action. Most Republicans sat behind the barricade of the embargo and avoided military preparations. But representatives from maritime regions were nervous, and called for naval expansion. Before dispersing in 1808, Congress did pass some military measures, but these were feeble. Republicans waited for another day to face war, momentarily content, but fearful for the future.[37]

By the fall, the Republicans were in confusion. Some argued for arming merchantmen in the expectation that when the embargo was removed, the ships would go out, be attacked, fight, and present the country with a *casus belli*. Others, like William Crawford of Georgia and Samuel Mitchell of New York, saw no middle ground between submission and war if the embargo were removed. When the Committee on Foreign Relations presented its report, it knew that Madison would be the next president. As chairman, George Campbell therefore reflected Madison's and Albert Gallatin's recommendations when he sketched the foundations for what later became the Non-Intercourse Act. War was the only "effectual mode" of resisting aggression, he noted. Since Congress could not repeal the embargo without taking some forward step, Campbell's committee recommended selected non-importation as a further buffer against war and avoiding submission to the belligerents.[38]

The committee did little to resolve congressional uncertainty. Nonimportation was, like the embargo, simultaneously a defensive and coercive measure. But it was not much of a step along the continuum from peace to war, and the militants began their revolt. Federalist Samuel Taggart thought that at this time a core of about thirty representatives favored full-scale war, which would involve campaigns against Britain. John Jackson of Virginia and John Taylor of South Carolina ventured that Canada would be ample compensation for America's unredressed injuries. Many balked at the prospect of their republic embarking on a war of conquest, and others such as Republican Matthew Lyon of Kentucky saw no virtue in dying for the country's honor. In company with other Republican moderates and Federalists, he helped defeat the Republican militant revolt.[39]

The militants tested the waters by having the initial resolution permit the president to arm merchantmen. This reflected the sequence of events Madison thought should unfold, suggesting that he was willing to support war if a congressional majority would agree on it. Madison wanted the embargo repealed, except against Britain and France. For the moment, he rejected the scheme of letting American vessels go out, be captured, and then using such seizures to justify war. But Wilson Cary Nicholas, John G. Jackson, and other militants were close political associates and confidants. Madison was probably prepared to accept a majority decision on limited defensive action. As a good republican he could do no less, for ideological and political reasons. The clause arming merchantmen was voted out, but Jackson moved to amend the final act so that the president would be authorized to seize Canadian territory and British vessels as prizes if England failed to withdraw the Orders in Council by a specified date. This proposal failed by a vote of 48 to 74. Nearly forty percent of those present were nevertheless willing to give President-elect Madison the power to present Britain with an ultimatum and wage a limited, offensive war if the British did not accede to American demands. Other 1809 militants tried alternative tactics, but these failed, and on 27 February, Republicans closed ranks and passed the Non-Intercourse Act by a two-to-one margin.[40]

The militant revolt was over, but the faction remained after the winter of 1809 and provided a core of agitation for more drastic measures against Britain until the final vote for war in June of 1812. The embargo and its successor, when added to the attack on the *Chesapeake,* constituted two more shocks which overcame the Republicans' half-way pacifism and helped to generate a congressional majority for war.

All Republicans agreed on the policy objectives as defined by Jefferson, and then Madison, as chief executives: an end to impressment, American exemption from the Orders in Council, and redress for past injuries (such as the *Chesapeake* losses) arising from Britain's maritime war against Napoleon. But Republicans clearly disagreed on how to achieve these objectives. And the sense of bruised national honor, reflecting a growing American nationalism, meant that whatever the British did, they would have to include some concession to American pride. The British eventually granted reparations for the *Chesapeake* affair. But they refused to settle on the other points, and remained arrogant. That only angered insulted patriots further, eventually eroded moderate strength and provided the final shocks that welded a Republican majority for a war of policy in 1812. But this took time, and moderates wanted to be certain that all peaceful alternatives had been tried in vain first. The moral restraints of Republican half-way pacifism remained strong.

The force and policy concept found overt expression against less formidable antagonists than Britain and France. The Republicans were not inhibited when it came to the Barbary pirates, for example, believing that the country had ample moral justification for a policy of war to protect trading interests in the Mediterranean. To be fair, Federalists thought so too, and as the Quasi-War had declined, America's naval commanders had received fresh orders to refit and proceed through the Straits of Gibraltar to protect Yankee traders. National interest and national pride dovetailed neatly, and the Barbary states were sufficiently weak to render a policy of force practical. So Jefferson picked up where John Adams had left off in this regard, and soon found himself waging a limited war of policy against Tripoli.[41]

Jefferson initially used his executive authority when he learned from the American consul in Tripoli, James Cathcart, that the Bashaw had broken the peace. He tried to isolate Tripoli by mollifying the other Barbary states, and at no point did Congress challenge his policy, even though the war lasted far longer than Jefferson had hoped. He underestimated the logistical difficulties of projecting even a small naval force so far from home, and he tried to fight as cheaply as possible. After some adventures — and misadventures — the navy vindicated his policy, and the treaty of 3 June 1805, while paying ransom for prisoners, stipulated no further tribute for the future. Republican applause drowned out the Federalists, who questioned why the war had taken so long and cost so much.[42]

The Republican majority in Congress understood what it was doing when it supported this limited war of policy. Legislation authorized Jefferson to order the navy to seize Tripolitan vessels and take all measures consistent with a state of war. Albert Gallatin devised a special Mediterranean fund, defrayed by the proceeds of a tax on salt, to sustain the twin policies of defense of trade and maintenance of American pride. And if James Field is correct in suggesting that behind such special interests lay an American belief that republicanism could be extended through the expansion of commerce, then war became a policy in support of ideological extension as well.[43] In this instance, Jefferson and the Republicans seemed more like than unlike the Federalists they replaced in power.

Secure boundaries constituted another policy objective which transferred to Republican keeping in 1800. Once again, Jefferson and his supporters implied or used force to add territory to the national domain. The Louisiana Purchase negotiations illustrate this point. Jefferson and Madison were alarmed to discover that France had coerced Spain into relinquishing title to Louisiana. Uncertain of Napoleon's intentions, but convinced that these included a resurrection of the Old French empire in North America, the administration initiated efforts to secure free navigation of the Mississippi River. At the same time, Jefferson hoped that he could persuade France to stay out of North America entirely. Spanish closure of the river by revoking the right of deposit supposedly guaranteed Americans by the Treaty of San Lorenzo in 1796 complicated the situation and added urgency to Jefferson's efforts. Westerners were outraged, the Federalists sought political capital from this incident, and Jefferson tried to transform the closure into a lever to assist his diplomacy with France.[44]

In Congress, Federalists called for a policy of force. James Ross of Pennsylvania argued that there was a just cause of war and that Congress must authorize vindication of the interests and honor of the country. His resolutions would have had the president seize New Orleans and other territory. Republicans easily defeated such efforts, pleading the need for restraint and arguing that if negotiation failed, then force could be employed to secure American interests and rights. Ultimately, a bill passed permitting Jefferson to call upon the state governors for 80,000 militia and accept volunteers, if he decided on military action.[45]

Meanwhile, Jefferson and Madison interwove the threat of war in their diplomacy with France. Jefferson was prepared to exchange American guarantees of Spanish territory west of the Mississippi River for Spanish cession of New Orleans and the eastern bank of the river to the Perdido, in West Florida. Robert Livingston and William Pinkney, the American ministers in Paris and Madrid, respectively, muttered darkly about a future conflict if American interests could not be insured by some such exchange. Jefferson pleaded with France that although he wanted to avoid war, the situation could slip out of his control. If France persisted in her reckless determination to keep Louisiana, war was inevitable, and America would perforce turn to an alliance with England.[46]

Henry Adams believed that Jefferson never intended to use force, but other scholars disagree. The evidence is clear that when James Monroe sailed to France to reinforce Livingston, he knew that the administration intended war if its diplomacy collapsed. In January 1803 Jefferson wrote Monroe that if the United States could not purchase a peace, "then as war cannot be distant, it behooves us immediately to be preparing for that course, without, however, hastening it." In April, Madison revealed the administration's plans in confidential instructions. France now held title to Louisiana. Free navigation on the Mississippi River was a vital American interest. If France refused to negotiate, and if Monroe and Livingston judged that she contemplated war or imperial projects which might threaten America, then the two diplomats were to sound out the British on a possible concert of policy, and even action. Jefferson and Madison did not say this lightly, nor were they bluffing. "The advantages to be derived from the cooperation of Great Britain . . . are too obvious and too important to be renounced," Madison related. Monroe was to keep America from too deep a commitment to Great Britain. Neither the president nor the secretary of state wanted his country so entangled that it would be compelled to take part in future conflicts where only British interests were at stake. The lesson of the French alliance was clear. But Monroe was to seek a military liaison rather than forfeit navigation of the Mississippi. The American agents could assume that war was inevitable and begin confidential talks with the British representative in Paris if the French were obdurate and denied American claims outright. And with these instructions, the American diplomats received letters of credence to British authorities.[47]

The picture of a republican America, with Thomas Jefferson, author of the Declaration of Independence, suggesting an alliance with monarchical Great Britain ruled by George III, is somewhat fantastic. But Jefferson's nationalism, his interpretation of America's vital interests, his fear of a dangerous potential neighbor, his concern for American political unity through the continued success of the Republican Party, his *Realpolitik*, and his suspicion on Napoleon — all of which he shared with Madison — combined to make this strange alliance a possibility. One cannot avoid pondering how Congress and the country might have reacted. The Federalists, advocates of a close Anglo-American accord and bitter about the recent Republican victory, would have been in an awkward position. The Republicans abhorred monarchism and had constructed a foreign policy around avoiding linkages with the British. But if advocated by a Republican president who enjoyed enormous prestige and the support of a unified party flushed with victory, a carefully limited alliance might well have been palatable. From a Federalist president, such a move would have been denounced as betrayal. Such speculation is idle, however, for Napoleon, discouraged by his fiasco in Haiti and marching to his personal drummer of destiny, sold all of Louisiana. After a brief hesitation, founded in constitutional scruples, Jefferson and Madison agreed to accept Napoleon's offer. The president boasted that his peaceful process had obtained what would otherwise have cost years of war with its accompanying lives and debt. In the euphoria of victory, one can forgive Jefferson his hyperbole. As Talleyrand termed it, Jefferson had struck a noble bargain, and he was fully aware of the fact.[48]

France had nominal title to Louisiana, but Spanish officials on the spot might balk about releasing the territory to American control. Force might still be required to consummate the deal. In the summer of 1803, with full cabinet support, Jefferson made military preparations. When Congress convened in the fall, it voted the funds to complete the transaction, and quickly passed other bills authorizing detachments of militia. Andrew Jackson exhorted his Tennessee troops to prepare to avenge national injuries, and young Henry Clay, chosen as a member of the Kentucky contingent, was delighted at the prospects of a military adventure and possible glory. He seemed almost disappointed when Louisiana fell peacefully under American control.[49]

In other ways too, the Republicans revealed that they adhered to the concept of force as an instrument of national policy. Jefferson and Madison continued to dally with schemes for annexing Spanish Florida, for example. Economic coercion was a variation on this theme, reflecting Republican ideals about attempting all peaceful measures before resorting to war. But as Virginia's William Burwell, a militant in 1811 and 1812, revealed, force was always in the minds of Republicans as the ultimate arbiter of Anglo-American differences if all else failed.

> It was by different means we should operate upon Great Britain and bring her to terms of justice; it would be by annoying her commerce with our privateers, expelling her from the continent and seizing upon her Canadian possessions, holding them as guarantees for indemnity, at a future pacification, by withholding provisions from her colonies in the West Indies, and raw materials from her manufacturers in Europe, and by forbidding consumption of her manufactures in this country, their most profitable market.[50]

This foreshadowed in broad terms the Republican approach to the War of 1812, even though it proved more difficult to apply force successfully than Burwell or others thought.

Thus American mercantilism, national interests, national ambitions, and American views of war combined to shape the contours of Republican foreign policy after 1800. Pacifism and Republicanism were superficially compatible companions, but underneath, the Republicans were always ready to move beyond restraint if vital interests were threatened. Nevertheless, Republicans believed that republics were inherently more peaceful than monarchies. When George Clinton of New York argued that nations were moral entities, he meant that their rulers should take moral factors into consideration in formulating policy. He reflected the way Americans wanted to think of themselves. But a growing nationalism created a gap between self-image and ambition and pride for country that made republican pacifism more mythological than real. A growing nationalism also strained at the moral barricades of the *jus ad bellum*. Throughout the Republican years, it was clear that war was a salve for wounded national honor, even though a breaking point was not reached in the minds of most Republicans until 1812. An old-fashioned Federalist like Timothy Pickering or a republican ideologue like John Randolph could not appreciate the power of a sense of national honor, but they were out of step with their times.[51] Pickering and Randolph reflected republican mythology about war. The march of events moved Republicans past mythology in practice, narrowing the ostensible gap between themselves and their Federalist predecessors in the application of the limited-war mentality to American affairs.

In 1811 and 1812, Madison's administration, sustained by congressional opinion, moved steadily toward a policy of force to settle Anglo-American differences. In 1809, Congress resolved overwhelmingly to support Madison in his squabble with the imperious "Copenhagen" Francis Jackson, "and to call into action the whole force of the nation if it should become necessary in consequence of the conduct of the Executive Government in this respect to repel such insults and to assert and maintain the rights, the honor, and the interests of the United States."[52] In February 1810, John Wayles Eppes, a Virginia militant who missed voting for war in 1812 only because he had tried to unseat John Randolph and failed, presented and then withdrew resolutions which again would have authorized Madison to wage a limited war of reprisal if the British did not accede to an American ultimatum. This was a shadow of the militant bid of 1809, but Senator Michael Leib, an "invisible" who opposed Madison's mild policies, made a similar attempt in the upper chamber in March 1810. Here, as a year earlier, Federalists combined with conservative Republicans to defeat such proposals, but a solid Republican majority nevertheless agreed that militia could be used outside the American borders, for it was now axiomatic that if war did come, the United States would attack Great Britain by way of Canada.[53]

By 1811 most Republicans were overcoming their ideological scruples about the use of force. Conservative Burwell Bassett noted that Americans would have to suffer the evils of war because it would be necessary to vindicate national interests and honor.[54] He reflected a growing trend among the moderate members of his party. So in the session of 1811-12, faced with continuing British obduracy and arrogance, exasperated Republican moderates and conservatives joined with their militant colleagues in sufficient numbers to adopt a policy of war in pursuit of national interests of redeeming wounded pride, sustaining a free and profitable commerce, and therefore preserving American independence.

After a decade of holding office, the Republicans were closer to the Federalists in their interpretation of the limited-war mentality than they would have admitted. Reality had overcome ideology, although partisan differences obscured that process. It therefore seems difficult to distinguish sharply between Federalist and Republican interpretations of the limited-war mentality. Certainly, Republicans had a deeper commitment to republican ideals than many Federalists, but both adopted similar courses of action in defending what they perceived as American national interests. A common nationalism insured a broad agreement, despite partisan criticism, about sustaining trade, defending the country, and maintaining national pride in the face of foreign insults and arrogance. All drew from the traditions of the law of nations, all agreed about the sources of war, and all used the rhetoric of the *jus ad bellum*. Restraint remained a watchword, even in the conflicts Americans waged during this time.[55] Republicans, like the Federalists before them, placed primary emphasis on national security in a threatening world, even though their political ideologies and styles in conducting foreign policy made them appear different. There was an American view of war after all, despite apparently divergent Federalist and Republican interpretations.

At the same time, hints arose that new perceptions could challenge the prevailing consensus of the limited-war mentality so cherished by the Revolutionary generation. Romantic nationalism emphasized self-righteousness which could sever the bonds of restraint so carefully established by humane and liberal thinkers in the eighteenth century. Nationalism led younger, more impatient politicians to confuse territorial ambitions with rights bestowed by nature. For example, Henry Clay from frontier Kentucky would have exploited alleged Spanish treaty violations as an excuse for seizing the Floridas. Clay also suggested Romantic nationalism in his reflections upon what a war between England and the United States would mean. It would encourage a "reproduction and cherishing of a martial spirit amongst us," but more importantly, "if we surrender without a struggle to maintain our rights, we forfeit the respect of the world, and what is infinitely worse, of ourselves."[56]

Most of the Revolutionary generation would agree with the second part of Clay's statement, but would be alarmed at the first. They viewed a resort to arms as a method of arbitrating international differences where diplomacy, entreaties, and ultimatums had failed to penetrate the arrogance of an aggressor. War was a limited instrument of state policy, in their view, and they believed that because of republican institutions the United States would avoid all save defensive struggles. Federalists and Repub-

licans alike drew from a common heritage, even though partisanship, the nature of the international crises they faced, and
whether they were in power or opposition frequently made it
seem that American views of war clashed. As the War of 1812
approached, it remained to be seen if the Revolutionary generation's ideals of restraint would prevail, or if the Romantic
nationalism of such men as Henry Clay would exert its influence
on the conduct of foreign and military affairs.

6

THE LIMITED WAR OF 1812

The Romantic nationalism exemplified by Henry Clay exerted a significant influence on United States foreign and military policy from 1811 to 1815. But the limited-war mentality of the Revolutionary generation remained the dominant guide for the use of force in world affairs. The War of 1812 was a limited war, despite contradictory currents and the dynamism that is inherent in all military conflict. To some extent, the War of 1812 marked a transition toward the newer, more forceful expressions of nationalism that would find later applicability in the Manifest Destiny movement and the Civil War. The Revolutionary generation was fast fading from prominence in national life, but it still held high office; the president was one of the principal architects of the Constitution of 1787.

British arrogance and disdain incensed and exasperated Americans, even while they disagreed about what to do. Many still viewed their venture in republicanism as an experiment, but by 1812 it was an experiment they did not want to fail. Federalists did not take this republican experiment quite so seriously as Republicans, and this, combined with convictions and partisanship, explains their opposition to the War of 1812. Further, they refused to believe that the Republicans would actually resort to force. They underestimated not only the power of nationalism in American life, but also James Madison's determination to achieve American policy objectives, as well as the way circumstances reinforced the arguments of the militants.

American opinion on the War of 1812 was divided and confused. Some Federalists supported military preparations and expansion of the navy after Madison called for preparedness in November 1811. In the House of Representatives, no Federalist would vote for war, but some in the Senate would. And a minority of Republicans in both houses broke with the party majority. The militants failed to convert all the moderates and conservatives, a failure that has made it difficult for historians to develop a convincing, all-embracing interpretation of the coming of the war. Moreover, economic interests, sectional loyalties, party discipline, nationalism, historical Anglophobia, and personal beliefs swirled together, at times within single personalities. The most persuasive interpretation seems rather old-fashioned. The majority vote for war stood upon a commitment to maritime issues rendered vital by a strong nationalism. This view is vague to the point where it nearly loses its utility as an explanatory device, but under the rubric of nationalism lay a commitment to the Republican party as the guardian of American republicanism. Thus partisan and national survival intertwined, linked in turn with American maritime grievances against Great Britain.

By the fall of 1811, many Americans believed that English insults constituted a just cause of war. With certain reservations, Madison concurred, and he planned a program of preparedness, diplomacy, and a resort to arms if the British would not redress past losses and exempt the United States from the Orders in Council and impressment.[1] He knew that Congress would be deeply divided, but called it together a month early to give more time for a consensus to emerge. His opening message stressed that humble petitions had been spurned. Therefore, "congress will feel the duty of putting the United States into an armor and an attitude demanded by the crisis, and corresponding with the national spirit and expectation."[2] Madison left the decision for war to Congress, realizing that it would likely take until the end of the session before a majority policy emerged. In the meantime, the British might yet relent, although Madison placed little faith in that possibility. A policy of coercion, he was clear, would have to arbitrate Anglo-American differences. In reaching this conclusion, Madison's mind had followed the guidelines of the limited-war mentality. The rational restraint of a Revolutionary leader still dominated policy-making in the United States.

At the same time, Madison was an indirect, rather than a forthright leader. Given his past performance, this November message seemed a cry for action. And it did carve a path for the militants. Combined with their energies and persuasive abilities, it showed the moderate and conservative Republicans the president's policy objectives and how he thought the country should achieve them. It embraced national honor because if the British settled on the Orders in Council and impressment, injured pride would heal and other matters could be dealt with in separate negotiations. And both Madison and James Monroe, by now secretary of state, stood convinced, as did the militants, that America's claims and ambitions were morally justified and realistic.[3] If the British refused to see reason, Madison and the militant Republicans had no qualms about pushing past diplomacy to war.

Most sections of the country smarted under British insults and understood the significance of maritime losses, but opinion varied on whether these were worth a war. To the business-minded New Englanders, aware that seizures in war and losses of trade would far exceed those occurring under the Orders in Council, hostilities seemed horrifying. Besides, many there believed that England stood in the front ranks of an Armageddon between civilization and Napoleonic barbarism. Republicans in New England, on the other hand, tended to side with the militants in Congress, while settlers in Michigan, Ohio, Tennessee, and Kentucky, strongly nationalistic, were genuinely outraged over impressment and Britain's efforts to shackle America's rights to free trade. Henry Clay reflected their views accurately.[4] South Carolina's militancy stemmed from the economic needs of foreign markets and a latent animus toward England dating from the patriot-loyalist clashes of the Revolution. In the far south and southwest, Georgia had ambitions for the Floridas. Settlers focused on local interests, such as control of Indian tribes, security of land claims, and free navigation of all rivers emptying into the Gulf of Mexico. Virginia was equally militant, but sheltered a minority of pacific Quids and Federalists, as did the Carolinas and Georgia.[5]

Other parts of the country were divided along partisan lines over the efficacy of war as an instrument of policy. New York's fourteen representatives voted eleven to three against war in June of 1812. The Clinton faction of Republicans, strongly opposed to Madison as well as Federalism, accounts for New York's opposition. Pennsylvania witnessed factional struggles within the Republican party, but the congressional delegation stood foursquare behind the drive for war. And Republicans throughout the United States argued for a more forceful policy. Submission would mean national degradation and political death to the party that permitted it. This raised the specter of a Federalist resurgence, with its intimations of a pro-British foreign policy and monarchical elitism. Elbridge Gerry of Massachusetts wrote to Madison that although the state Republicans had suffered in recent elections, "by war, we should be fortified, as by fire."[6] Despite divisions within the country, many would support a policy of war for a variety of reasons.

Congress reflected this diversity of local, state, and sectional views. Westerners and Southerners were militant; men from the Middle Atlantic states seemed ambivalent; and New Englanders were downright pacific, both skeptical and contemptuous of Madison and the militants. If a consensus outside New England existed in November 1811, it was for some stronger action than economic interdiction. Thus Madison's call for military preparedness reinforced the militants, who had been urging action for five years. Their greater, albeit not preponderant, strength, stood revealed in the election of Henry Clay as Speaker, and his subsequent appointment of leading militants, such as Felix Grundy, Langdon Cheves, John C. Calhoun, and Peter Porter, to the important committees. This did not mean that a decision for war had already been taken, but that Congress would face the issue squarely in contrast to past procrastination. Most Republicans had now shaken off the half-way pacifism of their republican ideology.

Many statements in debate reflected this transition. A Virginia resolution, for example, argued that since the British would not yield, the time had arrived when peace was disgraceful and war was honorable.[7] After consultation with James Monroe, Peter Porter reported for the House Foreign Relations Committee, perhaps the single most important group, next to the cabinet, for shaping American foreign policy in this period. Porter emphasized that "systematic aggression" undermined national independence. Americans must now submit or resist, for the "national character, misunderstood and traduced for a time by foreign and domestic enemies, should be vindicated." Porter knew that Madison would agree to war, provided a congressional majority would back him.[8]

The militants mounted their attack. Felix Grundy, for example, reminded the House that in 1808 the choice had lain among embargo, war, or submission. The embargo had been abandoned, and if Congress did not choose war, why, "I then say it with humiliation, produced by the degradation of my country, we have submitted." John C. Calhoun agreed, and Henry Clay summarized the issue as viewed by many Republicans by this time: "What are we not to lose by peace? — commerce, character, a nation's best treasure, honour!"[9]

This sense of national pride coupled easily with the principles of the *jus ad bellum* and specific national interests, not to mention partisan politics. These Republicans were serious, in part because their constituents were, but in part also because they thought of themselves as patriots. They assumed that their country would be acting in righteous self-defense. And older men, as well as the younger firebrands, seem to have feared that all they had struggled for through the agony of the Revolution and the uncertain times that followed might now be lost if a firm stand were not taken against Britain. The thesis of British hostility toward the United States had been a staple of Republican thought since the 1790s. Now, continued English arrogance and stubbornness born of the Napoleonic wars rendered such a view even more plausible.

The Federalists swam against an unbeatable tide. They remained largely silent from November 1811 to June 1812, hoping to shed their "Tory" image and playing to Madison's tune to try and expose what they thought was his hypocrisy about resorting to war. But with each bill, the Republican leadership repeated its case. The same arguments emerged again and again, with John C. Calhoun asserting on one occasion that a "war, just and necessary in its origin, wisely and vigorously carried on, and honourably terminated, would establish the integrity and prosperity of our country for centuries."[10] Such hyperbole cannot be taken at face value, yet it reflected the general mood of the militants and the Romantic nationalism that was coming to infect even the moderates as they marched together toward a war with Great Britain.

By June of 1812, Madison had every reason to believe that both Congress and the country would support a war. He interpreted the passage of tax measures as proof that the legislature was serious at last. The continuing silence of the Federalists contributed to underestimating the divisions in America over the issue, even though Clay told Monroe forthrightly that the president must ask for war, since a majority existed in Congress by March of 1812. Madison sent over a request for hostilities, buoyed by letters such as that from Captain Giles Kellogg: "We love peace, safety and our homes; but we prefer war with its calamities and privations, to the endurance of acknowledged injustice and wrongs, heaped upon us by foreign nations. We feel no ambition for foreign conquest."[11] Madison and Monroe felt precisely the same way.

There was little debate over the war bill. The Federalists were stunned and the militants saw no need to make a case they had been advancing for five years when they knew they had sufficient votes to win. Editorials in the *National Intelligencer,* many ghost-written by James Monroe, had intensified anti-British sentiment. On top of this, the alleged John Henry intrigue confirmed for many Republicans the depths of British perfidy. Actually, it did more to reveal the administration's gullibility. Henry and his accomplice, the fraudulent Comte de Crillon, bilked Madison and Monroe of $50,000 for papers of little value. But if Madison seems gullible in retrospect, he also seems determined to push on against the British. His call for a protective embargo was clearly a herald of imminent war. He thought that Britain had one more chance to settle, but did not expect that she would.[12]

Madison's war message of 1 June 1812 was a formal indictment of Great Britain in the court of world opinion. It demonstrated to a candid world the justice of America's cause much as the Declaration of Independence had justified secession from the British Empire in 1776. Great Britain was hostile to American independence and neutrality. All efforts at conciliation through diplomacy had been arrogantly rebuffed. British cruisers still harassed American commerce and coasts. Paper blockades assaulted the economy and impressment defied the law of nations. In addition, the British incited the Indians to savage warfare on the frontiers, thus violating the canons of civilization itself. As the Constitution directed, the legislature must now decide on using force and "commit a just cause into the hands of the Almighty Disposer of Events."[13] Madison freely employed the rhetoric and arguments of the *jus ad bellum*. His rationale for war lay in national pride and interests.

The war message went to John C. Calhoun's Foreign Relations Committee, which reported before a closed-door session of the House. Calhoun's committee approved of war. He drew a parallel with the Revolution. Then, there had been a British conspiracy against the people's liberty. Now, there was a British conspiracy against American independence. The House quickly passed a declaration of war, in which the Senate concurred, albeit after lengthier deliberation. Then the Senate asked the president to declare a day of fasting, humiliation, and prayer, since the country had been "compelled to resort to arms for the main-tenance and protection of those rights which have been achieved by the blood of their fathers."[14] The eighteenth-century character of the War of 1812 was clear.

This patriotic and formal veneer could not conceal the partisan core of the decision for war. Federalists, with a few exceptions, were steadfast in their opposition, once they recovered from the shock of the declaration. And Federalism was the principal force that made this conflict highly unpopular.[15] Privately, some wondered if the country would not be better off at war, which might prove less destructive than continuing economic restric-tions. But Rufus King reflected the broad view. This was not a national war, but a partisan one.[16] New Englanders adopted the role of conscientious objectors, denying that the war was just or prudent. This reflected the historical subjectivity of the *jus ad bellum*. In the end, partisanship rendered it ineffectual as a national criterion for judging when to resort to arms.

These partisan-regional divisions were by no means tidy. The war stirred national feelings among many Federalists. John Adams could not understand how a "rational, a social, or a moral creature can say that the war is unjust." Other Federalists accepted military commissions, and New England provided several regi-ments in the newly-raised American army. In the Senate, Charles Cutts, John Smith, and Joseph Varnum had voted with the Republican majority. Varnum later defended his decision against a detractor, arguing that Madison had done his best, but the situation had become critical. It was fight or surrender national

rights. Even Rufus King, after the invasion and burning of
Washington, D.C. in August of 1814, became a supporter of the
war and thought that the United States must now achieve a peace
consistent with its national rights.[17]

Republicans betrayed similar disagreements. Matthew Lyon of
Kentucky, admittedly something of a maverick of long standing,
had frequently criticized Republican foreign policy. Drifting
outside the party mainstream, he condemned the war because in
his view the militants sought only the conquest of Canada. Quids
John Randolph and Richard Stanford agreed. Randolph lectured
the House interminably about this war "of conquest, or aggran-
dizement, or ambition; a war foreign to the interest of this
country, to the interests of humanity itself." Randolph's republicanism was pure, and for him, even a trace of aggressiveness
sullied the country's reputation. Hugh Nelson, although he had
voted for war, feared that the lure of martial glory would subvert
republican simplicity and independence.[18] But such disclaimers
were few. For the most part, Republicans closed ranks and
sustained the war against Great Britain, despite the disappoint-
ments of the campaigns against Canada and the British control of
America's coastline.

The opposition remained strong and vocal throughout the
conflict. Nationalistic pressures for conformity existed, but could
not silence doubters and partisan critics. In Virginia the Quids
and some tidewater conservatives, along with local Federalists,
thought that the war would ruin the country's economy and
ideology. Others feared the damage from potential coastal raids
and slave uprisings. In Savannah, Georgia, Federalist editors who
spoke against the war were shouted down and intimidated, but
pockets of dissent punctuated North Carolina despite hostile
receptions. And Republican majorities in Vermont could not
eliminate an ambiguity arising from profitable trading with the
enemy in Canada. Finally, small groups of pacifists remained true
to their consciences and refused categorically any support for the
war effort.[19]

Dissenters drew from the same limited-war mentality as the
supporters of the conflict with Britain. In the case of New York
merchants who petitioned for continued embargo or nonimportation instead of war, economic interests were also evident. But
the Massachusetts legislature declared that the war was unjust

because it was aggressive and not defensive.[20] Both sides in this debate were heirs to eighteenth-century republicanism, and both saw themselves acting in the national interest, despite their partisan and ideological motivation. Their arguments reflected genuine convictions about the nature of their government and society, and their fears for its future.

The Federalist case found a typical expression in an editorial over the signature of Samuel Taggart. He argued that the war was unnecessary and impolitic, and aggressive because America planned invasion. Even if Canada could be conquered, this would not guarantee freedom of the seas or compensate for past seizures. Besides, the American coasts lay naked before Britain's naval might. National honor was not such a weighty thing, in Taggart's view, and if the country persisted in this course, it might lose everything except its honor before the struggle ended. Thirty-four sitting Federalists subsequently signed a minority report that constituted the official party perspective. Josiah Quincy wrote it, and he attacked what he saw as clandestine government ambition that threatened to plunge the country into the European maelstrom. And he echoed Taggart on the question of Canada, which would do nothing for either maritime rights or national honor.[21]

The Federalists discovered that it was too late to influence national policy. The Republicans were in control, and the opposition had kept secret counsel too long. By speaking out now, they appeared less as a responsible opposition than as exponents of treason. But in their speeches and letters, the Federalists revealed that they remained within the mainstream of the Revolutionary generation's interpretation of the limited-war mentality. In January 1813, Elijah Brigham of Massachusetts called the struggle a "war of conquest, totally inconsistent with the spirit and genius of our Constitution. . . . Republics, sir, ought never to be engaged in a foreign, offensive war; They are calculated only for defensive war." Others argued that those who supported foreign conquest under the banner of liberation were dissemblers at best. Some were bitter. Josiah Quincy, for example, likened Madison to an irresponsible monarch, distracting the people from the poverty of his leadership with the baubles of martial glory.[22]

The Federalist charges acquired greater credence when news arrived that the British had withdrawn the Orders in Council, and when the Canadian campaigns collapsed. The cause for war had vanished, and the administration should abandon the offensive. When Republicans called for larger bounties to entice volunteers, Cyrus King mocked them, and Samuel Shipherd of New York advanced a near pacifist argument. He denied that dissent meant treason. Individuals could determine the justice of a government's call to war on their own, for "the power to drag forth the Reluctant unconsenting citizen to a war of conquest is wholly inconsistent with the principles of civil and religious liberty." America's existence, her happiness, liberty, independence, and prosperity were not in peril, so this war was unjust. And to fight for principles was sheer folly, because win or lose, it made no difference. War was a trial of strength, so victory could not prove righteousness.[23] Apart from its partisan perspective, and assuming a leavening of personal conscience in such remarks, Shipherd was clearly some distance from the Romantic nationalist perspective of the Republican militants.

The Federalist assault may have made some Republicans squirm, but it did not dampen their support for the war effort. Madison won handily in the elections of 1812, which must be taken as a mandate and referendum combined for his foreign policy, as well as his record, Republican dominance notwithstanding. Quid John Randolph suffered the only defeat in his electoral career because of his opposition to the administration. Republicans also revealed that republicanism and American nationalism were intrinsically linked in their thought. Israel Pickens of North Carolina wrote to his constituents that the government approached a trial to determine if a republican society could preserve itself. And Hugh Nelson of Virginia stated that the war was to "shew that our republican government was competent to assert its rights, to maintain the interests of the people, and to repel foreign aggression." In 1814, following the British assault on Washington, D.C., even Federalists came to share this view. The Hartford Convention, infamous to some because of its implications of secession, focused upon regional defense since those New England moderates who dominated the proceedings believed that the states had been largely abandoned by the Federal government.[24] As the war's gloomiest hours approached, Americans tended to pull together despite partisan differences.

The principal pillar of the Federalist argument that the Madison administration had embarked upon an unjust war lay in the apparent Republican eagerness to invade Canada. And for some time following Julius Pratt's research, historians were inclined to accept this charge. Madison and Monroe clearly coveted Spanish territory, and a few hundred American volunteers crossed into Texas between 1810 and 1814 to aid early revolts against Spanish authority. The beaten survivors trickled back across the border in each case. The administration was aware of their actions, yet did nothing to discourage them. American troops briefly occupied Amelia Island, along the Florida-Georgia border, and even managed a skirmish with Spanish forces in 1812 before being pulled back because of the impending Anglo-American war. Suggesting Pratt's conspiracy thesis, Felix Grundy felt "anxious not only to add the Floridas to the South, but the Canadas to the North of this empire." To John A. Harper, it seemed that "the Author of Nature has marked our limits in the south, by the Gulf of Mexico; and on the north, by the regions of eternal frost." Zealous Republicans often sounded as though the expeditions to Canada sought only conquest, and William Bradley of Vermont boasted that this was one of the objectives of his constituents.[25] Superficially, there seems a case for the Federalist assertions.

Further evidence can be mustered to suggest a blossoming Manifest Destiny among Republicans. In late June 1812, Congress resolved that the president be empowered to tell Canadians that they would have all the rights and liberties of Americans if any of their territory became a permanent part of the United States as a result of the war. When General William Hull led his army across the Detroit River in July, his bombastic proclamation suggested a symbolic replay of the alleged liberation of the revolutionary invasion of 1775. Hull later surrendered Detroit to an inferior Canadian force, and in Madison's instructions to his successor as commander on the northern frontier, the principal disclaimer to the Federalist thesis arises. Henry Dearborn read over Madison's signature that the Americans must take and hold Canada as a "hostage for peace and justice."[26]

The administration did not mean that Canada was to be held
forever. Madison and Monroe waged a limited war in 1812 to
redress American grievances. It is here that the case for Manifest
Destiny begins to break down. In addition, once news that the
British had withdrawn the Orders in Council as they had applied
to the United States reached Madison, he offered to stop fighting if
the British would accept his position on impressment. But the
ministry refused, so the war continued. Madison and Monroe
rejected a cease-fire offer from the governor of Canada. He did not
speak for his government and the Americans concluded that a
truce could only work to the advantage of Britain by removing the
one point of pressure the United States could apply. Besides, the
governor said nothing about impressment, now the central reason
for the continuation of hostilities.[27]

The invasion of Canada was retaliation for past injuries and a
lever to gain concessions the administration desired. Even though
Monroe's early messages to the American agents sent to Europe to
negotiate with the British hinted that no peace settlement would
be durable without a complete withdrawal of the British from
North America, by the time discussion commenced at Ghent,
Belgium, the administration was content simply to stop the war.
John Quincy Adams and the other agents denied that Canada had
ever been an objective of the fighting. Only the maritime issues,
reduced now to impressment, stood between continued conflict
and renewed Anglo-American harmony.[28] Henry Clay summarized the majority view in Congress: "In making the war effective,
conquest may become necessary; but this does not change the
character of the war; there may be no other way of operating upon
our enemy but by taking possession of her provinces, which
adjoin us."[29]

One could argue that this was sophistry to mask ambition, but
if so, other militant Republicans adopted a similar guise of
innocence. Some were undoubtedly prepared to argue for keeping
Canada if it fell to American arms. But in January 1814 Perry
Humphreys suggested the perspective of the administration, and
probably a majority of Republicans:

The war was commenced for the defence of American rights, of
property, persons, and principles; in the prosecution of the war every
act may be considered as defensive, which will conduce to the
attainment of the objects for which hostilities were commenced. The

conquest of Canada, and the expulsion of the English power from the American continent, would operate most powerfully in depriving the enemy of the means of annoying our commerce and preying upon our citizens.[30]

For some, such an explanation may have been a gloss, intellectual gymnastics to harmonize war and expansion with republicanism. But for most it probably was not. They sincerely believed that they fought in self-defense. A few even concluded that provided Britain did America justice, she could keep Canada because it lacked any intrinsic value for Americans. To be sure, such conclusions emerged when two invasions had collapsed, but the main point is that charges of Manifest Destiny levelled at the Republican leadership in the War of 1812 were exaggerated both at the time and subsequently by historians seeking explanations of the conflict's origins.

American ambitions for Canada emerged, but as a result, rather than as a cause of, the war. The exhilaration of having finally embarked upon a course of direct action against the British tormentor combined with growing nationalism and the martial enthusiasm of the unbloodied. Republican half-way pacifism justified invasion as a form of retaliation, although Federalists and Quids did not agree. The tendency to see their country as the aggrieved party made the assaults on British territory defensive moves, inspired not by lust of conquest, which would have rendered the war unjust, but by a desire to preserve and protect. Strategic logic dictated offensive action, especially since America had declared the war. As it happened, Canada proved unconquerable because of a combination of American incompetence, British good fortune, and Canadian energy. But the administration nevertheless fought a limited war of state policy to settle maritime grievances. Utterly unable to challenge the British at sea, Madison and Monroe embarked upon an invasion of Canada as the only plausible way to press concessions from Great Britain. At best, the acquisition of new territory to the north was an ambition, a dream. At no time did it emerge from policy objectives of the administration.

At the same time, the internal dynamics of war generated forces that might have produced an impulse for conquest, even as the Revolution had acquired a crusading tinge. But in both cases, political objectives remained dominant — independence in the first, and a redress of grievances in the second. The French Revolution had presented alarming evidence on how a just war in defense of the homeland could become a crusade. During the Quasi-War, a few Federalists had extravagant ambitions for liberating Spanish America. These spasms had strained against the barricades of the limited-war mentality.

In 1812, Jefferson thought that it should take more to stop than to prevent a war, and Monroe reflected that Hull's apparently shameful surrender of Detroit would arouse national anger and pride, which in turn could fashion a war to erase all British influence in North America. Rufus King, writing to his son Charles, who was in London, suggested how nationalism and the dynamics of war could overcome partisanship. If Britain rejected the American peace offering in 1814, "we all say war must be continued until more just and moderate . . . policy prevails there." If England remained intransigent, she would convert Americans into a "military" people, the very thing Federalists and Quids had feared most.[31] Some Republicans undoubtedly saw the acquisition of Canada as an end in itself. For them the new territory would compensate for past injuries, as well as the immediate costs of the war. And if the initial invasions had been successful, instead of miserable failures, Congress, buoyed by the elation which flows from martial victories, might well have voted to retain Canada.

Dreams of conquest lingered to tease the ambitious and the proud, but on a more general level, Americans took solace from the mere act of fighting. Jonathan Russell in London and Richard Rush in America concluded that engaging in war at this point held inherent virtue and would go far to redeem the national character, which they both believed had sunk through humiliation at the hands of the British. Even men of letters evoked patriotic pride and a romantic view of war in defense of liberty. John C. Calhoun thought that Americans must "rejoice at the acquisition of those national qualities necessary to meet the vicissitudes of war when unavoidable."[32] Many Americans felt a throb of patriotism, which links their response to the war with their stated reasons for waging it. Such views occasionally went beyond the characteristic attitude of the Revolutionary generation, which saw the resort to armed force as a final method of arbitration, a form of legal contest. But for many patriots, war was national redemption.

These Romantic views emerged in other statements. Baptists and Methodists, not incidentally strong Anglophobes, frequently argued that the war was a holy endeavor. Even lukewarm clerics attacked the administration's policies, rather than the fact of war, trying to compromise their consciences for the sake of the continued support of their flocks. Nationalist spokesman Henry Wheaton believed that war developed man's best faculties, stimulated noble virtues, and encouraged a sense of honor. John Quincy Adams had a similar perspective and prayed, "God grant that in suffering the unavoidable calamities we may recover in all their vigor the energies of war."[33] It is impossible to determine how widespread such views were. But here was a concept of war alien to the modes of thought of the Revolutionary generation.

Here, as before, the war generated pressures for conformity which suggest how armed conflict can assail the civilized restraint with which men seek to conduct their affairs. Jefferson fumed at the Federalists and thought that a "barrel of tar in each state South of the Potomac will keep all in order." In New England, the opposition would be especially difficult, and he warned Madison that "you may there have to apply the rougher drastics of Govr. Wright, hemp and confiscation." Felix Grundy accused Federalists of trying to prolong the fighting just to ruin the administration, and in "The Olive Branch," in 1814, Mathew Carey blamed the ill fortunes of war on an opposition that forced Madison to wage two campaigns at once.[34] Federalists were often labelled "Tories" in newspapers and occasionally mob action silenced dissidents, as in Baltimore in June 1812. Two riots broke out because of editorials in the *Federalist Republican*. Several men were severely beaten. One died, and a hero of the Revolution, Henry "Light Horse Harry" Lee, became an invalid for the rest of his life.

The Madison administration was suspicious, but tolerant, of dissent. The president wrote privately about "seditious opposition," and James Monroe condemned the "inveterate Toryism" of New England.[35] Madison had the Hartford Convention watched closely, feared the worst, and was relieved when moderation prevailed in its councils. Throughout the war he resisted pressures for new forms of alien and sedition laws. The memories of 1798 remained real, and Madison was politically both liberal and prudent. The opposition was strong enough. It did not require martyrs condemned in Republican courts.

The wave of patriotism suggests a gap in attitudes between popular views and the perspective of the administration. For the latter, this was clearly a limited war, but for the former, a strategy of defense could become a design for conquest. Fiery Andrew Jackson believed that the "hour of national vengeance is now at hand." God's "will be done — our country calls — the god of battles cries aloud for vengeance — we are the means in His hands to punish the infamous Britons for their sacrilegious deeds."[36] Administration papers trumpeted a similar thesis for popular consumption, and William Hull's proclamation of 12 July 1812, upon setting foot on British soil across from Detroit, tendered Canadians "the invaluable blessing of civil, political and religious liberty." The *Military Monitor and American Register*, which began publication in New York 17 August 1812 to report the war, reprinted official documents and patriotic notices from all parts of the country. It even advertised a map so that readers could follow the course of the campaigns. It blasted Clinton Republicans as little better than Tories. The regional division of views implied that one part of the country favored foreign conquest and that the other exploited the invasion for partisan advantage.[37] This arousal of popular enthusiasm during wartime, with the resurrection of Revolutionary labels, suggests the context within which patriotic Americans understood this struggle. In turn, the enthusiasm assailed the restraint of the limited-war mentality, which dominated the attitudes of the administration.

Patriotism, the dynamism of war, romantic perceptions of struggle as redemption, popular enthusiasm: none of these seduced the Madison administration from its pursuit of state policy objectives. The war of 1812 was a limited war of policy that glanced backwards to the eighteenth century for its inspiration and character, and not toward the surging Romantic nationalism which fired the struggles of contemporary Europe. And this was not just a case of the administration holding a rearguard action against Romantic nationalism surging from the people. In June 1812, for example, the Senate nearly transformed an unrestricted war into reprisals at sea.[38] Andrew Gregg, a Pennsylvania Republican, wanted to amend the war bill from the House so that

American naval vessels and privateers could make reprisals on British ships. Gregg's, and Republican John Pope of Kentucky's amendments, would have made the war bill an act of reprisal only. Gregg's effort failed by a vote of fifteen to seventeen. The South-West alliance remained adamant about open war. But an effort to strike "war" from the bill and substitute "reprisal" lost only when the Senate divided sixteen to sixteen. And as finally passed, the war was to be against the government of Great Britain, but not "persons inhabiting within its territories or possessions." William B. Giles, one of the anti-Madison "invisibles," made one final exertion to block open war, but lost by fourteen to eighteen. He then voted for the war bill with the majority. A few days later, a separate marque and reprisal act passed swiftly, although the Senate rejected a resolution authorizing the president to acquire Canada and the Floridas.[39]

The Senate, in company with the administration, saw this as a limited war of policy. Both were prepared to run the risks of battle for the promise of a settlement of Anglo-American differences and the satisfaction of having resisted insults. This perspective was clearer in the Senate than in the House for several reasons. First, the Federalists were stronger there, and while they opposed unrestricted war, they had long thought that maritime defense was necessary. Second, the anti-Madison "invisibles" — Giles, Samuel Smith, Michael Leib — had a power which could tell in the voting because the Senate was small. Third, conservative and maritime interests found better representation in the Senate than in the House. Finally, Republicans disagreed among themselves about what kind of force should be applied to pursue the country's policy objectives. Some emphasized naval defense alone, but others opposed this on grounds of expense and effectiveness.[40]

The concepts of the *jus in bello* also found expression in this second Anglo-American conflict. British citizens in the United States received six months to settle their affairs and leave peacefully, but even after that, the administration did not hinder their departure. Englishmen who remained, like Americans in England, went about their business. The New York Supreme Court ruled that resident enemy aliens could sue in American courts. And the British financial house of Alexander Baring underwrote the expenses of the American peace commissioners in

Europe. Finally, eighteenth-century standards of civilized warfare emerged when the British granted generous articles of capitulation to protect private property and permit American prisoners to return home until duly exchanged after American garrisons surrendered. By 12 May 1813, a proper cartel for prisoner exchange had been drawn up. Authorized vessels ferried processed captives between America and England throughout the war.[41] Both the British and the Americans sought to restrict the impact of this war on their respective societies, the men in combat, and their economies, even as they strove to maintain gentlemanly standards of behavior.

Americans even boasted about their moderation. This was usually to highlight British abominations, as when the *Military Monitor* warned that "if the barbarous and savage policy of Great Britain be pursued, and the savages are let loose to murder our citizens and butcher our women and children, this war will be a war of extermination." British Admiral Cochrane, ordered to launch retaliatory raids because Canadians had suffered along the American border, wrote Monroe that he would stay his hand if the United States granted relief to the victims. The secretary of state was instantly indignant. The United States stood pledged to wage the war on humane principles. British atrocities had violated the law of war regarding civilians. Monroe disavowed American plundering in Upper Canada, as did a congressional committee. At no time, it concluded, had the country departed from the established rules of civilized combat.[42]

This conviction of righteousness involved the Americans in an unseemly squabble about retaliation on prisoners, which resembled similar incidents in the Revolution. Some Americans captured at the Battle of Queenstown were shipped to England to face trial for treason. British officials argued that these were British subjects who had defected, but had not jettisoned their true allegiance. In Upper Canada, recaptured Canadian deserters had been hanged, drawn, and quartered as an example to those who took up arms against their king and country. American authorities were alarmed about the possible fate of what they considered legitimate captives of war. In February 1813, therefore, Congress authorized Madison to retaliate on British prisoners in American hands if any of the disputed captives were to be executed. The United States documented its case, which revolved around the right of expatriation, and argued that such retaliation would be consistent with civilized warfare.[43] In any event, no prisoners suffered on either side. Apart from an unfortunate riot at Dartmoor prison in Britain at the end of the war, both sides behaved well and consciously strove to maintain the harmony between war and civilization that eighteenth-century humanists had thought so necessary for man's survival.

At the same time, atrocities stained the reputation of both British and American nationals. Some Americans living in Upper Canada deserted to the invading armies from the United States and then occasionally executed private vendettas reminiscent of the patriot-loyalist clashes of the Revolution. American troops were orderly while occupying York, the capital of Upper Canada. But public buildings were needlessly burned and private property of value disappeared if easily portable. Commander Henry Dearborn's failure to prevent this plunder contributed to his later removal from command. When British landing parties raided the Chesapeake Bay in 1814, they committed some vandalism and encouraged slaves to desert. Burning the American capital was conscious retaliation for York, but the looting of private property during the confusion of the brief British occupation was done not by unruly troops, but by servants of Washington citizens who had not fled. If England could be condemned for employing Indian allies, so could Andrew Jackson, George McClure, and John Armstrong, who found that Madison rebuffed his suggestion that this become part of the administration's policy.[44] Apparently, neither side possessed a monopoly on virtue in the war. For example, the House Foreign Relations Committee excused the burning of Moravian towns by dismissing them as collections of Indian huts, and asserting that Europeans had always waged such warfare against savages.

In short, the patterns of the colonial and revolutionary wars, and the attitudes of the *jus in bello,* survived as uneasy bedfellows. Americans still saw a sharp distinction between civilized and savage warfare, although in practice that line could blur. The dual tradition of limited war between European antagonists and unlimited war between Europeans and natives persisted. Europeans still considered it unnecessary to treat the natives as civilized enemies. Nevertheless, by adhering largely to the limited-war mentality, the Americans remained within the older, inher-

ited European tradition. Madison asserted in his second inaugural address that the United States had violated "no principal of
justice or honor, no usage of civilized nations, no precept of
courtesy or humanity." Madison's republican ideology and the
liberal humanism of the eighteenth century easily tempered his
nationalism and the dynamism of conflict when it came to his
view of war.[45]

A brief glance at the Napoleonic Wars suggests significant
differences between the nature of the contemporary struggles in
Europe and the character of the War of 1812. From the beginning,
the wars of the French Revolution had displayed savage qualities.
Ideological enthusiasm had masked and justified excesses against
domestic and foreign enemies alike for those in power. When
Napoleon took control of the engines started by the Revolution,
he tuned them to his own ambitions, compensating for diplo-
matic ineptitude with sheer military force. This evoked national-
istic responses in subject peoples who rebelled with patriotic fury.
In Spain in 1807, for example, when rebellion broke out against
French overlordship, neither side asked nor granted quarter. The
French murdered, burned, tortured, and looted with abandon.
The Spanish partisans responded with gruesome vengeance at
every opportunity. To take another example, one week after
Madison signed the American declaration of war against Great
Britain, Napoleon invaded Russia with over 600,000 troops. The
army viewed the Russian peasantry with contempt and ruthlessly
suppressed local revolts against the Russian aristocracy, for-
feiting any pretense of being liberators. When Napoleon's army
suffered and dwindled in the ensuing campaign, the partisans of
the steppes matched those of Spain's piedmont in the fury of their
reply. They scorched their earth and exacted a fearsome toll as
Napoleon's army disintegrated during the retreat from Moscow.[46]

A comparison of the War of 1812 with the Napoleonic struggles
seems absurd on the surface. Yet at the level of character and
attitudes, comparison is meaningful. The raids and retaliations
along the Canadian border were grim enough for the partici-
pants, but pale beside the fury of the people's wars in Europe. The
Americans and the British fought to arbitrate their differences; the
Russians, Spanish, and French for homeland and empire. The
differences in attitude toward their enemy are as striking as the
differences in scale between the vast armies of Europe and those
marching in the forests of America.

In some respects the War of 1812 involved commerce. Maritime depredations on American vessels had been a principal cause of Anglo-American discord, after all. But despite the advent of war, the Madison administration hoped that trade might flourish as usual. Jefferson, for one, saw no reason why some exchange should not continue with England, provided this was "mutually advantageous to the individuals, and not to their injury as belligerents." Much trade with Canada persisted, especially through Nova Scotia and along the lower Canadian border. Protests against an embargo to stop this proved sufficiently effective to have the restrictive legislation removed. When the British blockade became tighter in 1814, New Englanders funnelled their goods through Castine, Maine, where British forces established regular customs procedures during their occupation of this American territory. And the business of war itself emerged. Privateers sailed from all major American ports in search of prey. New Englanders were among those vessels of this maritime militia, which captured about 2,000 British merchantmen during the course of the war.[47] In many respects, patriotism and profit were convenient fellow travellers.

If economic attitudes suggest the limited character of the War of 1812, so too does the Madison administration's approach to making peace. From the beginning, the administration had been prepared to stop fighting if the British would settle the maritime grievances. Given moderate and conservative reluctance over declaring hostilities, and even militants' claims, Madison would likely have been able to muster a majority for peace if he had been able to go to Congress with a settlement. But the British were not helpful, and the war continued. In 1814, the cabinet abandoned impressment as a cause of war, leading Rufus King to conclude that the whole enterprise had been a failure, even though he expressed satisfaction over the Treaty of Ghent.[48] With England's great triumph in Europe and the dismal American performance through the summer of 1814, neither the administration nor its agents hoped for concessions from their British counterparts. The Plattsburgh and New Orleans campaigns allowed the war to end on a shining, if not utterly triumphant, note for the Americans, and the peace commissioners took the best terms they thought they could get. Henry Clay, a late addition to the American delegation at Ghent, was satisfied. He concluded that gains balanced losses.[49] Having fought, the Americans could make peace, even without having achieved all their declared objectives.

The national response to the treaty was almost wholly favorable. National pride infected even the Federalists, and Boston celebrated with artillery salutes, parades, and bells. The treaty had surrendered nothing except ambitions, and combined with the Plattsburgh and New Orleans victories, swept away the gloom of 1814. Madison was delighted, and justice Joseph Story wrote: "Peace has come in a most welcome time to delight and astonish us. Never did a country occupy more lofty ground; we have stood the contest singlehanded, against the conqueror of Europe; and we are at peace, with all our blushing victories thick crowding on us."[50] Story's euphoria seems overdrawn in light of the entire history of the war, but he did not stand alone in this judgment. James Monroe believed that the war had strengthened the nation and lent luster to its character. The treaty would enhance America's international stature, he ventured, as the commissioners at Ghent already thought. Jefferson concluded that it was significant that the country had been willing to fight for its self-respect. Israel Pickens told his constituents that the peace was "highly honorable" because Britain had abandoned its "arrogant demands." These expressions were typical of popular reaction. In retrospect, the War of 1812 spread and accelerated American nationalism, with its concomitant faith in republican ideology and structures.[51]

The relief that the war was over and that the country had survived drew a veil over the misfortunes of the War of 1812. As an instrument of policy, force had not been notably successful. The Indians had been cowed, defeated by Jackson in the southwest, and robbed of their British allies in the north. But these campaigns would have occurred regardless. More important, American speakers and writers conveniently overlooked the fact that the British had liquidated their American conflict because of continental and imperial interests. On the other hand, one of the objects of the fighting had been to redeem national honor; viewed in this light, the limited war of 1812 was a triumph of will for nationalistic Republicans who had feared that their country might collapse under the pressures of British arrogance and power and the war in Europe. They had exchanged material losses for psychological and ideological satisfactions. This, and gratitude that the ordeal had terminated without disaster, sparked American extravagance. Charles Ingersoll noted, "the nation now cannot be discredited. It has done its duty and is above disgrace. Within five and thirty years of our national existence, we have achieved a second acknowledgment of our national sovereignty."[52] For nationalists, this was a prize worth the effort.

These Republicans did more here than simply declare a victory. They revealed a significant strand in American attitudes toward war. In certain circumstances, such as had prevailed immediately prior to 1812, when the national sense of honor seemed bruised and ashamed, exertion, action, conflict, all generated a sense of redemption. And in eighteenth-century terms, the government had officially committed its cause to God in a trial by combat. Despite tribulations, the country, the government, and the Republican party had survived. To the extent that this had been a limited war for national honor, it was a success, even though British troops stood on American soil as the peace treaty was signed. The absence of defeat implied God's favor.

The mood throughout the country was similar and did not vary greatly with partisan perspectives. South Carolinians took satisfaction from merely having faced Great Britain. The republican system had proven itself in war and established American independence from European politics. Given the American commitment to republican theories and institutions, this seemed no mean accomplishment. For Jonathan Roberts of Pennsylvania, this was a victory of party, a "triumph of virtue over vice of republican men & republican principles over the advocates & doctrines of Tyranny." The War of 1812 increased the sense of distance Americans had between themselves and Europe. Clerics interpreted the coming of peace as a sign of God's pleasure and many others concluded that the struggle had helped to unify Americans. And from a greater distance in time, George Coggeshall, a former privateersman, reflected:

> And what is far above every other consideration, it has given us a national character, and caused our flag to be respected in every part of the world. It has inspired every individual American with a feeling of self-respect, and a stronger and deeper love for his country's honor and glory; and it continues to cherish a growing feeling of patriotism, which, after all, is a nation's surest and best protection.[53]

Even with allowances for the cleansing effect of distant memory, Coggeshall's remarks resembled closely those of nationalists such as William Pinckney, who had experienced the agonies of dealing with the British firsthand.[54]

It was just this self-respect that Republicans had feared was draining away immediately before declaring war against Britain in 1812. The long-range implications of the War of 1812 for American nationalism have been more often asserted than charted and documented. Yet there is little doubt that the prewar sense of national shame was erased by the act of fighting, even as a small child might gather pride and strength from having confronted the neighborhood bully, although he might be bloodied in the process. This too rendered the Anglo-American conflict of a different order from the wars that had raged in Europe. There, self-confident nations had engaged in tests of power. In America, republican half-way pacifism had yielded to a determination to fight, and Republican fears about the future of the country, and hence their party, were laid to rest by the absence of disaster. The self-confidence in themselves and their institutions that Americans gained by this relative success relegated republican pacifism to the status of a national myth. Henceforth, Americans would believe themselves far more pacific than they actually were.

The Republican view of the war found summary expression in Alexander Dallas's "Exposition on the Causes and Character of the War." Published anonymously before news of the peace arrived, this lengthy self-justification appeared in pamphlet form and in the *Annals* of Congress. It affirmed in self-righteous terms the Republican idea of the just war. The struggle had not been for conquest, but for the defense of national rights. Only imminent disgrace had driven Americans to take up arms, and even then they had simultaneously offered peace. This clear conscience and sincerity sustained the justice of the cause, much as classical writers had outlined. Just wars remained so only if peace was their principal object. Madison, who had contributed to Dallas's "Exposition," put America right with republican ideology by suggesting this rationale, and Dallas confirmed the lingering influence of the limited-war mentality by leaving them in, for the "Exposition" was essentially an eighteenth-century commentary on the War of 1812.[55]

In 1812, the Republicans viewed their struggle in purely defensive terms, which permitted them to dismiss charges of conquest arising from the invasion of Canada. One part of their

LIMITED WAR OF 1812

ideology salved another. And ultimately, James Madison, not congressional militants, or soldiers, or newspapers and their editors, controlled this limited war of policy. From Madison's perspective, a fight in defense of maritime rights would redeem national honor. Since the war had been voted by the people's representatives, it was clearly in the people's interests. Madison's policy was consistent with that of George Washington, John Adams, Thomas Jefferson, and other leading figures in the Revolutionary generation, because all drew from the same reservoir of thought on the origins, purpose, and meaning of war in human affairs.

Finally, the War of 1812 confirmed American attitudes toward the likelihood of future conflicts. To some extent, this overcame Republican parsimony and fear of standing forces. These forces would still remain small in contrast with European armies and navies, even given the population and resources of the country. But America was entering an era of "free security," as it has been described, and her military requirements were not great. Still, although Madison knew that America's immediate dangers had vanished with the close of the Napoleonic struggle, he noted when he sent the Treaty of Ghent to the Senate that Americans could not rely upon their own pacific character and institutions entirely. Experience revealed "that a certain degree of preparation for war is not only indispensable to avert disasters in the onset, but affords also the best security for the continuance of peace."[56] Before 1812, this had been a ritual expression; now it had profound meaning. And it embodied the emerging American war myth.

Others had a similar view. For his part, John Adams thought that the world stood in an era of struggle between despotism and republicanism. He agreed also with Richard Rush that wars sprang from flawed human nature. James Monroe, who as the next president would push relentlessly for a more effective military establishment, stressed that America must maintain forces for "every necessary national purpose." The concept of war and policy, as well as self-defense, appeared in these few words. In Congress, supporters of standing forces stressed anew their deterring impact, as well as the weight they gave to diplomatic protests.[57] In 1815, however, with the war over and with only vague threats to future security, a resurgent antimilitarism and

Republican parsimony resulted in the retention of 10,000 regulars, about half of what Monroe had requested.

The limited War of 1812 had shown all Americans that national honor and glory can be intoxicating. Although the tenets of the limited-war mentality retained a firm grip on the minds of the nation's leaders, younger nationalists, and all afflicted with emotional patriotism, discovered that rational restraint faces a serious challenge from the forces of nationalism, especially in time of war. Once troops march and clash, the heart can rule the head, and the balance between passion and reason in human beings can be upset. At the same time, the limited-war mentality shaped the character of the War of 1812 from the American perspective; and for the moment, it weathered the advent of nationalism in American thought. Even so, as the Revolutionary generation faded from power and national life, so did its world view. Eighteenth-century attitudes toward war and peace would not die, but they would no longer go unchallenged as James Monroe, the last Revolutionary veteran to hold high office, took over the presidency.

7

EMERGENCE OF THE AMERICAN WAR MYTH

Until 1815 the limited-war mentality and republican ideology had reinforced each other when crises arose in America's foreign relations. The rationale of the *jus ad bellum* had been applied against Great Britain during the Revolution, occasionally in formal statements on frontier conflicts with the Indians, against France in 1797, against the Barbary pirates, against Spain, and finally against Great Britain for a second time. Woven in with the legal and moral justifications for a resort to arms were American ambitions — for secure boundaries, protection of trade, added territory. A growing national pride helped to persuade Americans that the new republic could be rendered more secure only through the addition of new lands to the south and west.

Internal suspicions and dynamics had coupled with the external context of American foreign relations to produce frequent war crises from 1793 to 1815. Even after the Treaty of Ghent, some Americans feared that Napoleon's return from Elba and his spectacular Hundred Days' sweep would lead to renewed Anglo-American tensions. Americans had little faith in the Holy Alliance, which emerged later as a champion of reactionism, to keep the European peace, even after Napoleon was dispatched at the suitably climactic Battle of Waterloo. For American nationalists, an implacable hostility existed between republicanism and monarchism. Most of all, they continued to fear Great Britain, even though a succession of ministries worked out agreements with the United States that settled differences over boundaries, fisheries, commerce, and the threat of a naval armaments race on the Great Lakes.[1] The political configurations of Europe that had threatened the United States from the end of the War for Independence no longer pertained. Americans found themselves in a changed, and considerably more peaceful, world than they had known in the recent past.

As the Revolutionary generation sat largely in retirement, it observed a changing nation. The first party system disintegrated with the eclipse of the Federalist party as a result of the War of 1812. Younger, more nationalistic Republicans urged protection for America's infant industries, assistance to internal improvements, and a more stable financial system. Ambitions for Canada withered with successive Anglo-American agreements. But Andrew Jackson's victory at New Orleans riveted imaginations on the southwest and aroused further interest in the Floridas, and even Texas. What had been a regional ambition and a dream of Republican leaders prior to 1812 became national policy objectives after 1815.[2] Americans became more aggressive with their new self-confidence born of the war against Britain.

These forces encouraged new developments in American attitudes toward war. In many respects, the limited-war mentality remained. Political and military turbulence seemed likely to continue in Europe, and Americans expected future employment for armed forces. Furthermore, new territorial ambitions raised the need for troops to sustain national policy objectives. National interests were foremost for Americans guiding policy. Although republican, it was clear that the United States would not aid other republican movements, such as those in Spanish America or Greece, if such support raised any danger to national interests, which, as defined by men in Congress and the administration, remained secure borders, the protection and expansion of trade, and added territory. In the period after 1815, James Madison sent warships against Algiers when the Dey threw a tantrum, James Monroe sent forces to root out nests of freebooters in Amelia Island and Galveston, and he even had the navy chase pirates into Cuban jungles with the cooperation of local Spanish authorities.

After 1815, and indeed, during the War of 1812, the themes of the *jus ad bellum* became less topics for debate about the use of force than assertions of righteousness. America's republican nationalism led her policy-makers to conclude that their country would always be acting in self-defense. Republican thought assumed that republics were pacific because the people ruled. And the people had no interests in wars of ambition or glory. Americans had cited such arguments from the Revolution onward, but by the War of 1812, this faith had become a national myth. Americans embraced the delusion that their country would fight only defensive wars. Because their nationalism embraced republicanism, Americans subverted the *jus ad bellum,* unaware of what they were doing. Reasoned consideration of the merits of using force was replaced by patriotic assertions. James Madison made this clear in his last message to Congress. Americans believed their system benign, libertarian, and devoted to peace. The country always sought

> by appeals to reason and by its liberal examples to infuse into the law which governs the civilized world a spirit which may diminish the frequency or circumscribe the calamities of war, and meliorate the social and beneficent relations of peace; a Government, in a word, whose conduct within and without may bespeak the most noble of all ambitions — that of promoting peace on earth and good will to man.[3]

Given this kind of self-image, Americans could interpret their own expansion as a beneficial act, and rationalize aggression as the humane extension of civilization. Such tendencies became more significant after 1815. The success of the War of 1812, which temporarily eliminated competing visions of the nation's character and future by smothering the Federalist party, contributed to the emergence of this American war myth. This was little more than the Republican view of war transformed into an article of national faith.

This was why philosophical pacifism, or the utter rejection of force, made so little headway in the United States. Pacifism intensified and secularized after 1815 on an international scale in response to over twenty years of continuous warfare. This movement drew strength from revivalism in the United States and Evangelicalism in England. In continental Europe, pacifism remained confined to tiny, isolated sects.[4] In the United States, it grew out of the Quaker heritage, and the work of such men as Anthony Benezet. Then in 1814, Noah Worcester published his *Solemn Review of the Custom of War.* Conscious of the wartime atmosphere, Worcester carefully differentiated himself from Federalist dissenters and accepted the justice of a purely defensive struggle. In 1815 several small societies formed, among them

Worcester's Massachusetts Peace Society in Boston, and David Low Dodge's American Society in New York. As in England, Quakers and clerics provided the core of membership and enthusiasm, along with those of the middle classes who fired the antebellum reform movements. And like their British cousins, they operated as education organizations, spreading their message of peace through pamphlets, leaflets, and journals that included editorials and notices of progress in England as well as in America.[5]

Worcester's group proved to be the most influential in a largely ineffectual crusade. He worked to enlist such prominent members of the Revolutionary generation as Jefferson and John Adams to add prestige to his cause. And as propaganda, he published his correspondence with them in his journal, *The Friend of Peace*. Typical of republican half-way pacifists, Jefferson did not share all of Worcester's views, despite his optimism about human nature and his hopes for improving the lot of mankind. He argued, for example, that nations often legitimately redressed wrongs by force. And, as the War of 1812 had shown, even a weak nation could extract a sufficient toll from an aggressor to provide deterrence against future assaults. Jefferson agreed about reducing the occurrence of war through education, but despaired of ever eliminating resorts to arms. He accepted membership in Worcester's society nevertheless, not because he anticipated universal peace, but "if, by the inculcations of reason or religion, the perversities of our nature can be so far corrected" as to reduce "war, murder, and devastation, the benevolent endeavors of the friends of peace will not be entirely without remuneration."[6]

John Adams, largely because of his temperament, shot back a crusty refusal to Worcester's invitation. But his style made him seem more different from Jefferson than he really was. At one time, Adams wrote, he had agreed with advocates of peace, such as Erasmus, Fenelon, and the Abbe St. Pierre. But a "longer and more extensive experience has convinced me, that wars are as necessary and as inevitable, in our system, as Hurricanes, Earthquakes, and Volcanoes." Americans had ambitious, powerful, and unprincipled enemies. "Universal and perpetual peace appears to me no more nor less than everlasting passive obedience and non-resistance. The human flock would soon be fleeced and butchered by one or a few."[7] Like Jefferson and others of the Revolutionary generation, Adams was a half-way pacifist who balanced his hopes with a solid appraisal of the weaknesses of men and nations.

The peace journals had an optimistic, millennial tone, which reflected the overall reform movement. Worcester argued that even in monarchies, progress could be achieved because despots needed their subjects to wage their wars. And as people became more enlightened and Christianized, they developed a greater aversion to fighting that was not for their interests. Worcester incorporated American republicanism into his argument, and betrayed as well an anti- or non-nationalism. Like Timothy Pickering and Josiah Quincy, old Federalists, Worcester thought that national honor was not significant. Man was peaceful by nature and war was an acquired attribute. Since war had been learned, it could be unlearned.[8]

Elisha Bates's *The Moral Advocate,* published in Mount Pleasant, Ohio, beginning in 1817, covered many branches of reform. It, too, urged education to generate future progress and noted that war had gradually been weened from barbarism. Further efforts would remove more of its horrors so that eventually "no two nations may be found so uninlightened and depraved, as to be willing to destroy the general harmony." Bates reprinted Josiah Quincy's speech to the Massachusetts Society on its fifth anniversary. Quincy's remarks suggest a lingering bitterness over Madison and the War of 1812, but he nevertheless spoke from the heart about war. There was greater hope for peace in the United States because of its republicanism. Quincy assumed that a true republic would only fight defensive wars in the national interest as defined by the people. Bates sustained such views in his own writings, warning that human inclinations created self-delusions about war. Whether in monarchies or republics, the causes of war "are not identified with the interests of the great mass of the people, but they are drawn into it, by inflammatory declarations — by the prospect of individual advantage, and above all by the idea that the dreadful calamities of it, are to fall somewhere else, and not on themselves."[9] Bates's pacifism was pure, but he identified at the same time with the American war myth.

Indeed, this link between pacifism and the American war myth suggests why the peace advocates had so little impact. Nationalism, the support of unpopular sects, internal divisiveness, a New England base, and the darker elements of human nature all undercut pacifism. Yet in the United States more was at work. Worcester's optimism emphasized the nobler fibers of the American spirit, with its Enlightenment heritage. Bates linked these ideas more specifically to republican ideology than Worcester, but when pacifist petitions reached Congress, the prevailing republican ideology made congressmen assume that their country stood and worked for peace as it was.

In January of 1819, for example, William Lowndes of South Carolina rose as chairman of the House Foreign Relations Committee to report on memorials against privateering which had reached Congress. Abolition of private enterprise warfare was one goal of the pacifists, who assumed that greedy men simply cloaked their avarice in patriotism to prey upon private property. Lowndes understood the petitioners to request the "introduction of a system which shall confine the immediate injuries of war to those whose sex, and age, and occupation do not unfit them for the struggle." He and his committee fully concurred:

> The committee think that it will be right in the Government of the United States to renew its attempt to obtain the mitigation of a barbarous code, whenever there shall seem a probability of its success. They do not doubt that it will do so. Its first efforts at Negotiation were characterized by an anxiety to limit the evils of war.[10]

Lowndes expressed a commitment that many Americans already felt to Enlightenment goals about reducing the impact of war on society. He also reflected the practical conditions those idealists had placed upon their ambitions. The limited-war mentality had striven to reconcile war and civilization on the realization that conflict was an inevitable part of the human condition. But regarding free-ships–free-goods, if the United States were the only nation to practice this policy scrupulously, it could find itself at a disadvantage. American statesmen had learned to modify their ideals to circumstances. In a world where power ruled, humanity, reason, and Christian principles were frail barricades. The Revolutionary generation understood this, and it had become an article of faith with most Americans who considered questions of state policy. John Quincy Adams, for instance, took up the privateering clause with the British entirely on his own, not anticipating immediate acceptance, but hoping

for future progress.[11] In brief, most Americans thought themselves to be at least half-way pacifists because of their ideology.

The pacifist witness represented the most idealistic aspect of the
American self-image when it came to war. It grew out of the
limited-war mentality, with its Enlightenment roots, yet its
Christian purity would not permit compromise. The half-way
republican pacifism of the Revolutionary generation, on the
other hand, had adapted ideals to circumstances for the sake of
national interests. By juxtaposing Worcester, Quincy, Adams,
Jefferson, Lowndes, and the petitioners, we see the limited-war
mentality blending with republican ideology to produce variations on the same theme. Their points of difference revolved
around such variables as nationalism, temperament, pragma-
tism, idealism, experience, knowledge, ambitions, and perceptions of human nature. And the connecting links among them
suggest that Americans still broadly agreed about the nature of
war.

The American war myth included the natural rights of self-
defense and retaliation. Nationalism rendered definitions of these
entirely subjective. Judgment on the War of 1812, for example,
was largely positive. Albert Gallatin thought that Americans now
had "more general objects of attachment with which their pride
and political opinions are connected. They are more Americans;
they feel and act more as a nation." Madison asserted that national
rights were priceless and that the results of the war more than
compensated for the costs.[12] Disclaimers were few, and the
majority of Americans refused to believe that the war had been
either unjust or dishonorably concluded. Nationalism did not
permit Americans to entertain the idea that the struggle had been
in vain, and this separated them from the pacifists who saw only
the waste and futility of war.

The floor of Congress therefore heard much national self-
congratulation. Militant nationalist and peace negotiator Henry
Clay noted that a valuable lesson had been learned. In the last
analysis, independence could only be preserved by force of arms.
Clay and the other militants had maintained this view before
1812, and they saw no reason to alter their outlook. Richard M.
Johnson admitted that the decision to resort to arms had been
distressing, but how else was the nation to gain redress for
grievances and maintain independence? The only real calamity of

the war had been Federalist opposition, which had seemed to threaten the union. Both Clay and Johnson maintained that all Americans shared in the national glory acquired through military action. And as late as 1824, Robert Y. Hayne of South Carolina, in other respects an important Southern sectional champion, argued that at one time the United States seemed unable to protect its interests, its citizens, or its honor. The War of 1812 had changed all that.

> There is a debt of gratitude which we will never be able to pay, due to the Legislators who declared that war — to the statesmen who conducted it — but above all, to the heroes who, on the land and the sea, brightened our path by their victories, in the darkest hour of our national history. Ten years ago, we had a character to gain — now we have one to support.[13]

Pure pacifism could not dent American nationalism, nor could it persuade men that wars could be eradicated from human affairs. John Jay, responding to pacifist pamphlets, agreed that wars which arose from selfish motives were unlawful. Yet the law of nations permitted "war to be waged by an innocent against an offending nation, when rendered just and necessary by unprovoked, atrocious, and unredressed injuries." Rulers had a duty to defend the state. Until human morals and manners changed, war could never be abolished. This view emerged again when Spanish-American relations deteriorated over old claims, the control of the Florida Seminoles, and American ambitions for the acquisition of Florida. James Monroe noted to Congress that "the right of self-defence never ceases. It is among the most sacred, and alike necessary to nations and to individuals." Monroe also accepted that there was a general principle of reprisal, which John Quincy Adams evoked to defend Andrew Jackson's flaunting of Spanish rights in Florida in 1818.[14]

The limited-war mentality thus became a part of the American war myth combining with national interests to sustain a belief in the inevitability of war, in the defensive-mindedness of Americans, and in the need for force as an instrument of policy. Arguments for preparedness flowed naturally from this. The sorry spectacle of an unarmed United States confronting one of the martial behemoths of the age, and the pathetic American performance in two botched invasions of Canada, had sobered Republicans. Disunity had compounded the difficulties of inadequate direction at the center. Madison and James Monroe knew that the victory was somewhat trumped up and had only come after a painful and perilous trial. Even the British defeat at New Orleans had not persuaded the invaders to withdraw from America. British officers in the Gulf region were preparing new operations when word of the peace treaty compelled them to halt their efforts. The United States was difficult to conquer, but Britain had raided the coast at will, leaving troops on American soil north and south, repulsed but undefeated.

The Republican administrations in the postwar period believed that positive military programs would prevent future raids or invasions. Madison set the tone in December 1815. Tangible fortifications must buttress a love of peace and a respect for the rights of others. And in his first inaugural Monroe stated: "Experiencing the fortunes of other nations, the United States may again be involved in war." Distance from Europe and a just policy would not prevent friction with others. Monroe went on to present and insist upon a coherent defensive program, which he considered one of the important projects of his administration. Ideology might still make Americans half-way pacifists, but they erected solid ramparts as a second line of defense behind their assumption of American benevolence. Only a proper system of fortifications, a small but strong standing army, a well-maintained navy, and a refurbished militia could preserve American neutrality, protect citizens and property, and maintain national honor, in Monroe's mind.[15]

The American leaders had always been concerned with defensive self-sufficiency. In the past this had been associated with the Federalists, most notably Alexander Hamilton's suggestions for a standing army and his economic programs in the 1790s. Now, the Republican plans for military autarky moved far beyond the mythology of a nation of happy yeomen sustained by commerce, who would rush to the defense of an endangered homeland. Schemes arose for a network of roads and other internal improvements which would serve both civilian and military requirements. John Quincy Adams believed that along with a respectable navy, a sound revenue was one of the best guarantors of peace, suggesting fear of the bankruptcy that had beset the American government in the closing months of the War of 1812. John C. Calhoun, Monroe's brilliant, energetic, and ambitious secretary of war, suggested reforms of a similar nature. Calhoun suspected British good intentions which, when combined with a succession of Spanish crises from 1816 to 1821 and with sporadic Indian troubles, emphasized the need for defense against specific threats. And the tendency to relate force to foreign policy objectives, such as Florida or even Cuba, also underscored the need for standing forces.[16]

This new Republican military thought nevertheless betrayed American half-way pacifism. Madison and Monroe were liberal-thinking presidents who had a deep commitment to sustained diplomacy to avoid international collisions. The strains of the War of 1812, the domestic antagonisms, the near-bankruptcy, were vivid lessons of how republics could be crippled by war. The pursuit of naval disarmament on the Great Lakes was both to reduce expenditures and defuse the likelihood of armed clashes with the British.[17] And even though most Americans held the Spanish in contempt, official policy was forbearing. A fight could be costly and might tempt other European powers to support Spain, rather than see her defeated, thus precipitating a general war, which would prejudice America's present and future interests.

Members of Congress reluctantly voted funds for preparedness. They exhibited vestiges of republican antimilitarism, and realized only in a general way that the United States would have to face future conflicts. On the whole, apart from Spain, nuisance enemies such as Barbary and West Indian pirates, or Indian bands, the likely sources of war were too vague and distant to arouse much genuine fear. Entering what has been called an era of free security, Americans did not anticipate overt attacks, although they agreed to a more substantial fleet than they required. Robert G. Harper, in a rambling speech in April 1816, declared that since it was America's "destiny to fight," she must be prepared. Wars would arise "out of our habits, our pursuits, our character, our form of government, and our situation with respect to the great maritime Powers of the world. Our people were too enterprising, too active, too eager in the pursuit of commercial gain, to remain quietly at home." Harper understood that national interests, ambitions, and pride generated aggressive tendencies, apart from the antagonism between republics and monarchies. He also knew that human greed overcame conservative prudence. These many factors rendered future wars certain in his judgment. Others suggested that Britain was augmenting her forces in Canada, and the United States must remain vigilant. Look at "the vast extent of our maritime coast," Henry Clay commanded congressmen, and "recollect we have Indians and powerful nations coterminous on the whole frontier; and that we know not at what moment the savage enemy of Great Britain herself may seek to make war with us." Even though republics were not prone to war, other speakers suggested, enemies remained.[18]

The military system that emerged in the post-1815 period was a compromise among republican ideology, parsimony, and the apparent needs of the nation. Throughout, congressmen sought to balance competing fears. In 1817, for instance, Jeremiah Mason, a New Hampshire Federalist, thought that the army was too large. Yet he argued that a "nation, which should depend on its justice and moderation alone for protection, would be compelled to submit not only to degrading insults, but also in the end to surrender to foreign cupidity and ambition its essential rights." In 1818, Richard M. Johnson stated that "perpetual peace we cannot expect," no matter how "virtuous, how unambitious" Americans were. Johnson, more of a republican purist than some of his colleagues, wanted primary emphasis upon the militia, and a reduction in standing forces nevertheless.[19]

The American war myth therefore absorbed the thesis of the limited-war mentality that argued that conflict was inevitable among nations, just as it sustained the force and policy concept and subverted the *jus ad bellum* because of nationalism. The limited-war mentality of the Revolutionary generation was less replaced than reshaped. The Americans' conviction that theirs was a pacific system accounts for the failure of formal pacifism to make any headway as a reform movement, quite apart from the fact that it collided with nationalism. To deny a nation the right of self-defense, which the more extreme pacifists argued, was patently absurd. American nationalism had no room for an ideological variant that did not place the nation-state as a primary focus of loyalty.

Nationalism and national ambitions could also overcome the calls for restraint and prudence which had characterized the limited-war mentality. Andrew Jackson was a master of sophistry in such matters. Scarcely concealing his disdain for the Spanish, and a black angel of vengeance against Indians who had raided white settlements, he swooped into Florida in 1818. As with most Indian wars, the origins of this one lay with the collision of cultures, which the *jus ad bellum* could not adjudicate. And the first conflict with the Seminoles began with atrocities on both sides. Jackson, ready to wage a campaign of terror, brushed aside Spanish forces with ease and declared that "the immutable laws of self-defence, therefore compelled the American Government to take possession of such parts of the Floridas in which Spanish authority could not be maintained." Jackson defended his violation of Spanish sovereignty to President Monroe on the grounds of the laws of nations, justice, and, most effective with public opinion, "the innocent blood of our aged matrons and helpless infants." Richard M. Johnson noted in support that in the past, Americans had never surrendered the right of retaliation as a measure of self-defense. "When policy could, with safety, yield to mercy, our fathers were governed by the principles of humanity." Otherwise, defense and the survival of society took precedence. Faced with such choices, the Revolutionary generation had come to similar conclusions, albeit not without pangs of conscience at times. National policy interests had become paramount, even as nationalism itself distorted the perceptions policy-makers had of the country's interests involved.[20]

American concerns extended beyond mere defense of the homeland after 1815. And, in fact, this had been the case since the 1780s, but added strength and an altered external context meant that American administrations could pursue national interests more vigorously now. So Monroe's government sought protection and nurture of overseas trade, the control and acquisition of strategically significant territory, continued nonentanglement in European politics, and even neutralizing European influence in the New World. In short, American definitions of national interests mushroomed after 1815. American foreign policy became more offensive than defensive, more aggressive than passive, more self-righteous than studiously impartial. It reflected the changing American character.

American policy-makers seemed not to realize how aggressive and self-righteous they had become. James Madison and James Monroe set the pace. American merchantmen poked into the Mediterranean once again after the War of 1812, and Madison wanted to maintain an "elevated position" there for the United States. So when the Dey of Algiers attempted intimidation, Madison replied swiftly with a naval squadron and a recommendation that Congress declare war against the corsairs.[21] The application of force to protect national interests brought swift and favorable results. Later, freebooting nests in Amelia Island, off the Florida-Georgia coast, and Galveston, off the Texas coast, became troublesome. Monroe sent the navy and troops to clear them out. This simultaneously established American claims to hegemony in the region, protected trade, demonstrated neutrality in the Latin-American wars of independence, and placed Spain on notice that the United States could easily seize territory in its own interests.[22]

Madison and Monroe also pursued territorial ambitions in the Floridas. They had coveted this region since the Louisiana Purchase, and from time to time became alarmed at rumors that Great Britain might seize it. Admittedly, the Floridas were of immense strategic importance to the United States, but there was more than a trace of expansion for its own sake. This emerged in vague talk about national and natural frontiers and the destiny of geographical propinquity. Monroe and Madison had both dabbled in the settlers' revolt of 1810, which had carved a piece of West Florida away from Spain. Jackson's New Orleans victory confirmed the American presence in the Gulf of Mexico, and hence a continuing ambition for the entire Florida peninsula. Madison, and then Monroe, pressured Spain to surrender the territory, exploiting Jackson's 1818 invasion as a demonstration of American power and Spanish weakness.

Negotiation of the Transcontinental Treaty in February of 1819 seemed initially to resolve the problem. The Spanish had taken due note of Jackson's ferocity and American strength. If acquiring the Floridas was an American policy objective, they clearly had the will and power to achieve it. When Spain balked over ratification of the treaty, Monroe seemed patient. But he told Madison and others privately that he did not see how the United States could avoid simply taking Florida if the Spanish remained obdurate. He also glanced at Cuba, suspicious of English intentions, and perhaps because some southern slaveholders thought it might prove an ideal place to expand their labor system. Monroe had always concurred with Jefferson that "too much importance could not be attached to that Island, and that we ought, if possible, to incorporate it into our Union."[23] The storm of the Missouri controversy would dampen enthusiasm for any issue which threatened to revive the slavery debate after 1820, but control of the Gulf of Mexico remained a vital interest for American military and economic security.

John Quincy Adams was a tireless expansionist who combined grandiose dreams with a disciplined definition of immediate, realizable goals. Cuba was on the distant horizon. More important were establishing American claims in the far west and securing northern boundaries. He and Monroe made certain that Astoria, John Jacob Astor's fur post at the mouth of the Columbia River in Oregon, was returned according to the general terms of the Treaty of Ghent. He excluded Britain from Mississippi navigation by the Convention of 1817, even as he firmed the American-Canadian border and secured a further foothold in the Pacific northwest through joint occupation of the Oregon territory. Yet in response to European accusations that the United States was territorially ambitious, he wrote: "Nothing that we could say or do would remove this impression until the world shall be familiarized with the idea of considering our proper dominion to be the continent of North America. From the time when we became an independent people it was as much a law of nature that this should become our pretension as that the Mississippi should flow to the sea." For Adams, it was absurd that fragments of territory controlled by distant sovereigns should exist separate from the growing United States. There were laws of "political as well as of physical gravitation," and if Cuba became independent none could refuse if she requested to join the American union.[24] Adams's ambitions were both far-reaching and specific. Characteristically, while never losing sight of the former, he always tailored his diplomacy to the latter, reassured by an enhanced American strength which lent weight to his policies.

Not all expansionists had his vision, discipline, and patience. Madison thought that so long as Canada remained in British hands, it would be a source of future conflict. But he demurred about seizing territory on the grounds that its inhabitants were not making proper use of its resources. Such arguments could work to America's disadvantage, as well as in her favor. Henry Clay would have been more impetuous. He was cautious about seizing the Floridas, but only because he wanted to recognize the Latin American rebels and concentrate upon taking Texas.[25] Others were convinced that the United States would acquire Florida in good time, but if Spain began a war, then the Americans should not only capture Florida, but also go on to secure Cuba. Jackson agreed: "Texas for the present we could well do without. But without the Floridas our lower country cannot be made secure, and our Navy cannot afford protection to it in time of war."[26]

Taken to extremes, American expansionism had the potential for generating wars of conquest with a clear conscience because of the power of American ideology to cloud objectivity when it came to national interests. The American war myth convinced many nationalists that their ambitions were, in fact, rights. James Madison affirmed that the country's future conflicts would always be for national self-defense. Republican ideology persuaded politicians and citizens that the Constitution prevented Americans from fighting for glory, ambition, or injustice. Monroe concurred, and added that his government had no ambition in the European sense, but would always be guided by a "sacred regard for peace."[27] The Revolutionary generation failed to notice that its own ideology had weakened the restraining bonds of the limited-war mentality.

Members of Congress seemed less guarded. If Spain ever declared war on the United States, Samuel Smith of Maryland warned, her privateers might harry American commerce, but "in return . . . we would take Florida, might attack Cuba, and carry our arms into Mexico, through I know not how many hundred miles of wilderness." Senator Nathan Sanford and others wanted in 1820 to construct more frontier military posts to secure American interests in the interior against British competitors, expense notwithstanding. David Trimble of Kentucky, angry over Spain's refusal to ratify the Transcontinental Treaty, stated, "if the army comes in as finisher of treaties, let us have all the land, and hold it as we did West Florida, subject to negotiation." Treaties might limit American boundaries, but the "great Engineer of the Universe has fixed the natural limits of our country, and man cannot change them; that at least is above the treaty making power. To that boundary we shall go; 'peaceably if we can, forcibly if we must;' "[28] This was force and policy with a vengeance.

Such statements imply that Madison and Monroe were polite dissemblers and that the era of Manifest Destiny had arrived. But in reality they had a different perspective on expansionism from the more militant nationalists. The restraint of their eighteenth-century outlook was still at work. And from the center, where policy was made and executed, American statesmen tempered their ambitions better than congressmen anxious to make statements that might please their constituents or impress their colleagues. From Congress, and the press, therefore, a more strident note emerged than that customarily sounded by members of the administration.

Manifest Destiny had not yet arrived, but it grew out of this post-1815 period, and drew from the American war myth. The dual thrust of strident popular views and more restrained official policy would later confront President James K. Polk with a dilemma manufactured from his own party's rhetoric. Even though his territorial ambitions were specific — California and Oregon — spread-eagle hyperbole forced him to pursue a tortuous path combining force, bluster, demurring, and diplomacy in 1845. This would generate a confusing mélange of calls for conquest of all of North America, desire for specific territorial acquisition, and opposition to the Mexican War as an unjust conflict of aggression. The American war myth rendered debates over the country's moral position even more uncertain because the majority of the public refused to believe that the nation would fight any but defensive wars. The opposition's claim of a slaveholders' conspiracy seemed, therefore, much more satisfying and logical.[29]

From 1815 to 1823 the heralds of Manifest Destiny were few and muted. Calls such as Trimble's were remarkable for their isolation, and the continued American interest in neutrality at both official and popular levels suggests the continued strength of a sense of restraint. Old issues persisted, but lost much of their former fire. The United States came close to an agreement with Great Britain over impressment, for example, but ultimately failed to reach a compromise at the eleventh hour. In any event, this failure did not matter much. Americans refused to permit British access to vessels on the high seas flying the American flag. This violated the commitment of the United States to the eradication of the international slave trade, but impressment was too bitter a memory to have British naval officers inspecting American ships for any purpose. Despite their concern, however, the Americans would never again be compelled to use force to defend against this violation of national rights.[30] And while the Latin-American rebellions against Spanish rule raised the issue of neutrality once again, there was little likelihood that it would necessitate war, either.

Monroe and John Quincy Adams hewed a traditional path that blended national self-interest and a commitment to eighteenth-century principles in their policy toward these rebellions. Jefferson had initiated the American policy of recognizing *de facto* regimes, but for Monroe and Adams the rebellions seemed very much in the balance in the years just after the War of 1812. The American administration took the rebel side somewhat by viewing the struggle as a civil war and adopting a stance of neutrality. This in effect granted belligerent rights to the rebels. At the same time, Monroe's administration strengthened the neutrality laws to avoid antagonizing Spain, and Adams maintained to the Argentinian agent, Don Manuel H. de Aquirre, in 1818 that it had been a fixed American policy since independence to go to war only for strictly national interests. And Adams added that neutrals should not even attempt mediation unless invited to do so by both parties in a dispute.[31]

In 1793 popular sympathy had been with France, creating severe problems for the Washington administration's policy of neutrality. After 1815 emotions were not nearly so intense, nor the circumstances so dangerous for the United States. Henry Clay, genuinely sympathetic to the rebels, but also wanting to embarrass Monroe's government and further his own political career if he could, called repeatedly for recognition of the fledgling regimes. This would enhance American security, he claimed, because it would help to drive an old-world power forever from the new.[32] Solomon Sharp, another Kentuckian, ventured that "my most fervent wish and desire is, liberty and self-government to Main and South America; their cause is one that must and ought to be interesting to us; they are contending against tyranny and superstition of the most gloomy and hateful character." This reflected a prevailing anti-Spanish and anti-Catholic mood shared by many Americans. And John Floyd of Virginia argued that recognition of the rebels would testify to America's commitment to republicanism, suggest her strength, extend trade, and tug at the Spanish beard. Such statements in Congress drew upon the popular views expressed in editorials of the *Philadelphia Aurora*, the *Washington City Gazette*, the *Richmond Enquirer*, and Hezekiah Niles's *Weekly Register* through 1817. Baltimore became a center for rebel agents and their supporters. Merchants were eager to compete with the British, who were penetrating these emerging markets. And shipowners and unemployed sailors alike followed the lure of booty by privateering against Spanish merchantmen.[33] Opportunism, as well as ideological sympathy, colored many statements of support for the rebels. At the same time, the potential for a crusade seemed to build.

But as in 1793, administration policy contained tendencies to embark on militant republican adventures. Monroe extended an intelligence network into Spanish America, using such respectable politicians as Joel Poinsett, Theodorick Bland, Caesar A. Rodney, and John Graham. And he discovered that the revolutionary regimes were tottery, undemocratic, and indulged in caprice and excess. More important, their commitment to republicanism was superficial. When America's agents presented their reports, they dampened congressional ardor. And the United States still had more significant trading links with Spain than with the rebels, so not even financial interests would tempt policy-makers to abandon a course of strict neutrality. Besides, any precipitate action would have jeopardized the negotiations for the Transcontinental Treaty, might have unleashed Spanish privateers against American shipping in the Caribbean and points south, and could have aroused European nations to rally in Spain's defense. Monroe wanted none of this. So while the rebels found sympathetic American ears, the administration remained aloof and the hoped-for arms and funds did not pour forth. The Latin Americans justifiably became swiftly disillusioned about Yankee solidarity with the causes of self-government and republicanism.[34]

American national self-interest emerged here, as it had since the Revolution. However pristine in their republicanism, however democratic their system, the Latin Americans would not receive active help from the United States unless such aid would either assist, or not compromise, American interests. Congressmen made this clear in responding to Henry Clay's desire to extend recognition to the would-be republics to the south. Cyrus King of Massachusetts, for example, denounced Clay as a man "ready to 'cry havoc and let slip the dogs of war;' to devour thirty thousand more American citizens; to squander one hundred millions more of treasure." King's Federalist background colored his views, but the more stringent neutrality laws of 1817 passed easily. Some congressmen warned that ideological affinities must not sway sound judgments. When William Hendricks of Indiana wrote to his constituents, he noted that the rebels had only to learn the art of war effectively to win. And he thought that they would prize their liberty more dearly if they purchased it with their own blood. Lewis Williams of North Carolina wished the rebels well, but "the people in choosing representatives of the Fifteenth Congress, did not expect they would go crusading in defence of the liberties of the world."[35] As in the 1790s, expressions of republican enthusiasm were one thing; harnessing this to national policy objectives proved quite another. And majority opinion in Congress reinforced the views of Monroe's administration. The national orientation implied by the limited-war mentality and American self-interests prevailed.

The response of the United States to the Greek revolt of 1821 confirmed the pattern. This cause stirred American imaginations more than that of the Spanish-American rebels. If Spain was a despotic, imperial, Catholic power, Turkey, which controlled Greece, was worse. And Greece evoked memories of the origins of democratic thought and refined classical culture, which infatuated Americans in the early nineteenth century. Monroe reflected this partly in his 1822 address to Congress. He averred that "the United States owe to the world a great example, and, by means thereof, to the cause of liberty and humanity a generous support." But Monroe meant moral, not physical support, and he saw the United States as a passive champion of liberty by example, rather than as a crusader. John Adams seemed less dispassionate. He confessed to Jefferson that "my old imagination is kindling into a kind of missionary enthusiasm for the cause of the Greeks." The young, romantic nationalist George Bancroft, then touring Europe, saw the Greeks as "a nation rising against tyranny and vindicating the rights of man. Since the days of the American war for independence, there has been no scene of exertion so pure and so glorious as this." In 1823 and 1824, Americans demonstrated through Philhellenic societies, which channelled funds and volunteers, how much they agreed. The Boston physician, Samuel Gridley Howe, moved by Lord Byron's death on behalf of Greek freedom, made a pilgrimage to aid the rebels. Impassioned orators and writers, such as Daniel Webster, Henry Clay, and Edward Everett, through the pages of the *North American Review* encouraged popular enthusiasm, hoping for official support.[36] But once again, state policy diverged from public opinion. Assistance to Greece remained entirely private.

In Congress, Daniel Webster introduced a resolution to send an official American representative to the Greek rebels. Joel Poinsett agreed that "our sympathies are always with the oppressed — our feelings are always engaged in the cause of liberty," but warned that "any interference on our part, in favor of a cause which not even remotely affects our interests, could only be regarded in the light of a crusade, and might injure the Greeks by alarming the fears of the Allied Powers." Americans might be strong at home, but they could not project beyond their own sphere, where their strength would be dissipated. Poinsett reflected the American republican view that the United States was mighty in defense, but would forfeit its advantages and interests if it engaged in offensive action. George Cary of Georgia, another armchair sympathizer, thought that the United States had done enough for liberty by winning its own freedom and serving as an example to the world. Crusades would not prosper and would only erode liberty at home. Cary feared the impact of war on American society, and Silas Wood of New York put the case more bluntly. Nations owed other nations nothing save "the duties of humanity." Besides, the members of Congress derived no authority from the Constitution to engage in offensive wars of ambition, nor to embark on crusades for religion or secular ideologies.[37] The defensive emphasis of the American war myth was clear in all these remarks, as was the view of national self-interest. There was nothing to gain from intervention in Europe, and potentially a great deal to lose.

The rebels' causes in Latin America and Greece illustrated how ideological convictions were subordinate to national interests. Prudence, restraint, not some struggle between tyranny and freedom, motivated American policy-makers. These men believed that republicanism was unalterably opposed to monarchism. They also believed that European monarchs would trample on liberty whenever they could. At the same time, liberty had a dynamism which would lead it on to ultimate victory. The triumphs of reactionism would only be momentary in the span of history. Despotism would decay and sink into ruin through the forces of progress, but not because of what the United States did or did not do. By its very existence, America aided the cause of republicanism. Hence a sense of history, republican ideology, American nationalism, and the vital interests of the state proved mutually reinforcing for Americans concerned with policy-making. These republican Americans would not jeopardize the gains of liberty by gambling on causes removed from the vital interests of the United States. Liberty was a universal cause of truth, but history guaranteed its triumph. And in the meantime, American concerns took precedence because members of government had a duty to protect the society they represented and governed.

James Monroe therefore followed the tradition of the Revolutionary generation by submerging republican sympathies in a policy of nonentanglement. John Quincy Adams noted to Hugh Nelson that the causes of civil liberty and national independence linked America's own revolution with the current struggles. Americans could not be indifferent, but they must stand aloof. "The first and paramount duty of the government is to maintain *peace* amidst all the convulsions of foreign wars, and to enter the lists as parties to no cause other than our own." Foreign adventures would alter the thrust of the American system from "*liberty* to *power*," he told Edward Everett, when that writer pleaded for Adams's support for the Greeks. And to a Greek envoy, Mr. Luriottis, he was indulgent, but firm. Since the United States was at peace with all countries, interests of policy and international obligations prevented it from taking any action that might involve the country in war.[38]

National interests and the practical bent of the limited-war mentality held a firm check on impulsive sympathies. And Americans had been consistent in this regard from the Revolution onward. Although crusading tendencies emerged, national self-interests as defined by American leaders controlled popular enthusiasms, even when they ran counter to official policy. Although architects of a revolution, the Revolutionary generation retained the conservatism of enlightened eighteenth-century liberals. Proper and prudent government struck a balance between despotism and mob rule. Americans related the use of force closely to national policy objectives. Their clear sense of national self-interests held heady ambitions at bay. The American war myth after 1815 embraced and did not challenge such convictions.

An emerging national policy objective that might justify the use of force, on the other hand, was reducing European influence in the Americas, especially where that bordered on the United States. In theory, the Revolutionary generation had argued for separation of European and American spheres, since it considered the former a perpetual source of war.[39] When French troops marched across the Pyrenees to quash a Constitutionalist-Republican revolt in Spain, in response to the wishes of the Congress of Verona, the event not only confirmed monarchical tyranny, but also underscored the need for nonentanglement. Monroe noted that this intervention might lead to another war in Europe, but it was America's good fortune to be distant from such broils and John Quincy Adams strove to translate this conviction into policy.[40]

The American war myth intertwined with nonentanglement. Assuming the superiority of republicanism over monarchism, and seeing little hope for the present of republican success in Europe, separation was necessary. Alfred Gatlin told his constituents that America's tranquillity stemmed from its peaceful habits and character, as well as from nonentanglement. And Madison, reflecting upon Monroe's statements in the December 1823 message to Congress that came to be called the Monroe Doctrine, wrote that "this hemisphere must be protected agst the doctrines & despotisms which degrade the other."[41] Thus republicanism and the American war myth after 1815 continued the tradition of the limited-war mentality in shaping foreign policy.

Monroe's 1823 message packed diverse strands in American thought on war, peace, international politics, and the ambitions and character of the United States into a single thesis. Monroe exhibited a broad self-consciousness, a sense of independence, and an aggressive nationalism that capsuled the emerging American way. His message defined the nation's vital interests and expressed its self-proclaimed role as the premier state of the New World, as well as its moral leadership of republicanism.[42] The

Monroe Doctrine drew from general attitudes and specific circumstances, especially Great Britain's overture to Richard Rush
that the United States join in a declaration that would discourage
rumors that France might assist Spain to recover her lost colonies
under the umbrella of the Holy Alliance. Monroe cast a wide net
to construct a consensus in cabinet on what to do. Andrew
Jackson, as America's leading military luminary, had always
urged Monroe to develop an aggressive, nationalistic policy.
Monroe also sought the advice of Madison and Jefferson, as the
retired Republican sages. When Monroe wrote to Jefferson that
"we would view an interference on the part of the European
powers, and especially an attack on the Colonies, by them, as an
attack on ourselves," Jefferson concurred and suggested joining
England:

> Not that I would purchase even her amity at the price of taking part in
> her wars. But the war in which the present proposition might engage
> us . . . is not her war but ours. Its object is to introduce and establish
> the American system, of keeping out of our land all foreign powers, or
> never permitting those of Europe to intermeddle with the affairs of
> our nations.[43]

Jefferson's distinctly proprietary view reflected a broad outlook
—the republicanism and nationalism which lay behind the
Monroe Doctrine.

Although the Americans did not know it, the circumstances
that produced the initial British overtures altered swiftly. Just the
same, John Quincy Adams favored transforming a bilateral into a
unilateral statement. He toned down some of Monroe's language
expressing sympathy with the Greek revolt, but emphasized
American defiance of European intrusion into the New World.
"We owe it, therefore, to candor," Monroe warned, "and to the
amicable relations existing between the United States and those
powers to declare that we should consider any attempt on their
part to extend their system to any portion of this hemisphere as
dangerous to our peace and safety." The United States would
apparently resist new colonizing ventures, such as those by Russia
down the northwest coast from Alaska, as well as attempts at
reconquest, as the false rumors of the Holy Allies' intentions had
suggested. The message implied that force would sustain this
policy, but privately, Monroe revealed his flexibility. He explained to Jefferson why no joint declaration had been made with

Britain. Speaking alone would elevate national prestige, he believed, and "besides, it does not follow, from what has been said, that we should be bound to engage in the war, in such event."[44]

The Monroe Doctrine illustrates also the emerging American war myth. The nation would act in self-defense only, and the justice of its cause was clearly implied, even though aggressive national pretensions poked through the mild language of the statement. Cautious restraint still tempered the ostensibly bold declaration, indicating that the prudence of the limited-war mentality in relating force to policy still pertained, at least in the mind of James Monroe.

This underlying current of restraint ran through the foreign policy of the Monroe administration. In 1816, for example, congressmen digressed while discussing a new commercial treaty with Great Britain. Those who considered the matter saw force as a limited instrument of policy, closely controlled by law, whether it was the law of nations, as some asserted, or municipal regulations, as others preferred to believe. And, as John G. Jackson stated, "the laws of war are essentially humane and liberal, and every civilized nation that respects the opinions of the world, and the faithful award of posterity, will keep them sacred."[45] This was the eighteenth century speaking. And it spoke on other occasions, as when John Quincy Adams denied that the War of 1812 had cancelled existing international obligations. He argued that wars had only a limited impact on human affairs, and specific treaty agreements must take precedence.[46] Although war was inevitable, although force could be used in self-defense or to pursue national policy objectives, control, restraint, and limitation must remain bywords to harmonize war and civilization.

Andrew Jackson's invasion of Florida in 1818 harnessed the most aggressive tendencies of the emerging American war myth to challenge this tradition. When the first Seminole War flared up, Jackson received orders to march against the Indians. Monroe told Congress in March that he did not expect the fighting to extend beyond that season. But American troops could pursue the enemy into Florida as part of the policy of self-defense. If hot pursuit became necessary, those involved would act in accord with "the highest obligations and privileges of this great and sacred right." This message has the ring of a prepared excuse, because in Jackson, Monroe had a commander who would scarcely feel inhibited by liberal ideals if his blood was up. And John C. Calhoun, as secretary of war, had ordered the general to do whatever proved necessary to conclude the campaign successfully. At the same time he had warned that Americans must always seem to have justice on their side so that if war did come, the United States would be maintaining its rights, and not engaging in conquest.[47] This exposed the darker potentials of the American war myth. The appearance of justice would serve as well as its substance. Further, conquest could be conducted under the rubric of defense of rights. National policy objectives, in short, could be masked by rhetorical assertions.

When Jackson marched against the Seminoles, he epitomized the frontiersman's contempt for the Spanish and for any Indian who dared to attack white settlers. He carried out a *de facto* conquest of Spanish Florida and hanged two Britishers, Alexander Arbuthnot and Robert C. Ambrister, who had been captured with the Indians. Jackson also occupied Spanish St. Marks, and his army became the sole power of the region. He seems to have assumed that he had the tacit complicity of Monroe's administration, although he could not obtain official sanction for a scheme he had concocted to have this reach his ears by a third source to avoid outright executive involvement. Still, Jackson instructed General Edmund P. Gaines to proceed against St. Augustine and collar its garrison unless direct orders to the contrary arrived from the War Department. Monroe was alarmed when he discovered what Jackson had done. The law of nations permitted pursuit of an enemy, he wrote to the general, but it could not authorize seizure of a Spanish post because that was an act of war. "Congress alone possess the power." Besides, if America did go to war against Spain, "it is of the greatest importance that our people be united, and with that view, that Spain commence it; and, above all, that the government be free from the charge of committing a breach of the Constitution."[48]

Jackson had concluded the Seminole War, as ordered, but he had generated the possibility of a conflict with Spain, which might compromise American interests. Monroe called the cabinet to consider the crisis. In the end, the administration restored the captured Spanish posts and sought to exploit the incident to press its foreign policy objectives regarding a settlement of all Spanish-

American differences over old claims, the Floridas, and a boundary to the Pacific. Not even the American war myth permitted
members of the administration to launch a conflict against
common sense, the laws of nations, and constitutional restric-
tions. John Quincy Adams tried simultaneously to conciliate and
pressure the Spanish minister to the United States, Don Luis de
Onis. Adams termed the executions of the Englishmen as
"retributive justice" which in a war with uncivilized peoples
permitted the elimination of "leading warriors taken in arms,
and, still more, the lives of their foreign white incendiaries."[49]
This was how Jefferson had viewed British Major Henry Hamilton during the Revolution, and how Americans had traditionally
distinguished civilized from savage warfare. The Spanish duly
noted how easily Jackson had brushed aside their forces in
Florida, but proclaimed their honor satisfied with the return of
the posts. Diplomacy plastered the crack Jackson's fist had made
in Spanish-American relations.

But Jackson was the American war myth incarnate. Personally,
he had little sense of restraint. His nationalism and fiery
temperament led him to believe that his country was always just.
Any action that furthered the national interest as he defined it was
therefore right. Summary executions became moral acts through
the citation of vague laws of nature or nations wrenched from
context. Jackson was the antithesis of a George Washington who
reflected the refined and liberal restraint of the limited-war
mentality at its finest. And Jackson embodied American attitudes
toward warfare against the Indians. When fighting savages, it was
not necessary, it was even foolish, to be civilized.

Although Monroe and the cabinet decided that Jackson acted
on his own authority, and did nothing except soothe Spanish
pride to contradict the general, a group in Congress in January
1819 wanted more. In the Senate, Abner Lacock of Pennsylvania,
one of William Crawford's political allies and therefore a Jackson
antagonist, condemned the general as a military adventurer.
Spain's failure to control the Seminoles could not sanction the
invasion. The United States now stood exposed as a nation
willing to sweep away neutrals' rights by sheer might. The
Executive had properly disavowed the seizures of the posts. But
the executions of Ambrister and Arbuthnot had been "cold
blooded," and even though savages who paid no attention to the

law of nations could expect vengeance in kind, any civilized nation that resorted to such measures would stand degraded and debased. Besides, this violated Christian precepts and moral rectitude alike. "Retaliation in the United States has always been confined to specified acts of cruelty."[50] Whatever his motivations, Lacock clearly invoked the canons of the limited-war mentality.

Members of the House of Representatives reacted variously to Jackson's invasion. Some were scandalized. Some thought that both the Constitution and Spanish territory had suffered. Southerners supported the invasion because it cleared out what had been sanctuaries for runaway slaves. Still others saw Jackson as a man on horseback, a Cromwell or Caesar in an American uniform. There were those who cheered, and those who recoiled from the strident national emotions aroused by the incident. More than a few sought to exploit it to embarrass the Monroe administration. Henry Clay's motivation was clear in this regard. But Thomas Nelson of Virginia, speaking for a bare majority of the House Military Committee, which brought down resolutions of censure on Jackson, spoke for the limited-war mentality.

Nelson began with a piece of sophistry. The law of nations permitted retaliation in kind on a savage enemy, he argued, to educate them into humanity. But if such severity was not necessary, then mercy became a duty. By his acts, Jackson had violated the laws of the United States, of nations, and of humanity. When Nelson had finished, Richard M. Johnson, of the same committee, delivered a "minority" report that exonerated the general. For Johnson, the law of nations sanctified Jackson's behavior. He had justifiably sought to crush brutal savages and had seized the Spanish posts because Spain had been unable or unwilling to control the Indians. Progress had eliminated many of war's worst abuses, but if a nation departed from proper conduct, reprisals could be carried out to teach the offenders to behave better in the future. And Ambrister and Arbuthnot deserved their fate because they had fought with savages.[51]

A debate ensued between what can be characterized as champions of the limited-war mentality and advocates of the American war myth. Two camps emerged, and attitudes toward Jackson and politics had more to do with how congressmen sorted themselves out than attitudes toward war. Nevertheless, the debate symbolized diverging American perspectives on the nature of human conflict. John Holmes, a Massachusetts Federalist, defended the general; Henry Clay did not. Retaliation was only justified, Clay stated, if it affected the outcome of the war. Otherwise, humanity and justice demanded moderation. Many agreed with Clay, despite his partisan and self-seeking motivations, and frequently because of them. Alexander Smyth of Virginia, on the other hand, believed that a war waged by Indians sought only plunder, massacre, destruction, and revenge. "A nation attacked by such enemies is under no obligation to treat them as lawful enemies. They may be hanged as robbers or banditti." Ambrister and Arbuthnot stood condemned because they were allied to savages, Philip Barbour argued, but Charles Mercer cautioned that if this practice ever became widespread, it would plunge the world into barbarism. "In refusing to wage a war for revenge, and blending martial courtesy with valor, a nation advances her true glory." Finally, John Rhea, an old militant from Tennessee, Jackson's home state, summarized what became majority opinion in this debate, and captured the spirit of the American war myth at the same time:

> General Jackson was authorized by the supreme law of nature and nations, the law of self-defence, corresponding with the great national maxim, namely, the safety of the people . . . to enter the Spanish territory of Florida in pursuit of, and to destroy, hostile, murdering savages, not bound by any obligation, who were without the practice of any moral principle reciprocally obligatory on nations.[52]

If Rhea's speech stated the summary for the defense, Timothy Fuller of Massachusetts epitomized the case for the prosecution. In a just war, the enemy must not be made to suffer any more than was required by the object of the resort to arms. And the object was to "conquer the enemy and compel him to do justice." War was a method of arbitration. Further, one could not distinguish between civilized and savage enemies. "In all cases, the evils of war must be limited to a reasonable probability of effecting the purpose for which war was commenced." To do otherwise would make "wanton cruelty and useless bloodshed" legal. Moderation and humanity, even against savages, "are beheld and pointed out by foreign nations as tokens of future triumph — as emblams of republican virtue — infallible omens of speedy ascendency over the naval tyranny of our enemy. It well becomes our great Republic, and should be cultivated as a precious gem of our national character, to mitigate the horrors of war." Fuller's eloquence reflected the humane attitudes and aspirations of the eighteenth century, but to no avail in this instance. The censure resolutions were resoundingly defeated.[53] The American war myth seemed triumphant.

This debate and its outcome cannot be seen entirely in terms of a symbolic clash between old and new American perspectives on war. The issue embraced many facets. Jackson was a national hero, seen as a coming man in politics. Rivals thus sought to forestall his political rise. But Jackson had done what many Americans would cheerfully have accomplished themselves in scattering the Seminoles and humbling the Spanish. Partisan politics and frontier arrogance were far more important for the fate of the censure resolution on Jackson than competing philosophies on war. And yet the outcome reflected the future of American attitudes. The emerging war myth would prevail over the traditions of the limited-war mentality which the Revolutionary generation had cherished and sought to propagate.

The threat of force continuously underlay American policy toward Spain, and the Americans never doubted the justice of their claims. In December of 1815, some seizures in the Gulf of Mexico conjured a brief war scare for the following year. Monroe had discovered then that European nations did not want to see a Spanish-American conflict, but swift Spanish disavowals had satisfied the United States, and the scare evaporated.[54] Boundary disputes provided another example of how force might sustain policy. After Jackson's invasion, the Spanish proved more accommodating and granted American demands for the Floridas and the long-sought boundary to the Pacific Ocean in February 1819. Generally popular, the Transcontinental Treaty muted anti-Spanish feelings and smothered overt sympathies for the Latin-American rebels.

But Spain balked over ratifying the treaty and the administration considered military action. John C. Calhoun did not expect trouble in August 1819, but by November his War Department had begun planning. In his December message to Congress, Monroe stated that Spanish behavior provided a foundation for action on the grounds of injustice and national rights and interests. He then evoked the American war myth to sanction future contingencies:

> Our national honor must be maintained, and a new and distinguished proof afforded of that regard for justice and moderation which has invariably governed the council of this free people. It must be obvious to all that if the United States had been desireous of making conquests, or had even been willing to aggrandize themselves in that way, they could have had no inducement to form this treaty.[55]

Monroe spoke for broad American opinion on this issue. Jackson hoped for a campaign and had retained his commission in part because of a possible war with Spain. But he did not expect that Congress would act. The administration remained reluctant to employ force, and John Quincy Adams told William Lowndes, chairman of the House Foreign Relations committee, that military action would not be required unless negotiations with Spain broke down completely. At the same time, Monroe and Adams wanted the authority to move swiftly if necessary, and Lowndes's committee obediently recommended a bill authorizing the president to take possession of East and West Florida and establish a government there.[56]

The drift toward a Spanish-American war slowed, and then stalled. By March of 1820 it was over. The Spanish sent a new minister, and their internal turmoil arising from the Constitutionalist revolt made the American administration pause. Besides, Monroe discovered that Great Britain and France, while they would not assist Spain, would look askance at any American use of force. Nearly another year, and a second ratification by the United States Senate, passed before the Transcontinental Treaty took effect, but by the summer of 1821, Jackson could report the peaceful "surrender" of Florida to American control.[57] Throughout, the Americans had been prepared to use troops to achieve their policy objectives. And if it had been necessary, Jackson would have performed a speedy encore of his 1818 conquest with full administration blessing and congressional support. For his part, James Monroe had blended the restraint of the limited-war mentality with the nationalistic self-righteousness of the American war myth.

Monroe was a transition figure in the evolution of American attitudes toward war. Even as the American war myth emerged, it retained many eighteenth-century elements. Ideas are not linked with behavior in a lock-step manner. Yet attitudes toward military conflict, its likelihood, its functions, and the manner of its application after 1815, came directly from the outlook of the Revolutionary generation. New elements related to American nationalism and ambitions. But at the center of affairs and policy-making, a sense of restraint prevailed. The American war myth contributed to this impression through its conviction that repub-lics were pacific and would only fight in self-defense, and then only because of manifest injustice. The division of powers in the Constitution proved a further brake upon aggressive impulses.

The American war myth was thus Janus-faced. On one side, it could be aggressive, imperious, self-righteous because of the powerful nationalism which prompted its expressions. On the other, it was restrained, forbearing, reluctant to resort to force. Alfred Cuthbert of Georgia gave this myth, with its ambiguities, full expression, capsuling American ideas about war as they had developed by the time the Revolutionary generation had all but disappeared from the national scene:

> Monarchy can go to war from policy or ambition, and if they do not find it suits their views they can, with almost equal ease, withdraw from the contest. But it is far otherwise with Republics. In these, before you enter a war, you must convince the mass of the nation that the war is virtuous and just in its principles, and unavoidable without disgrace. When a free people have become, by reflection, convinced of this, they become reckless of consequences; you rouse a deeper spirit; you concentrate a mightier wrath than a despotic Government can even know. There is a moral force that mingles with the physical, and propels it with redoubled energy. But, if the war is unreasonable, unjust, unnecessary, when any calamity happens in its prosecution they at once look back to its origin, re-examine its principles; they ask, in a spirit of discontent and indignation, why it was not avoided; and they wreak their vengeance on its authors.[58]

Cuthbert's commentary has been cited at length because it reveals persistent nuances of the American war myth that have great significance for continuing American ideas. The view that popular majorities must support military action; the view that republics are pacific by nature; the cynical perspective on the motivation of monarchs; the faith that the people will recognize whether a war is unjust or unnecessary; the faith that the popular will can control executive adventurism — all are themes in

twentieth-century American history. But this perspective over-
looks that national indignation and pride can smother rational
reflection, and that ideological convictions can so grip popular
enthusiasm that considerations of justice seem irrelevant because
of a sense of self-righteousness. At the same time, Cuthbert's
statement shows why Americans have historically considered
themselves a peaceful people.

Another difficulty with the American war myth is that it relied
upon second thought instead of prior reflection. It is true that
popular passions can be deflected and a government that embarks
on an unwise war may, from a political standpoint, rue its
decision. But such popular transformations occur slowly and take
time to emerge as a counterweight to unwise policy. Much evil
can be perpetrated in the interim, even precipitating an erosion in
the faith in national values, as the Mexican and even Vietnam
wars would suggest. Exponents of the *jus ad bellum* from St.
Augustine to Emmerich de Vattel, on the other hand, focused on
prior restraint to reduce the number and severity of wars. The
American war myth embraced the alleged pacifism of republics
and the institutional distribution of powers in the Constitution as
an alternative. Nationalism and the growth of executive power
have eroded both foundations of limitation.

During the Revolutionary and Early National periods of
American history, however, those at the center of policy-making
balanced passion and reason. This dualism was at the core of their
philosophies of life, not to mention their views on social and
political organization. The Revolutionary generation faded in
time, but left a significant legacy in the tenets of the limited-war
mentality, which became incorporated into American national
doctrines on war and peace. This restraint succumbed to other,
newer forces, reflected in the ambitions and attitudes of younger
generations of politicians and national leaders — expansionism,
a sense of national superiority and destiny, an increasing tendency to equate ambitions with rights — which harnessed the
view that war is an instrument for achieving policy objectives.
Despite the American war myth, therefore, the United States has
not historically behaved markedly differently from other nation-
states pursuing self-defined interests and rights. American universalist rhetoric, held over from the eighteenth century and the
Revolution, created a gap between self-image and reality that
emerged only spasmodically in the period after 1815.

Silas Wood of New York and Alfred Cuthbert presented this strident self-delusion in sharp relief. Wood argued that Providence intended the American people for "high destinies." The United States was a "great moral empire" and God had "connected our felicity with an incapacity for wars of ambition or conquest which would impair it." Cuthbert agreed. "The sustaining energy of a free Government pervades the land, and raises and strengthens the character of all who inhabit it. In such a country, wars can never be waged for glory or empire."[59]

Wood and Cuthbert used eighteenth-century terminology to understand nineteenth-century circumstances. They did not see how the implications of their assertions contradicted their thesis of a peaceful United States. For it was nationalism which transformed the restraint of the limited-war mentality into the assumed inhibitions of the American war myth. By taking such ideological invocations for granted, instead of constantly exerting their will to match theory with reality as the Revolutionary generation had done, Americans would henceforth not entirely understand themselves when it came to employing force. After 1815 a sense of realism remained in American thought, but national ambitions, self-righteousness, and a universalist rhetoric at a popular level created a gap between intentions and behavior. Men often lose their innocence when confronted by the demands of the real world. When the Revolutionary generation faded, Americans, on the other hand, acquired an innocent perception of war and their military role which they would not lose until the atomic age.

8

LEGACIES AND LEGENDS:
AN AMERICAN VIEW OF WAR

The limited-war mentality of the Revolutionary generation dominated American ideas about the origins, application, justice, and objectives of the use of force in world affairs from the mid-eighteenth century to the second decade of the nineteenth century. This mentality gathered elements of thought and experience from Christian precepts, Enlightenment ideals, European statecraft, concepts about the nature of man, historical evidence, views of the nature of international law, convictions about the nature of states, America's own colonial experience, and finally the apparent needs of the United States, which emerged from the imperial crisis of 1763-83 in the old British Empire. This attitude of mind toward war emphasized restraint and the exertion of reason in a realm where human passions normally display great power. Americans discovered that the same forces that had produced the age of limited wars in Europe — the need to gain the consent of parts or the whole of a populace, the costs, the vulnerability to retaliation, the scarcity of resources, the fear of defeat, the moral inhibitions about the use of violence, and the calculation of objectives — acted upon them. The Revolutionary leaders knew that war is a human act, premeditated and purposive, and while fearing its excesses, they employed it in the belief that it could be controlled. There were flaws in their reasoning, and contradictions brought about by the nature of war itself. But regarding European antagonists at least, the Revolutionary leaders assumed that nations in war stood as moral equals, subject to civilized practices. In conducting wars, suffering must be restricted, especially upon the innocent. The possibility of peace being swiftly restored must always be apparent, reprisals must be used sparingly as a deterrent to barbarism, and above all, statesmen must never forget that war is a method of arbitration between sovereign equals defending their self-defined interests, and not a crusade.[1]

Although it is sometimes difficult to weld an amalgam of thought on the one hand to behavior or policy decisions on the other, there is no doubt that the Revolutionary leaders drew upon and applied the precepts of the limited-war mentality as they cultivated the interests of the United States, especially after 1783. In many ways, despite their republicanism and their moral idealism about international relations, they were typical eighteenth-century statesmen. The tenets of the *jus ad bellum* are evident in their foreign policy. The guidelines of the *jus in bello* operated during their conflicts with English, French, and even Indian enemies. Without succumbing to cynicism, they anticipated war in the future, just as they expected a republican democracy to be less aggressive and reluctant to fight, even when provoked. Crusading impulses interwove through the period of this generation's political domination of American affairs, yet these ideals never breached the barricades of restraint when it came to war. To a significant degree, the conflicts of the United States from 1775 to 1823 were limited wars of policy in the eighteenth-century tradition.

Contrasting forces worked against such restraint nevertheless. Human passions emerged in debates over the rights and applications of retaliation. Americans generally distinguished sharply between "civilized" and "savage" warfare as well. Against Indians, the inhibitions of the limited-war mentality exercised less control over American behavior.

And new trends arose which generated illusions about certain aspects of the limited-war mentality, culminating in the American war myth. This lay within eighteenth-century thinking about war and peace, but was dormant until an increasingly self-confident nationalism, combined with a greater sense of national security and self-righteousness regarding national ambitions, gave it shape. The American war myth emerged after 1815 as a developing American philosophy of war.

Another, and more significant point, was the tension which frequently existed between popular conceptions and those of the Revolutionary leaders when cast in their roles as policy-makers. American zeal for the French Revolution led to both popular and congressional opposition to George Washington's policy of strict neutrality in 1793. Building upon fear and suspicion of Great Britain, this enthusiasm contributed to the rise of the first party system, and carried into the Quasi-War with France. After Thomas Jefferson's triumph in 1800, such tensions subsided, but only for a time. They arose again, albeit in partisan form, during the Embargo of 1808 and during James Madison's administration over the policies that preceded the War of 1812 and the decision to fight. And the people disagreed among themselves, as well as with policy-makers, about whether and how force should be used.

These ideas carried beyond 1815, to popular responses to James K. Polk's campaigns to acquire Oregon from Britain and California from Mexico. He exploited the rhetoric of Manifest Destiny so well that he nearly found his country in a confrontation with the British. But diplomacy eased Oregon from partial to full ownership of the United States. Such was not the case with Mexico, and while the west and south supported Polk's limited war of policy for territory, significant segments of opinion in the midwest and northeast did not. Opposition spokesmen employed arguments drawn from the *jus ad bellum* to condemn the Mexican War of 1846 as unjust and immoral, a struggle for conquest and not for national rights.[2]

The elements of the limited-war mentality survived in American thought, a legacy for generations following the Revolution. Albert Gallatin and John Quincy Adams were still present in 1846 to articulate it in old-fashioned terms. But the significant point is that they reflected a segment of American opinion about the just use of force as an instrument of policy. And despite the power of the antebellum reform movement in the United States, pacifism remained a trivial, if noble, effort in terms of both numbers and influence. Among literary and intellectual circles, a strongly moralistic, even millennial view of war developed, which led to perceptions of the Civil War as a moral crusade and a positive force in the advancement of civilization.[3] Against such convictions, pacifism made little headway, even as it failed to penetrate nationalism. The American war myth convinced many Americans that their system was peaceful, evidence to the contrary notwithstanding.

The influence of the limited-war mentality on the Civil War is less certain than on the conflicts of the Revolutionary generation, but it was nevertheless there. Many of America's leading soldiers and politicians took up arms with an eighteenth-century mentality that resisted crusading impulses. Among soldiers, the writings of the Baron Henri de Jomini had been widely known and absorbed. Jomini's military manual was highly technical, but it contained an underlying philosophy which accepted war as an integral part of civilization subject to control through the application of human reason. Jomini, horrified by the abandon of the Napoleonic struggles, deplored their fanaticism openly, preferring the order, harmony, and restraint of the previous age. Because of Jomini's influence, Civil War strategy betrayed elements of this fundamental perspective. Winfield Scott's anaconda plan, for example, sought to subdue the Confederacy with a minimum loss of life and destruction to property through the application of superior resources, rather than the Napoleonic wastage of superior manpower in furious battle. William Tecumseh Sherman and Philip Sheridan, renowned as practitioners of modern, even total warfare, did not lust for vengeance or view their cause as a crusade.[4]

A case can also be made that both Abraham Lincoln and Jefferson Davis had limited objectives. While subjugation of the Confederacy and Southern independence could not be compromised, Lincoln understood that if the conquest of the South were not done with restraint, reunification might prove a hollow triumph rendered bitter by prolonged military occupation. And Davis wanted to have the Confederacy live in peace with its neighbor, assuming his country could make good its claims to sovereign status. Such an argument cannot transform the nature of the Civil War, but it does illustrate the need to define terms cautiously and examine attitudes closely. Total war is best confined to those conflicts which engulf a country's entire citizenry and resources in the struggle for victory. This effort may or may not be related to unlimited policy objectives. For example, Rome employed only part of her resources against Carthage, yet her objective was to reduce her enemy to a memory. And she did just that. After their armies collapsed, the Carthaginians were rounded up and sold into slavery, their city was razed, and their lands sewn with salt. Few defeats in history have been so complete. Unlimited ends and unlimited means are separate elements in war, as are restricted ends and restricted means. While war is risky, statesmen and soldiers can manipulate these elements, despite the chaos which often accompanies a decision to resort to arms.

Karl von Clausewitz understood this perhaps the best of any of the philosophers of war in the modern world. Grappling with the inner dynamics of conflict, he created a scale with limitation at one end and the absolute at the other. But absolute war proved more an intellectual construct than an achieveable reality. He emphasized the will and judgment of statesmen, and wrote of limited aims, restricted means, and "friction" that prevented war from reaching a plateau of absolute intensity. Most important, war was an instrument of policy. Men created it.[5] The Revolutionary generation also understood this, and, like Clausewitz, it saw no sharp dividing lines between peace and war, since elements of force always played on human affairs in a world of self-responsible nation-states.

The origins of war are complex and vary with circumstances. But scholars past and present have by no means agreed on this. Some emphasize mankind's inner nature, others his systems of social and political organization, or his economic interests. And one cannot omit the power of ideology, ignorance, and greed operating both on individuals making policy and populations at large in accounting for the occurrence of war.[6] An untidy rhythm emerges in western history from the Renaissance onward, which suggests that war has moved from a limited to an unlimited nature. The United States has existed within this rhythm, subject to many of the forces that have produced its pulsations. The limited-war mentality, to take the example which influenced the Revolutionary generation, was in large part a reaction to the excesses of the Religious Wars. In part, an act of will collectively maintained by European sovereigns, and reinforced by circumstances, did produce an age of limited wars. The apparent effectiveness of their efforts may have so lulled Europeans that they failed to guard against the excesses which could flow from a new outburst of ideological fervor with the French Revolution. Frenchmen in 1793 had taken up arms convinced that republics were peaceful and fought only in self-defense. But France marched swiftly over the frail barricades of the limited-war mentality to topple the *ancien régime* and convulse Europe for over twenty years. The United States remained on the fringes politically, economically, militarily, and intellectually. For Lazare Carnot and the decree of 23 August 1793, which called for total war, had no American counterpart.[7]

The French wars had been neither foreseen nor wanted. European liberals had not anticipated the explosion that national ideology and "defensive" war could create. Immanuel Kant and Jean Jacques Rousseau, like Thomas Paine and James Madison, assumed that republican revolution would foster a more peaceful world. Instead it spawned a monster.[8] And following Napoleon's defeat in 1815, the fragments of the old ruling classes scrambled to prevent future armageddons. The rhythm had returned to restraint, even though the ideological power of nationalism and liberalism dominated European thought in the nineteenth century. The reactionary monarchs, symbolized in the Holy Alliance, carefully contained their wars, so much so that continental armies for the next century spent more time fighting street rioters and recalcitrant natives than one another. Europe's politics smouldered and frequently threatened war, just as Americans suspected, but all the conflicts from 1815 to 1914 were limited — the Turks and the Greeks in 1821, which sprang from revolution; the Austrians and the Piedmontese in 1848, 1859, and 1866; the Russians and the Turks in 1828 and 1877; the Polish and Hungarian troubles in 1831 and 1848-49; the Russians and the Anglo-French in 1854-56; the French and the Austrians in 1859; the wars of Italian unification in the 1860s; and the wars of Prussia with Denmark, Austria, and France from 1864 to 1871.[9] Throughout, European armies pushed imperial possessions and controls into remote regions, such as the Atlas Mountains of North Africa or through the Khyber Pass in India, even as American troops consolidated the sovereignty of the United States against dwindling Indian tribes. Andrew Jackson's expedition into Florida in 1818 has its counterparts in threatened clashes of European rivals as they divided Africa and Asia among themselves. And later in the nineteenth century, Americans fell prey to more familiar imperial impulses in the aftermath of the Spanish-American War.[10]

American views of and experiences with war have important
parallels with Europe which scholars have not always appreciated. The notion of American uniqueness has much validity.
But regarding understanding of the American view of war,
scholars have argued that Americans perceive war with liberal,
democratic eyes, as a human aberration, which must not be used
to pursue mere policy objectives, but only to defend the homeland
or great principles. In brief, scholars agree that Americans have
been anti-Clausewitzian in outlook. To a great extent, however,
this is an illusion which has built upon the rhetoric of nationalism and the American war myth.

Alexis de Tocqueville initiated the trend. Even though democracies would experience wars, like all societies, their social and
political systems induced feelings of equality and created a strong
sense of community which would mute military passions. He
implied that democracies would tend to wage crusades once they
had embarked on war: "There are two things that a democratic
people will always find very difficult, to begin a war and to end
it." De Tocqueville took American professions in this regard at
face value. Emory Upton, a late-nineteenth-century reforming
army officer, was more penetrating. Americans had always
believed that their wars were in the interests of the people. But the
people's interests usually proved more a reflection of the interests
of legislators than of the people themselves. Upton cited the
difficulties of the volunteer system as proof of his claim. It was
Upton's object to have America discard the militia and volunteer
systems for a more professional army, but in penetrating the war
myth, he collided with the republican antimilitarism that had
survived from the eighteenth century. In an obscure post-World
War I pacifist tract, C. H. Hamlin took Americans to task for
believing that their wars were always defensive. The United States
had been as bellicose as any other country in history.[11] These early
statements probably had little influence on historiography, but
they illustrate different aspects of the way the American war myth
drew attention.

More significant are two statements by prominent diplomatic
historians just after World War II. Thomas A. Bailey accepted
that popular government provoked wars just as frequently as
monarchies or even totalitarian states. But he also believed that
the forces which drove other peoples to fight — scanty resources,

overpopulation, lack of land — did not apply in the United States. This brief foray into the origins of war lacked penetrating power and led to little understanding of the subject. But in its context, it implied again that the United States was exempt from the usual historical forces which produced conflict. Dexter Perkins was more explicit. Americans had in the past fought for more than mere defense of the homeland, but as a people they were slow to anger. No single incident could precipitate a conflict. Democratic statesmen had to establish popular support for policies of force. Even American territorial expansion had been "strangely mingled with a respect for the democratic process that, in and of itself, makes conquest a little absurd."[12] Bailey and Perkins reflected both the vestiges of the American war myth and the perceptions of World War II that characterized the response of many liberal scholars in the United States, even while they attempted to be critical of their country's past performance in international affairs.

The onset of the Cold War, with its concomitant emphasis on ideological distinctions between variations of Marxism-Leninism and liberal-democratic theories, combined with the dread of nuclear weapons to intensify this historiographical view. On the one hand, containment signalled a return to eighteenth-century or post-Napoleonic concepts of limited wars and maintenance of a balance of power. On the other, this proved baffling to most Americans and constituted a challenge to the nation's accepted strategic doctrines. A stream of studies emerged, many of which built upon traditional perceptions of an American view of war. For instance, T. B. Kittredge, an American officer, argued that the United States had "always been critical of the policy of countries like Britain, which have fought wars for the attainment of specific political or economic purposes." Americans had historically rejected such a view and fought for total victory and peace as the only legitimate objectives. Robert Osgood agreed with this thesis, but argued that such concepts could no longer guide American policy. A return to limited-war doctrines would be necessary in nuclear and Cold-War circumstances. Osgood drew a close parallel with European practices in the eighteenth century, but like so many others did not appreciate the significance of the legacy of the Revolutionary generation and its limited-war mentality.[13]

The concerns of Osgood and most other scholars in this area were contemporary. Historical research was less to trace unfolding trends than provide case studies for advocacy of particular doctrines. Samuel P. Huntington tackled civil-military relations, which also gained a new significance in the context of the Cold War, but he accepted without serious question what was by now a historiographical consensus on the American view of war. Liberalism had been the dominant ideology in the United States, in Huntington's view, and this led to a rejection of war in accord with the "liberal view that men are rational and that consequently they should be able to arrive at a peaceable solution of difficulties." Further, "American idealism has tended to make every war a crusade, fought, not for specific objectives of national security, but on behalf of universal principles" until 1950 and Korea: "Since liberalism deprecates the moral validity of the interests of the state in security, war must be either condemned as incompatible with liberal goals or justified as a movement in support of those goals. American thought has not viewed war in the conservative-military sense as an instrument of national policy."[14] The Cold War, nuclear weapons, and especially the Korean experience, combined to produce a more precise articulation of the American philosophy of war than had ever appeared before.

Interpretations of this philosophy blurred historical nuances and the singular circumstances of America's wars. The War for Independence, the Quasi-War, the War of 1812, actions against the Indians, the Mexican War, the Civil War, the Spanish-American War, interventions in the Caribbean, pacification of the Philippines, the world conflicts of 1914-18 and 1939-45, and finally Korea, cannot be lumped together without careful consideration of the nature of each. But liberal scholars in the 1950s developed a homogeneous view. Edward McNall Burns, for example, was concerned with tracing the idea of mission in American history. He waved aside the delusion that the United States had been a peace-loving nation. But Americans had been crusaders from the Revolution until the 1950s:

> The idea that resort to force is the most efficient means of disposing of national problems is one of the strongest of our national myths. Force has likewise always been considered a justifiable instrument for the attainment of those noble purposes which Destiny has thrust upon

us. As the Israelites of the modern World we could hardly think otherwise. The Chosen People have a God-given right to put to the sword those who would prevent us from extending the sphere of our blessings.[15]

On the one hand, Burns implied that Americans had used force as an instrument of national policy. But he then made it clear that this had always been perceived through the spectacles of crusaders.

War is a complex phenomenon. People respond to it in an even more complex manner. To view Americans as a people who have always taken a crusading approach to war violates such complexities. When he approached military doctrine, Walter Millis was more careful. He showed how the Revolution initiated a significant shift in perceptions. Americans democratized war because they drew upon the military resources of an armed populace. Yet George Washington and others did not want a people's war. They wanted an eighteenth-century army which could meet British troops and mercenaries on their own terms, and which would be disbanded once the conflict was over. Despite similar needs in 1812 and 1846, neither conflict threatened to become a people's war, either. And this was true up to the Civil War, in Millis's view.[16] Although they entered the initial phases of the transformation of war, which took place in Europe in the 1790s, the Americans stopped short, retaining an eighteenth-century outlook for nearly another hundred years.

Apart from shifts in historical cadence, individual responses to war swirl and alter with variations in personal temperament and ambition, partisan perspectives, ideological persuasion, religious convictions, economic interests, and region or locale of origin. Educational background, reading habits, and even attitudes toward family life are additional factors. It is not possible to create a useful generalization about American attitudes toward war taking all such factors into account in all cases. Such an effort would reduce historical understanding to a meaningless mosaic. But it must be clear that the remarks of Alexander Hamilton or John Jay about man's dark passions producing war, or the selfish motivation of Baltimore shipowners supporting the republican revolutions of Spanish America so that they could prey upon commerce, present particular aspects of American views of war, and not foundations for all-embracing generalizations. So is it with crusading rhetoric.

Despite the growing sophistication of scholarship on war, the anti-Clausewitzian generalizations did not appreciably alter in the 1960s. Laurence Epstein examined the American philosophy of war for changes in the period after 1945. From the Revolution to the end of World War II, he found great consistency. Only when the United States began to engage in power politics on a daily basis did policy-makers develop an appreciation of the potential of limited war. And despite this shift, the American public remained crusaders.[17] While probing American millennial thought, Ernest Lee Tuveson ventured that an apocalyptic attitude lay behind the American tendency to seek final solutions to problems. Tuveson then skipped easily to argue that "the great wars of our history have all to a considerable extent been regarded as Armageddon — which surely was near. After the war had been won, and evil conquered, a permanent era of peace and prosperity would begin."[18]

Traces of such a perspective can be found among colonials immediately prior to and during the Great War for Empire from 1754 to 1763, during the struggle for independence, and to a limited degree among clerics who supported the War of 1812. But early Americans rarely entertained such views, much less held them with any consistency. And even if the public does wish to pretend that a particular struggle is a crusade, this does not mean that policy-makers view it that way. Statesmen shape and direct the national energies that sustain wars. They may exploit popular moods or employ rhetoric with a crusading tinge. But they are still a buffer between the nation and an antagonist, applying force as an instrument of policy even while they project national views and aspirations. The Revolutionary leaders exercised this power as much as Woodrow Wilson or Franklin D. Roosevelt in the twentieth century.

John Spanier, in an interpretation of American foreign policy since World War II based on realpolitik, nevertheless began with a familiar view of the American approach to war. He argued that Americans entered the twentieth century largely unaware of the role of power in international affairs. So "resort to the evil instrument of war can be justified only by presuming noble purposes and completely destroying the immoral enemy who threatens the integrity, if not the existence, of these principles." The United States had historically "rejected the concept of war as a political instrument and the Clausewitzian definition of war as the continuation of politics by other means.''[19] This was not true of the Founding Fathers, and not true of Polk in the Mexican War. One could dispute it concerning Lincoln or Davis in the Civil War, or even William McKinley in the Spanish-American War of 1898. If it applies, such a generalization characterizes popular attitudes. But just as professional soldiers can at a given time have differing views of war — Winfield Scott and Zachary Taylor, Robert E. Lee and William Tecumseh Sherman, George Patton and Dwight D. Eisenhower, Douglas MacArthur and George Marshall are examples — so too can segments of the public — intellectuals, clerics, politicians, cabinet members, and less easily identifiable citizens.

A study of the attitudes of the Revolutionary generation toward war, and a brief survey of other aspects of the American experience with war in the nineteenth century, suggest that scholars have been working from a legend about the American view of war, rather than with legacies.[20] More detailed study must be done before the legends and the legacies can be unravelled and clarified, but for the early period of its national existence, the United States had a cluster of leaders who had a firm grasp of the role of power in international affairs. And the evidence indicates that they reflected a broad consensus among Americans in which liberal-crusading attitudes played an insignificant part. It is unclear how and when this legend of the liberal-crusading, or anti-Clausewitzian, view of war arose. Although the American war myth suggests traces of it as early as the period just after 1815, it reflects more a national self-righteousness in combination with ambitions transformed into grants from Heaven. And such attitudes, however they arose, are distinct from the development of total war in the modern world, and from the emergence of distinctive American strategic doctrines.[21]

To say this is not to deny that Americans have ever fought on behalf of liberal principles. Mere defense of their society, which embodies liberalism, is not, however, a contradiction of Clausewitz's doctrine that force is an instrument of policy. The two concepts can coexist without clashing. The many components of the American character suggest that the American view of war is really a collection, and historically therefore a series of collections, of views. For example, the United States has always had a

bourgeois character, with a strong emphasis on private ownership and the protection of property. Without accepting economic
determinism, this character is reflected in the Revolutionary
leaders' efforts to limit the impact of war on private property
through strict rules for searches and seizures and later opposition
to privateering. To take another example, Americans, although
religiously heterogeneous, have been a dissenting, protestant
people, with a strong Calvinistic strain in their view of mankind.
It is not surprising, therefore, that the Revolutionary generation
frequently saw humanity's flawed nature as a source of war.
Finally, Americans have been known as an optimistic people,
with high hopes for future progress. Again, the Revolutionary
generation's view of war reflects this. Both sectarian and non-
sectarian pacifism is an extreme example of this general belief.

   The Revolutionary generation drew from the legends and
legacies of the past in composing and developing its views of war.
In turn, it created legacies, some of which have become so
distorted by subsequent generations that they became legends,
only tenuously linked with the original thought and experience.
The limited-war mentality had clear echoes through the nineteenth century, and even in the modern period with the advent of
the Cold War and nuclear weapons. The limited-war mentality,
while derivative of a distant time and set of circumstances, retains
significance because it suggests the clear possibility of controlling
war, although it offers little encouragement toward war's elimination from human affairs. It is the Revolutionary generation's
legacy, and not the legend, which must inform our understanding
of the American view of war. Only then will the nuances and
complexities of mankind's attempts to grapple with the anoma-
lies of armed forces, civilization, and national ambitions in the
context of United States history become apparent.

ABBREVIATIONS USED IN NOTES

JOURNALS

AHR	*American Historical Review*
AN	*American Neptune*
APSR	*American Political Science Review*
EIHC	*Essex Institute Historical Collections*
HLQ	*Huntington Library Quarterly*
IMH	*Indiana Magazine of History*
JAH	*Journal of American History*
JCS	*Journal of Church and State*
JSH	*Journal of Southern History*
KHSR	*Kentucky Historical Society Register*
MA	*Military Affairs*
MVHR	*Mississippi Valley Historical Review*
NEQ	*New England Quarterly*
PMHB	*Pennsylvania Magazine of History and Biography*
PSQ	*Political Science Quarterly*
RP	*Review of Politics*
VMHB	*Virginia Magazine of History and Biography*
VQR	*Virginia Quarterly Review*
WMQ	*William and Mary Quarterly* (Unless otherwise noted, all citations are from the third series.)

PUBLIC DOCUMENTS

AC	*The Debates and Proceedings in the Congress of the United States* (Annals of Congress) (Washington, D.C.: Gales and Seaton, 1834), 42 vols.
ASP:FR	Walter Lowrie and Matthew St. Clair Clarke, eds., *American State Papers: Foreign Relations* (Washington, D.C.: Gales and Seaton, 1832), 5 vols.
ASP:MA	Walter Lowrie and Matthew St. Clair Clarke, eds., *American State Papers: Military Affairs* (Washington, D.C.: Gales and Seaton, 1832), 5 vols.

CMP   James D. Richardson, comp., *Compilation of the Mes-*
             sages and Papers of the Presidents 1789-1908 (Wash-
             ington, D.C.: Bureau of National Literature and Art,
             1908), 11 vols.
DC:CR   William R. Manning, ed., *Diplomatic Correspondence of*
             the United States: Canadian Relations 1783-1860 (Wash-
             ington, D.C.: The Carnegie Endowment for International
             Peace, 1940-45), 4 vols.
DC: ILAN   William R. Manning, ed., *Diplomatic Correspondence of*
             the United States Concerning the Independence of the
             Latin-American Nations (New York: Oxford Univ. Press,
             1925), 3 vols.
DCUS   Francis Wharton, ed., *The Revolutionary Diplomatic*
             Correspondence of the United States (Washington, D.C.:
             Government Printing Office, 1889), 6 vols.
JCC   Worthington C. Ford, ed., *Journals of the Continental*
             Congress (Washington, D.C.: Government Printing Of-
             fice, 1904-37), 34 vols.
LMCC   Edmund C. Burnett, ed., *Letters of Members of the*
             Continental Congress (Washington, D.C.: The Carnegie
             Institution, 1921), 8 vols.
ND:BW   Dudley W. Knox, ed., *Naval Documents Related to the*
             United States Wars with the Barbary Powers (Wash-
             ington, D.C.: Government Printing Office, 1940), 5 vols.
ND:QW   Dudley W. Knox, ed., *Naval Documents Related to the*
             Quasi-War with France (Washington, D.C.: Government
             Printing Office, 1936), 7 vols.

MANUSCRIPT COLLECTIONS

AP   *The Adams Papers,* Massachusetts Historical Society,
             Microfilm copy, Library of Congress, Manuscript Divi-
             sion, Washington, D.C.
MP   *Madison Papers,* Library of Congress, photocopies in the
             James Madison Papers files, Alderman Library, Univer-
             sity of Virginia
PCC   *Papers of the Continental Congress,* National Archives,
             Washington, D.C.

WRITINGS AND PAPERS

AFC   L. H. Butterfield, ed., *Adams Family Correspondence*
             1761-1728 (Cambridge, Mass.: The Belknap Press of
             Harvard Univ. Press, 1963), 4 vols.

AJL   Lester J. Cappon, ed., *The Adams-Jefferson Letters: The Complete Correspondence between Thomas Jefferson and Abigail and John Adams* (Chapel Hill: Univ. of North Carolina Press, 1959), 2 vols.

CAJ   John Spencer Bassett, ed., *Correspondence of Andrew Jackson* (Washington, D.C.: The Carnegie Institution, 1926), 7 vols.

CPPJJ   Henry P. Johnston, ed., *The Correspondence and Public Papers of John Jay* (New York: G. P. Putnam's Sons, 1890-93), 3 vols.

LRHL   James Curtis Ballagh, ed., *The Letters of Richard Henry Lee* (New York: Macmillan, 1911), 2 vols.

PAH   Harold C. Syrett, ed., *The Papers of Alexander Hamilton* (New York: Columbia Univ. Press, 1960-), 26 vols.

PDW   Charles M. Wiltse and Harold D. Moser, eds., *The Papers of Daniel Webster* (Hanover, N. H.: Univ. Press of New England, 1974), Correspondence, I.

PHC   James F. Hopkins, ed., *Papers of Henry Clay* (Lexington: Univ. Press of Kentucky, 1959-), 5 vols. to date.

PJC   Robert L. Meriwether and W. Edwin Hamphill, eds., *The Papers of John C. Calhoun* (Columbia: Univ. of South Carolina Press, 1959-), 10 vols. to date.

PJM   William T. Hutchinson and William M. E. Rachal, eds., *The Papers of James Madison* (Chicago: Univ. of Chicago Press, 1962-), 11 vols. to date. Now edited by Robert Rutland and published at Charlottesville: Univ. of Virginia Press.

PTJ   Julian P. Boyd, ed., *Papers of Thomas Jefferson* (Princeton: Princeton Univ. Press, 1950-), 21 vols. to date.

TWJM   Gaillard Hunt, ed., *The Writings of James Madison* (New York: G. P. Putnam's Sons, 1906), 10 vols.

WAG   Henry Adams, ed., *The Writings of Albert Gallatin* (New York: J. B. Lippincott, 1879), 3 vols.

WBF   John Bigelow, ed., *The Complete Works of Benjamin Franklin* (New York: G. P. Putnam's Sons, 1887-88), 10 vols.

WGW   John Fitzpatrick, ed., *The Writings of George Washington* (Washington, D.C.: George Washington Bicentennial Commission, 1931-34), 39 vols.

WJM   S. M. Hamilton, ed., *The Writings of James Monroe* (New York: G. P. Putnam's Sons, 1901), 7 vols.

WJQA   Worthington C. Ford, ed., *Writings of John Quincy Adams* (New York: Macmillan, 1913), 8 vols.

WJW   James DeWitt Andrews, ed., *The Works of James Wilson*
               (Chicago: Callaghan and Co., 1896), 2 vols.
WTJ   Paul Leicester Ford, ed., *The Works of Thomas Jefferson*
               (New York: G. P. Putnam's Sons, 1905), 12 vols.
WTP   M. D. Conway, ed., *The Writings of Thomas Paine* (New
               York: G. P. Putnam's Sons, 1894-96), 4 vols.

NOTES

1. LEGENDS AND LEGACIES:
THE OLD WORLD AND THE NEW

1. Michael Kamman, *People of Paradox: An Inquiry Concerning The Origins of American Civilization* (New York: Alfred Knopf, 1972); Henry F. May, *The Enlightenment in America* (New York: Oxford Univ. Press, 1976).

2. James J. Walsh, *Education of the Founding Fathers of the Republic: Scholasticism in the Colonial Colleges* (New York: Fordham Univ. Press, 1935).

3. H. Trevor Colbourn, *The Lamp of Experience: Whig History and the Intellectual Origins of the American Revolution* (Chapel Hill: Univ. of North Carolina Press, 1965); Charles G. Fenwick, "The Authority of Vattel," *APSR*, 7 (1913), 395-410.

4. John U. Nef, *War and Human Progress: An Essay on the Rise of Industrial Civilization* (New York: W. W. Norton, 1958), pp. 182-267.

5. Henry Guerlac, "Vauban: The Impact of Science on War," in *Makers of Modern Strategy: Military Thought from Machiavelli to Hitler*, ed. Edward M. Earle (Princeton: Princeton Univ. Press, 1941), pp. 26-48.

6. F. H. Hinsley, *Power and the Pursuit of Peace: Theory and Practice in the History of Relations Between States* (Cambridge: The University Press, 1967), pp. 153-85; Felix Gilbert, *To the Farewell Address* (Princeton: Princeton Univ. Press, 1961).

7. Roland Bainton, *Christian Attitudes Toward War and Peace* (New York: Abingdon Press, 1960), pp. 174-82; James T. Johnson, *Ideology, Reason, and the Limitation of War: Religious and Secular Concepts 1200-1740* (Princeton: Princeton Univ. Press, 1975).

8. Peter Gay, *The Enlightenment: An Interpretation* (New York: Alfred Knopf, 1969), 2:40-41, 50-51, 401-4.

9. Hugo Grotius, *The Rights of War and Peace,* trans, A. C. Campbell (New York: M. Walter Dunne, 1901), p. 32.

10. Voltaire, "Philosophical Dictionary," *The Works of Voltaire,* ed. John Morley (New York: E. R. DuMont, 1901), 14:194-200; Charles de Secondat, Baron de Montesquieu, *The Spirit of Laws,* trans. Thomas Nugent (Chicago: Encyclopaedia Britannica, 1952), vol. 1, pt. 3, p. 2; vol. 10, pt. 2, p. 61.

11. Stanley Hoffman, *The State of War: Essays on the Theory and Practice of International Politics* (New York: Frederick A. Praeger, 1965), pp. 54-87.

12. Stephen S. Webb, "Army and Empire: English Garrison Government in Britain and America, 1569-1763," *WMQ,* 34 (1977), 1-31; Keith Kavenagh, ed., *Foundations of Colonial America: A Documentary History* (New York: Chelsea House, 1973), 2:760; John Ferling, *A Wilderness of Miseries: War and Warriors in Early America* (Westport, Conn.: Greenwood Press, 1980), chaps. 1-3.

199

13. Joshua Moodey, *Souldiery Spiritualized or the Christian Souldier Orderly and Strenuously Engaged in the Spiritual War* (Cambridge, Mass.: Samuel Green, 1674), pp. 33, 39; Jon A. T. Alexander, "Colonial New England Preaching on War as Illustrated in Massachusetts Artillery Election Sermons," *JCS,* 17 (1975), 423-42.

14. Thomas Balch, *A Sermon Preached to the Ancient and Honourable Artillery Company* (Boston: Edes and Gill, 1763), p. 34; poem by Rowley, *War, Temporal and Spiritual, Considered* (Boston: Fowle and Draper, 1762), p. 1.

15. Gerald Stourzh, *Benjamin Franklin and American Foreign Policy* (Chicago: Univ. of Chicago Press, 1959), pp. 7-12, 47-53, 59-60.

16. Nathanael Appleton, *The Origins of War Examined and Applied* (Boston: T. Fleet, 1733), p. 25.

17. M. H. Keen, *The Laws of War in the Late Middle Ages* (London: Routledge and K. Paul, 1965), pp. 189-97, 243-47.

18. William B. Ballis, *The Legal Position of War: Changes in its Practice and Theory from Plato to Vattel* (The Hague: Martinus Nijhoff, 1937), pp. 40-104.

19. See for examples Samuel Pufendorf, *D. Officio Hominis et Civis Juxta Legem Naturalem Libri Duo,* trans, Frank G. Moore (New York: Oxford Univ. Press, 1927), and Cornelius van Bynkershoek, *Quaestionum Juris Publici Libri Duo,* trans. Tenney Frank (Oxford: The Clarendon Press, 1930).

20. Grotius, *War and Peace,* p. 83.

21. Emmerich de Vattel, *The Law of Nations,* trans. Charles G. Fenwick (Washington, D.C.: The Carnegie Institution, 1916, pp. 3, 6-8, 223-29, 244-59.

22. Jay Luvaas, ed. and trans., *Frederick the Great on the Art of War* (New York: Free Press, 1966), p. 44.

23. William Blackstone, *Commentaries on the Laws of England: Of Public Wrongs* (Boston: Beacon Press, 1962), 4:62-66.

24. Edwin Canaan, ed., *Lectures on Justice, Police, Revenue and Arms delivered in the University of Glasgow by Adam Smith, reported by a student in 1763* (Oxford: The Clarendon Press, 1896), p. 266.

25. Montesquieu, *Spirit of Laws,* 1:3, p. 3; and *ibid.,* pp. 59, 60, 62-65.

26. Douglas Edward Leach, *Arms for Empire: A Military History of the British Colonies in North America 1607-1763* (New York: Macmillan, 1973).

27. Samuel Nowell, *Abraham in Arms* (Boston: John Foster, 1768), pp. 4, 10; Benjamin Wadsworth, *Good Souldiers a Great Blessing* (Boston: B. Green and J. Allen, 1701), pp. 6-7.

28. Peter Clark, *The Captain of the Lord's Host Appearing with his Sword Drawn* (Boston: S. Kneeland and T. Green, 1741), p. 26; Ebenezer Gay, *Well-accomplish'd Soldiers, a Glory to their King and Defence to their Country* (Boston: T. Fleet, 1738), pp. 6, 8-9.

29. Nathaniel Walter, *The Character of a Christian Hero* (Boston: J. Draper, 1746), passim; Gad Hitchcock, *A Sermon* (Boston: Edes and Gill, 1757), pp. 8-9, 16.

30. John Winthrop, *A Declaration of Former Passages* (Cambridge, Mass.: 1645).

31. John Lowell, *The Advantages of God's Presence with his People in an Expedition against their Enemies* (Boston: J. Draper, 1755), pp. 10-13.

32. Alan Heimert, *Religion and the American Mind from the Great Awakening to the Revolution* (Cambridge, Mass.: Harvard Univ. Press, 1966), pp. 85-86, 324-27, 330, 338.

33. Solomon Williams, *The Duty of Christian Soldiers When Called to War, to Undertake it in the Name of God* (New London: T. and J. Green, 1755), p. 4.

34. Kavenagh, *Foundations*, 1:33-34, 58, 117; Leonard Woods Labaree, ed., *Royal Instructions to British Colonial Governors 1670-1776* (New York: Octagon Books, 1967), 2:463-64, 735-39.

35. Richard H. Marcus, "The Militia of Colonial Connecticut: An Institutional Study" (Ph.D. diss., University of Colorado, 1965), pp. 149-52.

36. *Speech of Chief Justice Samuel Chew of Delaware* (Philadelphia: R. Aitken, 1742), passim; Ralph L. Ketcham, "Conscience, War and Politics in Pennsylvania 1755-1757," *WMQ*, 20 (1963), 416-39.

37. Harry Ward, *"Unite or Die:" Intercolony Relations 1690-1763* (Port Washington, N.Y.: Kennikat Press, 1971), p. 250.

38. "A Ballad Concerning the Fight between the English and the French at Lake George" (Boston: 1755).

39. Richard Shelly Hartigan, "Noncombatant Immunity: Reflections on its Origins and Present Status," *RP*, 29 (1967), 214-17; Hawkins cited by Gay, *Enlightenment*, 2:41.

40. Nef, *War and Human Progress*, pp. 182-267.

41. Count Saxe, *Reveries or Memoirs upon the Art of War* (Westport, Conn.: Greenwood Press, 1971), p. 93; Canaan, *Lectures by Smith*, pp. 267-74; Sydney Bailey, *Prohibitions and Restraints in War* (London: Oxford Univ. Press, 1972), pp. 31-34.

42. Montesquieu, *Spirit of Laws*, 1:3, p. 3; Blackstone, *Commentaries*, 4:62; Vattel, *Law of Nations*, pp. 280-91.

43. Bynkershoek, *Quaestionum*, pp. 16-18.

44. Lewis K. Gann, *Guerrillas in History* (Stanford: Stanford Univ. Press, 1971), pp. 6-14; Peter Brock, *Pacifism in Europe to 1914* (Princeton: Princeton Univ. Press, 1970), pp. 306-7, 321-25.

45. Daniel J. Boorstin, *The Americans: The Colonial Experience* (New York: Alfred Knopf, 1958), pp. 345-52.

46. Kavenagh, *Foundations*, 1:126, 2:769-71, 800-802.

47. William Hobby, *The Soldier Caution'd and Counsel'd* (Boston: J. Draper, 1747), pp. 26, 31.

48. Kavenagh, *Foundations*, 1:100-101, 116, 405; 2:927, 1060, 1745, 1746; 3:1832-33, 2031.

49. Winthrop, *Declaration*, p. 7; Moodey, *Soldiery Spiritualized*, p. 12; William McClenachan, *The Christian Warrior* (Boston: D. Gookin, 1745), pp. 12, 15.

50. Jonathan Ellis, *The Justice of the Present War against the French . . .* (New Port: J. Franklin, 1755), pp. 7-8; Samuel Davies, *Religion and Patriotism*, pp. 3-5.

51. A. H. Buffinton, "The Isolationist Policy of Colonial Massachusetts," *NEQ*, 1 (1928), 164, 169-70; Albert Harkness, "Americanism and Jenkins' Ear," *MVHR*, 37 (1950-51), 61-90.

52. George Rawlyk, *Yankees at Louisbourg* (Orono: Univ. of Maine Press, 1967), pp. 149-51, 156-57.

53. Gwenda Morgan, "Virginia and the French and Indian War: A Case Study of the War's Effects on Imperial Relations," *VMHB*, 81 (1973), 28-29, 38-40; Sharp cited in Ward, *"Unite or Die,"* p. 196.

54. Douglas Edward Leach, *Flintlock and Tomahawk: New England in King Philip's War* (New York: W. W. Norton, 1958), pp. 58, 93, 144, 190, 225.

55. I. K. Steele, *Guerrillas and Grenadiers: The Struggle for Canada* (Toronto: Ryerson Press, 1969), p. 133.

56. M. C. Jacob, ed., *Peace Projects of the Eighteenth Century* (New York: Garland Publishing, 1974); Sylvester John Hemleben, *Plans for World Peace through Six Centuries* (New York: Garland Publishing, 1972), pp. 52-58.

57. Johnson, *Ideology and Limitation of War*, p. 162; R. R. Palmer, "Frederick the Great, Guibert, Bülow: From Dynastic to National War," in *Makers of Modern Strategy*, ed. Earle, p. 68.

58. Kavenagh, *Foundations*, 1:58.

59. Labaree, *Royal Instructions*, 1:444-47; 2:717-20.

60. Charles Chauncey, *Character and Overthrow of Laish Considered and Applied* (Boston: S. Kneeland and T. Green, 1734), pp. 5, 13.

61. Bernard Bailyn, *The New England Merchants in the Seventeenth Century* (Cambridge, Mass.: Harvard Univ. Press, 1955), pp. 131-32.

62 Boorstin, *Americans*, pp. 352, 358-62; Paul Varg, *Foreign Policies of the Fou ıding Fathers* (East Lansing: Michigan State Univ. Press, 1963), pp. 2-5; Fer̃ ng, *Wilderness of Miseries*, "Conclusion."

2. THE LIMITED-WAR MENTALITY
AND THE AMERICAN REVOLUTION

1. Reginald C. Stuart, "The Origins of American Nationalism to 1783: An Historiographical Appraisal," *Canadian Review of Studies in Nationalism*, 6 (1979), 1-12, and following essays.

2. Pauline Maier, *From Resistance to Revolution: Colonial Radicals and the Development of American Opposition to Britain, 1765-1776* (New York: Alfred Knopf, 1972), chaps. 1-2.

3. Benjamin F. Wright, *American Interpretations of Natural Law: A Study in the Historical Process of Political Thought* (Cambridge, Mass.: Harvard Univ. Press, 1931); Charles Mullett, *Fundamental Law and the American Revolution 1760-1776* (New York: Columbia Univ. Press, 1933).

4. Gordon S. Wood, *The Creation of the American Republic 1776-1787* (Chapel Hill: Univ. of North Carolina Press, 1969).

5. Winthrop Jordan, "Familial Politics: Thomas Paine and the Killing of the King, 1776," *JAH*, 60 (1973), 294-308.

6. R. H. Lee to Gouverneur Morris, 28 May 1775, *LRHL*, 1:140-41.

7. Mason, "The British American," no. 9, Williamsburg, 28 July 1774, in *American Archives*, ed. Peter Force (Washington, D.C.: Gales and Seaton, 1837), Fourth Series, 1:653. Charles Royster, *A Revolutionary People at War: The*

Continental Army and American Character, 1775-1783 (Chapel Hill: Univ. of North Carolina Press, 1979), chap. 1.

8. Jefferson, "Draught," July 1774, *PTJ*, 1:133; Gadsden in *Diary and Autobiography of John Adams*, ed. L. H. Butterfield (Cambridge, Mass.: Belknap Press, 1961), 2:139.

9. Franklin to Mr. Strahan, 5 July 1775, *WBF*, 7:79-80. This is part of what Royster, *A Revolutionary People*, terms the "rage militaire."

10. *JCC*, 2:70, 181, 218; for Hostile Acts Committee see John Adams to James Warren, 19 Oct. 1775, *LMCC*, 1:235.

11. Tom Paine, "Thoughts on Defensive War," July 1775, *WTP*, 1:55-58; "Declaration," *PTJ*, 1:187-217.

12. Washington, "To Canada," *WGW*, 3:478-80, and "General Orders," 2 July 1776, *ibid.*, 1:211.

13. Morris to Joseph Reed, 21 July 1776, *LMCC*, 2:10.

14. Reginald C. Stuart, " 'For the Lord is a Man of Warr': Colonial New England Views of War and the American Revolution," *JCS*, 23 (1981), 519-32.

15. Zabdiel Adams, *The Grounds of Confidence and Success in War Represented* (Boston: 1775), pp. 25-27.

16. Cushing, *Divine Judgment upon Tyrants* (Boston: 1778), p. 23.

17. Hamilton to Catherine Livingston, May 1777, *PAH*, 1:260; Gilbert Lycan, *Alexander Hamilton and American Foreign Policy: A Design for Greatness* (Norman: Univ. of Oklahoma Press, 1970), pp. 17-19, 46-47, 54-55.

18. "Instructions to Virginia Delegates in re Confiscated Property," 17 Dec. 1782, *PJM*, 5:409.

19. Maier, *Resistance to Revolution*, pp. 280-86; Washington to the Massachusetts Legislature, 9 July 1776, *WGW*, 5:239.

20. Adams to Abigail Adams, 3 July 1776, *AFC*, 2:28, and *ibid.*, 2, 28, 227; 3:141; 4:266; to Mr. Calkoen, 4 Oct. 1780, *WJA*, 7:269-73.

21. Paine, "The Crisis," nos. 2 and 5, *WTP*, 1:190-92, 249; A Moderate Whig, *Defensive Arms Vindicated and the Lawfulness of the American War Made Manifest* (Privately printed, 1783), pp. 11, 15, 19, 20-24.

22. Milton Klein, "Failure of a Mission: The Drummond Peace Proposal of 1775," *HLQ*, 25 (1971-72), 343-80.

23. David Ramsay, *The History of the American Revolution* (Dublin: W. Jones, 1795), 1:230. See also *JCC*, 4:85-86; R. H. Lee to George Washington, 22 Oct. 1775, *LRHL*, 1:153.

24. Dave R. Palmer, *The Way of the Fox: Strategy in the War for America 1775-1783* (Westport, Conn.: Greenwood Press, 1975); John Shy, *A People Numerous and Armed: Reflections on the Military Struggle for Independence* (New York: Oxford Univ. Press, 1976), pp. 138-61; Royster, *A Revolutionary People*, pp. 114-20.

25. Shy, *People Numerous*, pp. 216, 223-24; Paul Smith, "The American Loyalists: Notes on their Organization and Numerical Strength," *WMQ*, 25 (1968), 269.

26. Philip Davidson, *Propaganda and the American Revolution 1763-1783* (Chapel Hill: Univ. of North Carolina Press, 1941), pp. 365-84.

27. William Stinchcomb, *The American Revolution and the French Alliance* (Syracuse: Syracuse Univ. Press, 1969), pp. 10-12, 14-31.

28. For privateer commissions see *JCC*, 16:403-4, 407-8; 19:361-63; 22:99-100. Model Treaty in *ibid.*, 5:585-86; Hamilton to George Clinton, 22 Dec. 1777, *PAH*, 1:368.

29. For cartels see *PAH*, 1:466-72, and 2:380-81; Jefferson to John Page, 5 Aug. 1776, *PTJ*, 1:485-86.

30. Charles H. Metzger, SJ, *The Prisoner in the American Revolution* (Chicago: Loyola Univ. Press, 1971).

31. Gage to George Washington, 23 Nov. 1777, Jared Sparks, ed., *Correspondence of the American Revolution* (Boston: Little, Brown, 1853), 2:48; Jefferson to Henry, 27 Mar. 1779, *PTJ*, 2:242.

32. "Advice of Council Respecting Henry Hamilton and Others," 29 Sept. 1779, *PTJ*, 3:94-95; Madison, "Report on Retaliation," 1 Oct. 1781, *PJM*, 3:271-72.

33. Washington to William Howe, 18 Dec. 1775, *WGW*, 4:171; on André *ibid.*, 20:86-87; Charles Royster, " 'The Nature of Treason': Revolutionary Virtue and American Reactions to Benedict Arnold," *WMQ*, 36 (1979), 163-93.

34. Peter Brock, *Pacifism in the United States: From the Colonial Era to the First World War* (Princeton: Princeton Univ. Press, 1968), pp. 183-284; Roger E. Sappington, "North Carolina and the Non-Resistant Sects During the American War of Independence," *Quaker History*, 60 (1971), 29-47.

35. James Madison, "Motion for Complete Non-Intercourse with Great Britain," 16 Mar. 1781, *PJM*, 3:22-24; "Report on Illicit Trade with the Enemy," 19 June 1782, *ibid.*, 4:351-52.

36. John Carmichael, *A Self-Defensive War Lawful* (Lancaster: Francis Bailey, 1775), pp. 8, 16, 22, 24; Pendleton to James Madison, 9 Sept. 1782, *PJM*, 5:109-10.

37. Christopher Ward, *The War of the Revolution*, ed. John R. Alden (New York: The Macmillan Co., 1952), 2:603.

38. "Secret Foreign Journals," 14 July 1779, Records of Congresses, in *PCC*, RG 360, M 247, Roll 19.

39. *JCC*, 21:977-78; 14:916. On 22 Nov. 1780 Congress accused the British of waging a predatory war "regardless of their rank among civilized nations." *Ibid.*, 18:1081; see also *WGW*, 3:415.

40. Chaplain cited in North Callahan, *Royal Raiders: The Tories of the American Revolution* (Indianapolis: Bobbs-Merrill, 1963), p. 72; Lynn Underwood, "Indian and Tory Raids in the Otter Valley, 1777-1782," *Vermont Quarterly*, 5 (1947), 195-221.

41. Russell F. Weigley, *The Partisan War: The South Carolina Campaigns of 1780-1782* (Columbia: Univ. of South Carolina Press, 1970), pp. 15-25, 69; Jac Weller, "The Irregular War in the South," *MA*, 24 (1960), 124-36.

42. "Instructions to Virginia Delegates," 17 Dec. 1782, *PJM*, 5:409-10.

43. Adams to Abigail Adams, 14 Mar. 1777, *AFC*, 2:175.

44. For Washington's views see *WGW*, 7:210; American Commissioners to Prisoners in Britain, 20 Sept. 1778, *WJA*, 7:41; Hamilton to George Clinton, 12 Mar. 1778, *PAH*, 1:441, and *ibid.*, 460-62; also *WGW*, 9:183; 12:466; 13:28; 16:175; 26:9-10.

45. John Adams to Comte de Vergennes, 19 July 1781, *WJA*, 7:448, and *ibid.*, 100, 544; Hamilton to Hugh Knox, July 1777, *PAH*, 1:301; 3:362.

46. Washington to Jonathan Trumbull, 28 Nov. 1781, *WGW*, 23:360.

47. "Reports of Committee on Foreign Affairs," 6 Sept. 1777, Records of Congresses, in *PCC*, RG 360, M 247, Roll 32, 1, p. 25; "Plan for Invasion of Canada, 1778," *ibid.*, p. 41.

48. Mason to Lee, 21 July 1778, cited in Richard W. Van Alstyne, *The Rising American Empire* (New York: Oxford Univ. Press, 1960), pp. 54-55; "Secret Foreign Journals," Records of Congresses, *PCC*, RG 360, M 247, Roll 19, pp. 245-47.

49. Gerald Stourzh, *Benjamin Franklin and American Foreign Policy* (Chicago: Univ. of Chicago Press, 1959), pp. 127-234.

50. Cooke to George Washington, 21 Jan. 1776, Sparks, *Correspondence*, 1:132.

51. Washington to President of Congress, 13 June 1776, *WGW*, 5:128; Madison to Edmund Pendleton, 7 Nov. 1780, *PJM*, 2:165-66; "Powers of Congress," 3 Oct. 1780, *JCC*, 18:897.

52. "Report on the Rights of Neutral Nations," 12 June 1783, *PJM*, 7:138.

53. Morris to John Jay, 23 Sept. 1776, *LMCC*, 2:197n; "On Mississippi Navigation," *JCC*, 18:935-47.

54. Paine, "Common Sense," *WTP*, 1:75, 89, 96-97, 117; Witherspoon, *LMCC*, 3:511.

55. Hamilton to George Clinton, 3 Oct. 1783, *PAH*, 4:468; Jay to Gouverneur Morris, 24 Sept. 1783, *CPPJJ*, 3:83-84.

56. Franklin to Burke, 15 Oct. 1781, *WBF*, 9:36; to Joseph Priestly, 7 June 1782, *ibid.*, 214-15.

57. Adams to Abigail Adams, 23 Oct. 1775, *AFC*, 1:312.

58. Benezet, *Thoughts on the Nature of War, & c* (Philadelphia: 1776), p. 2; Elisha Fish, *The Art of War Lawful* (Boston: Thomas and John Fleet, 1774), pp. 9-13.

59. "Peace Army," 10 Sept. 1783, *JCC*, 25:722-44; Washington to Fielding Lewis, 6 July 1780, *WGW*, 19:133; Hamilton, "The Continentalist," *PAH*, 2:655-57, 660-61; 3:102, 378-95.

60. Jay to John Adams, 17 July 1780, *CPPJJ*, 1:380; Adams to John Quincy Adams, 11 Aug. 1775, *AFC*, 2:307.

61. Jefferson to Abigail Adams, 25 Sept. 1785, *PTJ*, 8:548.

62. The "Retaliation Report," 11 June 1781, *JCC*, 20:620-21.

3. CONFEDERATION PROBLEMS
AND THE CONSTITUTIONAL SOLUTION

1. Frederick W. Marks, III, *Independence on Trial: Foreign Affairs and the Making of the Constitution* (Baton Rouge: Louisiana State Univ. Press, 1973).

2. William Jackson, *An Oration to Commemorate the Independence of the United States of North America* (Philadelphia: Eleazer Oswald, 1786), pp. 7, 12, 14.

3. Alexander Hamilton, "Phocion Letters," and Otto Zeichner, "The Rehabilitation of Loyalists in Connecticut," *NEQ*, 11 (1938), 308-30.

4. *JCC*, 26:180-83; Gilbert, *Farewell Address*, pp. 87-88.

5. Julian P. Boyd, "Editorial Note" to Jefferson's "General Form of a Treaty," 4 Sept. to 10 Nov. 1784, *PTJ*, 7:463-70, 476-78.

6. The American Commissioners to De Thulemeier, 10 Nov. 1784, *ibid.*, 490-91, and "Enclosure," *ibid.*, 491-92; Benjamin Franklin, "Observations on War," *WBF*, 12:55-57.

7. Lee to Adams, 14 Mar. 1785, *LRHL*, 2:342-43; Jay, "Secret Foreign Journals," *PCC*, RG 360, M 247, Roll 19, pp. 1272-73; Washington to Rochambeau, 31 July 1786, *WGW*, 28:493.

8. Washington to Newenham, 29 Aug. 1788, *ibid.*, 30:71.

9. Jay to Gouverneur Morris, 24 Sept. 1783, *CPPJJ*, 3:84.

10. *JCC*, 27:475; "Circular," 13 Apr. 1787, "Secret Foreign Journals," p. 1598; Adams to John Jay, 6 Aug. 1785, *DCUS*, 4:279; Madison to Monroe, 7 Aug. 1785, *PJM*, 7:334.

11. Robert Seller, "The American Museum, 1787-1792, as a Forum for Ideas of American Foreign Policy," *PMHB*, 93 (1969), 184, 187-88; R. H. Lee to Sam Adams, 14 Mar. 1785, *LRHL*, 3:342-43; Jay to John Adams, 16 Oct. 1787, *CPPJJ*, 3:259.

12. George Washington to La Luzerne, 7 Feb. 1788, *WGW*, 29:406.

13. Jefferson to James Madison, 11 Nov. 1784, *PTJ*, 7:502, and *ibid.*, 12:33, 107-12, 145.

14. Jefferson to G. K. Van Hogendorp, 13 Oct. 1785, *ibid.*, 7:633.

15. John Adams to President of Congress, 20 Oct. 1784, *DCUS*, 2:145; John Jay to same, 13 Oct. 1785, *CPPJJ*, 3:171; James Monroe to Thomas Jefferson, 12 Apr. 1785, *WJM*, 1:74-75.

16. Jefferson to John Jay, 23 Aug. 1785, *PTJ*, 8:427; New Hampshire Delegates to Mesech Weare, 5 May 1784, *LMCC*, 7:514; Monroe to James Madison, 15 Nov. 1784, *WJM*, 1:49.

17. Adams to John Jay, 3 May and 6 Dec. 1785, *DCUS*, 2:177; 4:453; "Reports of John Jay, 1785-88," 22 Sept. 1785, *PCC*, RG 360, M 247, Item 81, Roll 107, 1:398-99.

18. Marks, *Independence on Trial*, pp. 45-49, 97, 115.

19. Massachusetts Delegates to Massachusetts Assembly, 4 June 1784, *LMCC*, 7:453; Richard Kohn, *Eagle and Sword: The Beginnings of the Military Establishment in America 1783-1802* (New York: Free Press, 1975), chap. 4.

20. Jefferson to Monroe, 11 Nov. 1784, *PTJ*, 7:511-12; Jay to President of Congress, 20 Oct. 1785, *JCC*, 29:843-44; Jay to Jones, 13 Oct. 1785, *DCUS*, 7:319.

21. Jones to Jefferson, 31 July 1785, *PTJ*, 8:334.

22. For the Adams-Jefferson discussion see *PTJ*, 8:123-24, 176-78; 9:64, 611-12; 10:176-78; Adams to Jay, 15 Dec. 1784, *DCUS*, 2:152; Franklin, "Extract from Private Journal," 10 July 1784, *WBF*, 10:353-54.

23. *JCC*, 27:65; 30:11-12, 152-53; *LMCC*, 8:234-36, 348, 360-61.

24. Jay to President of Congress, 20 Oct. 1785, *JCC*, 29:843-44; motion, *ibid.*, 33:419-20; Lee to Marquis de Lafayette, 30 Oct. 1785, *LRHL*, 2:405.

25. American Commissioners to Vergennes, 28 Mar. 1785, *PTJ*, 8:62; Jefferson to Adams, 27 Nov. 1785, *ibid.*, 9:64; to James Monroe, 11 Aug. 1786, *ibid.*, 9:64.

26. Lafayette to Jefferson, 6 Mar. 1786, D'Estaing to Jefferson, 17 May 1786, *PTJ*, 10:560-70; Jefferson, "Proposed Convention against the Barbary States," 4 July 1786, *ibid.*, 566-70.

27. Jay to Congress, 2 Aug. 1787, *JCC*, 32:451-53; Washington to Lafayette, 25 Mar. 1787, *WGW*, 29:185; *LMCC*, 8:582, 674.

28. *PTJ*, 10:585-86; 12:500-501; 14:506.

29. Reginald Horsman, *Expansion and American Indian Policy* (Michigan State Univ. Press, 1967).

30. James Monroe to Thomas Jefferson, 1 Nov. 1784, *WJM*, 1:44; Address by Nathan Dane, 9 Nov. 1786, *LMCC*, 8:503-4; "Report on Frontier Posts," 6 Apr. 1784, *JCC*, 26:202-7.

31. "Report," 26 May 1784, *ibid.*, 27:433-34, 456.

32. Knox to Congress, 13 Feb. 1786, *PCC*, RG 360, M 247, Item 150, 1:137-39, and "Report," 10 July 1787, *JCC*, 32:330.

33. Knox, "Report," 10 July 1787, *JCC*, 32:332.

34. St. Clair, 14 Sept. 1786, *JCC*, 31:657; committee report, 9 Aug. 1787, *ibid.*, 33:479; Jay to Thomas Jefferson, *CPPJJ*, 3:224, and to John Adams, 4 July 1787, *ibid.*, 249.

35. St. Clair, 14 Sept. 1786, *JCC*, 31:657; Committee on Indian Affairs, 3 Aug. 1787, *ibid.*, 33:459, and *ibid.*, 30:189, 192, 194.

36. Horsman, *Expansion*, chs. 1-3.

37. Washington to Benjamin Harrison, 10 Oct. 1784, *WGW*, 27:475; Marks, *Independence on Trial*, pp. 6-9.

38. Jay to Congress, 24 Sept. 1785, *JCC*, 29:753.

39. *LMCC*, 7:622; 8:263.

40. Hardy to Patrick Henry, 5 Dec. 1784, *ibid.*, 7:620; Madison to Thomas Jefferson, 20 Aug. 1784, *PJM*, 8:105-6, 220.

41. Jay to Congress, 13 July 1786, *JCC*, 30:400-401; 21:480-83; 32:192-93, 202-4.

42. *LMCC*, 8:381, 408, 429-30, 458, 620-21.

43. Madison to James Monroe, 7 Aug. 1785, *PJM*, 8:333; Monroe to Thomas Jefferson, 16 June 1785, *WJM*, 1:84; St. Clair, 14 Sept. 1786, *JCC*, 31:656; Pinckney, 13 Mar. 1786, *LMCC*, 8:322; "Resolve," 13 Apr. 1787, *JCC*, 32: 178-80.

44. United States Constitution, Article I, Sections 8, 10; Article II, Section 2, in *The Records of The Federal Convention of 1787*, ed. Max Farrand (New Haven: Yale Univ. Press, 1911), 2:655-59; Abraham Sofaer, *War, Foreign Affairs and Constitutional Power: The Origins* (Cambridge, Mass.: Harvard Univ. Press, 1976).

45. Two examples are Merlo J. Pusey, *The Way We Go To War* (Boston: Houghton Mifflin, 1971); Jacob Javits, *Who Makes War? The President versus Congress* (New York: William Morrow, 1973).

46. Pinckney Plan, Farrand, *Records*, 3:558-60; Hamilton, *ibid.*, 1:307; 3:622, 624; Madison, *ibid.*, 1:70, 285, 292; Benjamin Franklin, "Proposals," 6 June 1787, *WBF*, 11:341.

47. "Reports of Committee on Detail to 23 July," Farrand, *Records*, 2:143, 145, 147, 168-69.

48. *Ibid.*, 182, 185, 318-19.

49. Gerry, 18 Aug. 1787, *ibid.*, 326; Madison and McHenry, 21 Aug., *ibid.*, 361-62; "Report," *ibid.*, 508, 540-43, 548-49.

50. Jonathan Elliot, comp., *The Debates in the Several State Conventions on the Adoption of the Federal Constitution as Recommended by the General Convention at Philadelphia, in 1787* (Philadelphia: J. B. Lippincott, 1896), 1:328, 335; 2:62; 3:611.

208   NOTES FOR CHAPTER 4

51. *Ibid.*, 1:501; 2:185, 189, 209-12, 485-88, 520-23, 526-28, 536; 3:132, 337-38, 634-35.

52. Washington to Thomas Jefferson, 1 Jan. 1788, *WGW*, 29:378; Wilson in Elliot, *Debates*, 2:521, 528; 3:227.

53. Elliot, *Debates*, 2:407, 528, 536; 3:611; 4:107-8, 263; "Letters of Agrippa," 28 Dec. 1787, Paul Ford, ed., *Essays on the Constitution of the United States Published During its Discussion by the People 1787-1788* (New York: G. P. Putnam's Sons, 1892), p. 79.

54. Jefferson to Madison, 6 Sept. 1789, *PTJ*, 15:397.

55. Benjamin F. Wright, ed., *The Federalist* (Cambridge, Mass.: Harvard Univ. Press, 1966), no. 3, pp. 97-99; no. 4, pp. 101-2; no. 6, pp. 109-11; no. 10, p. 131, no. 15, p. 159; no. 24, pp. 206-8; no. 34, pp. 250-51.

56. *The Federalist*, no. 41, pp. 295, 299; no. 62, p. 411.

57. *The Federalist*, no. 3, pp. 98-99; no. 8, pp. 116-20; no. 16, pp. 163-64.

58. *The Federalist*, no. 6, p. 112; no. 11, pp. 138-39; no. 16, pp. 164-65, no. 22, p. 195; no. 25, p. 211; no. 69, pp. 446, 450; no. 79, p. 473; Edward Meade Earle, "Adam Smith, Alexander Hamilton, Friedrich List: The Economic Foundations of Military Power," in Earle, *Makers of Modern Strategy*, pp. 130-39.

59. Wright, *The Federalist*, no. 3, p. 99; no. 4, pp. 103-4; no. 41, p. 295; no. 43, p. 314.

60. Marks, *Independence on Trial*.

4. FEDERALISM, FORCE, AND POLICY

1. Richard Buel, Jr., *Securing the Revolution: Ideology in American Politics, 1789-1815* (Ithaca: Cornell Univ. Press, 1972).

2. Alexander de Conde, *Entangling Alliances: Politics and Diplomacy under George Washington* (Durham: Duke Univ. Press, 1958), and *The Quasi-War: The Politics and Diplomacy of the Undeclared War with France 1797-1801* (New York: Charles Scribners, 1966).

3. Thomas Barnard, *A Sermon Preached at the Request of the Ancient and Honourable Artillery Company in Boston* (Boston: Benjamin Russell, 1789).

4. Jay to John Hartley, 8 Jan. 1795, *CPPJJ*, 4:153-54.

5. Madison, "Universal Peace," 1792, *TWJM*, 6:88-91; Jefferson to James Madison, 1 Jan. 1797, *WTJ*, 8:264.

6. Washington to Secretary of State, 29 Aug. 1797, *WGW*, 36:19; Goodrich, *AC*, 5th Cong., 2d Sess., p. 935.

7. Dwight cited in James A. Field, Jr., *America and the Mediterranean World 1776-1882* (Princeton: Princeton Univ. Press, 1969), p. 11; Jay, *CPPJJ*, 4:115-16; Adams to Timothy Pickering, 10 Sept. 1798, *WJA*, 8:593.

8. *AC*, 4th Cong., 2d Sess., p. 2125; 6th Cong., 1st Sess., p. 290.

9. Jefferson to Edward Rutledge, 4 July 1790, *PTJ*, 16:601; 17:116; Gallatin, *AC*, 5th Cong., 2d Sess., p. 1129.

10. Harper, *AC*, 4th Cong., 2d Sess., p. 2126, and *ibid.*, p. 2120; 2d Cong., 2d Sess., p. 271; 3d Cong., 1st Sess., pp. 548, 590-92; Timothy Pickering, 1796, *ASP:MA*, 1:112.

11. Henry Knox, *ASP:MA*, 1:112; Edmond Randolph, *DC:CR*, 1:64-65; *AC*, 2d Cong., 2d Sess., pp. 1046-52.

12. Hamilton to George Washington, 14 Apr. 1794, *PAH*, 16:267-69, 18:495-96; Jefferson to Thomas Lomax, 12 Mar. 1799, *WTJ*, 9:63; Smith, *AC*, 3d Cong., 1st Sess., pp. 201-2; Adams to George Washington, 19 Feb. 1799, "Letterbook," *AP*, Reel #117.

13. E. M. Coulter, "The Efforts of the Democratic Societies of the West to Open the Navigation of the Mississippi," *MVHR*, 2 (1924-25), 376-89.

14. Pinckney, *AC*, 6th Cong., 1st Sess., pp. 56-57; Madison to Jefferson, 2 Apr. 1798, *TWJM*, 6:312-13; "Helvidius" papers in *ibid.*, 148, 174.

15. Jefferson to David Campbell, 27 Mar. 1792, *WTJ*, 6:455; Jackson to John McKee, 30 Jan. 1793 and 16 May 1794, *CAJ*, 1:12, 13.

16. *WGW*, 31:491-94; 32:35; 34:99-100; *AC*, 2d Cong., 1st Sess., pp. 762-65.

17. Jefferson to William Pinckney, 11 Sept. 1793, and 27 Nov. 1793, *DC:CR*, 1:58-60; *AC*, 3d Cong., 2d Sess., pp. 1072-80, 1123-24, 1168-70.

18. John A. Logan, *No Transfer: An American Security Principle* (New Haven: Yale Univ. Press, 1961), pp. 33-47.

19. Jefferson, "Outline of Policy," 2 Aug. 1790, *PTJ*, 17:113-16; Hamilton to George Washington, 15 Sept. 1790, *PAH*, 7:36-57; Adams to Washington, 29 Aug. 1790, *WJA*, 8:498-99.

20. Charles D. Hazen, *Contemporary American Opinion of the French Revolution* (Baltimore: The Johns Hopkins Press, 1897).

21. Harper to Constituents, 5 Jan. 1797, Elizabeth Donnan, ed., *Papers of James A. Bayard 1796-1815* (Washington, D.C.: American Historical Assoc., 1913), 2:27-28.

22. Madison to Archibald Stuart, 1 Sept. 1793, *TWJM*, 6:188-91; Donald H. Stewart, *The Opposition Press of the Federalist Period* (Albany: State Univ. of New York Press, 1969), chaps. 4-5.

23. Jefferson to Marquis de Lafayette, 16 June 1792, *WTJ*, 7:109, and 283-301; Washington to Cabinet, 18 Apr. 1793, *WGW*, 32:419-20; Hamilton to Washington, 2 May 1793, *PAH*, 14:398-99, and *ibid.*, 403, 405-6, 458.

24. Lee to Richard Bland Lee, 5 Feb. 1794, *LRHL*, 2:565-74; Jay, 22 May 1793, *CPPJJ*, 3:482-84; Madison to Horatio Gates, 24 Mar. 1794, *TWJM*, 6:209; Philip Foner, ed., *The Democratic-Republican Societies 1790-1800: A Documentary Sourcebook of Constitutions, Declarations, Addresses, Resolutions and Toasts* (Westport: Greenwood Press, 1976), p. 283.

25. Giles, *AC*, 3d Cong., 1st Sess., p. 544; Lee to Richard Bland Lee, 5 Feb. 1794, *LRHL*, 2:567.

26. Herman Kahn, *On Escalation: Metaphors and Scenarios* (New York: Frederick A. Praeger, 1965), chaps. 3-4.

27. Jay, *CPPJJ*, 3:484-85; Hamilton, *PAH*, 16:132-36, 18:494, 19:91.

28. Charles G. Fenwick, *The Neutrality Laws of the United States* (Baltimore: The Johns Hopkins Univ. Press, 1913), pp. 27-30.

29. Adams to Knox, 30 Mar. 1797, *WJA*, 8:535, and *CMP*, 1:236-37, 264-65; Jefferson to Madison, 24 Mar. 1793, *WTJ*, 7:250-51.

30. Stephen G. Kurtz, *The Presidency of John Adams: The Collapse of Federalism 1795-1800* (Philadelphia: Univ. of Pennsylvania Press, 1957), pp. 132-34, 288-91.

31. Lawrence Kaplan, "The Consensus of 1789: Jefferson and Hamilton on American Foreign Policy," *South Atlantic Quarterly*, 71 (1972), 91-105.

32. Washington, 3 Dec. 1793, *CMP*, 1:140.

33. Adams, 8 Dec. 1798, *CMP*, 1:273, 306-7.

34. For Indians, *AC*, 2d Cong., 1st Sess., pp. 785-90; for Algiers, *ibid.*, pp. 433-47, and *ND:BW*, 1:23-26, 44-45, 296-97, 378-79.

35. Hamilton to Washington 15 Sept. 1790, *PAH*, 7:36-57; Jefferson, "Outline of Policy," 2 Aug. 1790, *PTJ*, 17:113-16, 129-32.

36. The cabinet meeting is 19 Apr. 1793, in *PAH*, 14:328; for Jefferson see *WTJ*, 7:302.

37. Harry Ammon, *The Genet Mission* (New York: W. W. Norton, 1973), pp. 62-75.

38. Stuart G. Brown, ed., *The Autobiography of James Monroe* (Syracuse: Syracuse Univ. Press, 1959), p. 54.

39. Hazen, *American Opinion of Revolution*, pp. 253-54, 266-75.

40. Jefferson to James Monroe, 24 Apr. 1794, *WTJ*, 8:143.

41. William Glenn Moore, "Economic Coercion as a Policy of the United States 1794-1805" (Ph.D. diss., University of Alabama, 1960), chap. 3.

42. *AC*, 3d Cong., 1st Sess., pp. 535-41.

43. *Ibid.*, pp. 567-70, 571, 590.

44. Washington to Gouverneur Morris, 25 June 1794 and 22 Dec. 1795, *WGW*, 33:414, and 24:401.

45. Washington's address, *CMP*, 1:222; Hamilton, "Pacificus," *PAH*, 15:33-135, passim.

46. Adams to Gerry, 3 May 1797, "Letterbook," *AP*, Reel #117.

47. Jeanne Ojala, "Ira Allen and the French Directory, 1796: Plans for the Creation of the Republic of United Columbia," *WMQ*, 36 (1979), 436-48; *AC*, 5th Cong., 1st Sess., p. 102; 2d Sess., pp. 1128, 1442.

48. Jefferson to Aaron Burr, 17 June 1797, *WTJ*, 8:310-11.

49. Tazewell to Jackson, 20 July 1798, *CAJ*, 1:51-53; Adams to Heads of Departments, 24 Jan. 1798, *WJA*, 8:561-63.

50. De Conde, *Quasi-War*, chaps. 7, 10.

51. *DC:CR*, 1:101-2, 138, 507; *ASP:FA*, 2:20-21, 66-67; Marshall Smelser, "George Washington Declines the Part of El Libertador," *WMQ*, 11 (1954), 42-51.

52. Otis, *AC*, 5th Cong., 3d Sess., p. 2874; Adams to Murray, 22 July 1798, *WJQA*, 2:344.

53. Kirkland, *A Sermon Preached Before the Ancient and Honourable Artillery Company*, (Boston: Joseph Belknap, 1795), pp. 19-24; Jefferson to Thomas Pinckney, 7 May 1793, in Carleton Savage, *Policy of the United States Toward Maritime Commerce in War* (Washington, D.C.: Government Printing Office, 1934), 1:163; Madison, *TWJM*, 6:88-91.

54. *AC*, 5th Cong., 2d Sess., pp. 1785-86.

55. Washington and Adams, *CMP*, 1:152, 288; Jefferson to James Madison, 24 Mar. 1793, *WTJ*, 7:250-51.

56. Adams to Joseph Pitcairn, 10 Feb. 1797, *WJQA*, 2:116; *AC*, 3d Cong., 1st Sess., pp. 313, 325, 502-4, 508.

57. Hamilton to Jefferson, 13 Jan. 1791, *PAH*, 7:426, and 11:439-40; 18:494; Adams to John Adams, 24 June 1796, *WJQA*, 1:499-507; Giles, *AC*, 4th Cong., 2d Sess., p. 1331. Harper to Constituents, 13 Mar. 1797 and 9 Mar. 1798, 10 Feb. 1799, *Papers of Bayard*, 2:38-39, 52, 78-79.

58. Rutledge and Otis, *AC*, 5th Cong., 2d Sess., pp. 1325-26, and *ibid.*, 3d Sess., p. 2475.

59. James B. Scott, ed., *The Controversy Over Neutral Rights Between the United States and France 1797-1800: A Collection of American State Papers and Judicial Decisions* (New York: Oxford Univ. Press, 1917), pp. 104, 107, 109, 112-15.

60. *ND:QW*, 1:77, 187, 198, 204; 2:347-48, 352-54, 377-78, 405-11; 3:129, 199, 277, 370; 4:29, 429.

61. Adams, "Proclamation," 9 May 1798, *CMP*, 1:268-70; Kirkland, *A Sermon*, pp. 18-20.

62. Jay to Lindley Murray, 22 Aug. 1794, *CPPJJ*, 4:53; Hamilton, "Defence #20," *PAH*, 29:344, and 20:339-40; Pickering to John Quincy Adams, 17 Mar. 1798, *ASP:FR*, 2:251; Harper to Constituents, 5 Jan. 1797, *Papers of Bayard*, 2:27-28, 38, 67-68; Tazewell to Andrew Jackson, 20 July 1798, *CAJ*, 1:53.

63. Paul C. Nagel, *This Sacred Trust: American Nationality 1798-1898* (New York: Oxford Univ. Press, 1971).

5. REPUBLICAN ALTERNATIVES AND HALF-WAY PACIFISM

1. John A. Logan, *No Transfer: An American Security Principle* (New Haven: Yale Univ. Press, 1961), pp. 74-124; James A. Field, *America and the Mediterranean World, 1776-1882* (Princeton: Princeton Univ. Press, 1969), pp. 49-68.

2. Norman K. Risjord, *The Old Republicans: Southern Conservatism in the Age of Jefferson* (New York: Columbia Univ. Press, 1965), pp. 1-17; Richard Hofstadter, *The Idea of a Party System: The Rise of Legitimate Opposition in the United States 1780-1840* (Berkeley: Univ. of California Press, 1972), pp. 105-80.

3. Mary P. Adams, "Jefferson's Military Policy with Special Reference to the Frontier, 1805-1809" (Ph.D. diss., University of Virginia, 1958).

4. Jefferson, *CMP*, 1:316-17, 367; *WTJ*, 9:309.

5. Duane, *The American Military Library* (Philadelphia: 1809), 1:iii.

6. Williams in *Extracts from the Minutes of the United States Military Philosophical Society*, 28 Dec. 1809, pp. 6-7, 13. For examples of congressional views see *AC*, 6th Cong., 2d Sess., pp. 827-28, 830-33.

7. Jackson to John Sevier and Jefferson, 20 Apr. 1808, *CAJ*, 1:186-87, 188-89; Madison, *DC:CR*, 1:174, 179.

8. Jefferson to Benjamin Rush, 4 Oct. 1803, *WTJ*, 10:32; Madison, *TWJM*, 7:204-375; Smith cited by John Pancake, "The 'Invisibles': A Chapter in the Opposition to President Madison," *JSH*, 21 (1955), 24.

9. *CMP*, 1:372, 377; *WTJ*, 10:30-31; *TWJM*, 7:58-59, 75-78, 194; *WAG*, 1:152-53, 162-66.

10. Webster, "Argument for Acquisition of the Floridas," *PDW*, 1:29-30; Jackson to Claiborne, 12 Nov. 1806, *CAJ*, 1:153; Monroe, "Notes on Differences with Spain," *WJM*, 4:439-41.

11. Madison, "Proclamation," 27 Oct. 1810, *CMP*, 1:465-66; Isaac Cox, "The American Intervention in West Florida," *AHR*, 17 (1912), 290-311.

12. *AC*, 11th Cong., 3d Sess., pp. 44-47, 61-64, 374-75, 1121-23.

13. Jefferson and Madison to Congress, *CMP*, 1:373 and 407-8, 461, 463, 471-72; *AC*, 12th Cong., 1st Sess., p. 822.

14. Hofstadter, *Idea of a Party System*, p. 176.

15. Otis, *AC*, 6th Cong., 2d Sess., p. 828; Morris, *ibid.*, 7th Cong., 2d Sess., pp. 198-200; authorization, *ibid.*, pp. 255-62.

16. *Ibid.*, 9th Cong., 1st Sess., pp. 103, 864, 952, 1265-66, 1272-73, 1287, provides examples.

17. *Ibid.*, 10th Cong., 1st Sess., pp. 27-33, 988-95, 1000, 1036, 1916-17.

18. Jefferson, *WTJ*, 9:220; Gallatin, *WAG*, 1:339.

19. Clinton, *AC*, 7th Cong., 2d Sess., pp. 131-33; Jackson, *ibid.*, pp. 149, 242; bill, *ibid.*, pp. 371-74.

20. Worthington, *ibid.*, 9th Cong., 1st Sess., p. 108; Key, 10th Cong., 2d Sess., p. 1355.

21. Rutledge, *ibid.*, 7th Cong., 1st Sess., p. 418; Ross, *ibid.*, 2d Sess., p. 94.

22. Monroe to General Armstrong, 11 Mar. 1806, *WJM*, 4:428; Madison to Monroe and William Pinckney, 20 May 1807, *TWJM*, 7:444-45; Jackson to Generals, 4 Oct. 1806, *CAJ*, 1:150, 192.

23. Senate Resolution, *AC*, 9th Cong., 1st Sess., p. 91.

24. Edwin M. Gaines, "Outrageous Encounter! The Chesapeake-Leopard Affair of 1807" (Ph.D. diss., University of Virginia, 1960), chap. 5; Jefferson, *WTJ*, 1:140; 10:436, 439-40.

25. Noble E. Cunningham, Jr., *Circular Letters of Congressmen to their Constituents 1789-1829* (Chapel Hill: Univ. of North Carolina Press, 1978), 2:522-40, passim, 551, 556, 580-85, 596, 605-14.

26. Johnson, *AC*, 10th Cong., 2d Sess., p. 589; December Resolve, *ibid.*, p. 855; Williams, *ibid.*, p. 1238.

27. Jackson to Madison, 5 July 1807, *MP*; Nicholas to Madison, 6 Feb. 1809, *ibid.*

28. Jefferson to Pierre de Nemours, 2 Mar. 1809, Dumas Malone, ed., *Correspondence Between Thomas Jefferson and Pierre Samuel Du Pont de Nemours 1798-1817*, trans. Linwood Lehman (Boston: Houghton Mifflin, 1930), p. 121.

29. Madison, *CMP*, 1:457-58.

30. Lawrence Kaplan, "Jefferson, the Napoleonic Wars, and the Balance of Power," *WMQ*, 14 (1957), 196-217.

31. Madison, notes, 29-30 Oct. 1808, *MP*, and letters to William Pinckney, 10, 25 Nov. 1808, to Wilson Nicholas, 6 Feb. 1809, and Jan.-Feb. 1809, *ibid.*; Robert A. Rutland, *Madison's Alternatives: the Jeffersonian Republicans and the Coming of War 1805-1812* (Philadelphia: J. B. Lippincott, 1975), pp. 1-48.

32. Monroe to John Taylor, 13 June 1812, *WJM*, 5:206.

33. Breckenridge, *AC*, 7th Cong., 1st Sess., pp. 115-17; Noah Webster, "Rights of Neutrals," in *A Collection of Papers on Political, Literary and Moral Subjects*

(New York: Webster and Clark, 1843), pp. 42-118; Madison, *TWJM*, 7:207, 268-69.

34. *AC*, 9th Cong., 1st Sess., pp. 555-74, 582, 625-27.

35. Jefferson to James Madison, 11 Mar. 1808, *WTJ*, 11:12-13, 15-17; to James Bowdoin, 29 May 1808, *ibid.*, 69; to William Cabell, 29 June 1807, *ibid.*, 10:433; Madison to William Pinckney, 3 Jan. 1809, *MP*; Gallatin to Jefferson, 18 Dec. 1807, *WAG*, 1:368.

36. Henry Adams, *History of the United States During the Administration of Thomas Jefferson* (New York: Albert and Charles Boni, 1930), vol. 2, pt. 4, p. 277.

37. Alston and Stanford, *AC*, 10th Cong., 1st Sess., pp. 1035, 2018.

38. *Ibid.*, 2d Sess., pp. 20-27, 42-47, 64-73, 78-93, 1312-16; Campbell's report pp. 519-21.

39. Taggart to John Taylor, 27 Apr. 1810, "Letters of Samuel Taggart," *Proceedings of the American Antiquarian Society*, 33 (1923), 347-48; Jackson and Taylor, *AC*, 10th Cong., 1st Sess., pp. 1402, 1201, 1210-11; Lyon, p. 1414.

40. Cunningham, *Letters*, 2:623-74 passim, suggest the belligerence of southern congressmen. Madison to Wilson Cary Nicholas, 6 Feb. 1809; Resolution, 9 Feb. 1809, *MP*; voting in *AC*, 10th Cong., 1st Sess., pp. 1428-29, 1523-32, 1541.

41. *ND:BW*, 1:454-55, 460-61.

42. Cathcart to U.S. Consuls and Agents in Europe, 15 May 1801, *ibid.*; Jefferson, *WTJ*, 9:454-55; *AC*, 7th Cong., 1st Sess., pp. 327-29, 432, 1303-04.

43. *ND:BW*, 2:51-52; Field, *America and Mediterranean*, pp. 59-68.

44. Mary P. Adams, "Jefferson's Reaction to the Treaty of San Ildefonso," *JSH*, 21 (1955), 173-88; Stuart S. Sprague, "Jefferson, Kentucky, and the Closing of the Port of New Orleans, 1802-1803," *KHSR*, 70 (1972), 312-17.

45. *AC*, 7th Cong., 2d Sess., pp. 83-88, 93-95.

46. Madison to William Pinckney, 11 May 1802, *TWJM*, 6:455; Jefferson to Livingston, 18 Apr. 1802, *WTJ*, 9:364-66; to de Nemours, 25 Apr. 1802, Malone, *Correspondence*, pp. 49-61.

47. Jefferson to James Monroe, 13 Jan. 1803, and to Robert Livingston, 3 Feb. 1803, *WTJ*, 9:419, 442; Madison to Monroe, 1 Mar. 1803, *TWJM*, 7:30-31n; and *ibid.*, 37-41, 47-48n; Adams, *History*, vol. 1, pt. 1, p. 445.

48. Jefferson to John Bacon, 30 Apr. 1803, *WTJ*, 9:464.

49. Jackson, "Orders," 7 Aug. 1803, *CAJ*, 1:68-69; Clay to John Breckenridge, 21 Nov. and 30 Dec. 1803, *PHC*, 1:122, 124-25.

50. Burwell, *AC*, 10th Cong., 1st Sess., p. 1128.

51. Pickering, *ibid.*, 2d Sess., pp. 175-92; Risjord, *Old Republicans*, chap. 5.

52. Resolves, *AC*, 11th Cong., 2d Sess., pp. 481, 509, 1151-52.

53. Eppes, *ibid.*, pp. 1453-57, 1482, 1484; Leib, *ibid.*, p. 594.

54. Bassett, *ibid.*, p. 1962.

55. *ND:BW*, 1:463-69; 2:55-56, 60-61, 475-76.

56. Clay, *PHC*, 1:514; Nagel, *Sacred Trust*, pp. 39-42.

6. THE LIMITED WAR OF 1812

1. Madison to Thomas Jefferson, 18 Mar. 1811, and to Elbridge Gerry, 21 June 1811, *MP*; Harry Ammon, *James Monroe: The Quest for National Identity* (New York: McGraw Hill, 1971), pp. 292-303.

2. Madison, "Proclamation," 24 July 1811, *CMP*, 1:476-81.

3. Madison to John Quincy Adams, 15 Nov. 1811, *TWJM*, 8:166-67, and *ibid.*, 169-72.

4. William Barlow, "The Coming of the War of 1812 in Michigan Territory," *Michigan History*, 53 (1969), 92-100; Stephen M. Millett, "Bellicose Nationalism in Ohio: An Origin of the War of 1812," *Canadian Review of Studies in Nationalism*, 1 (1974), 221-40; Ellery Hall, "Canadian Annexation Sentiment in Kentucky Prior to the War of 1812," *KHSR*, 28 (1930), 373-80.

5. Robert Hayne, "The Southwest and the War of 1812," *Louisiana History*, 5 (1964), 51; Sarah Lemmon, *Frustrated Patriots: North Carolina and the War of 1812* (Chapel Hill: Univ. of North Carolina Press, 1973), chap. 1; Norman K. Risjord, *The Old Republicans: Southern Conservatism in the Age of Jefferson* (New York: Columbia Univ. Press, 1965), pp. 126-40.

6. Gerry to Madison, 19 May 1812, *MP*.

7. Virginia Resolution, *AC*, 12th Cong., 1st Sess., pp. 113-14.

8. Porter, *ibid.*, pp. 374-76, 414-17.

9. Grundy, *ibid.*, pp. 423-26; Calhoun, pp. 476-81; Clay, p. 599.

10. Calhoun, *ibid.*, p. 1399.

11. Kellogg to Madison, 1 June 1812, *MP*; Madison to Jefferson, 6 Mar. 1812, *ibid*; Clay to Monroe, 15 Mar. 1812, *PHC*, 1:637.

12. On Henry Affair, *CMP*, 1:483, 484, and Madison to Jefferson, 3, 24 Apr. 1812, *MP*.

13. Madison to Congress, 1 June 1812, *CMP*, 1:485-90.

14. *AC*, 12th Cong., 1st Sess., pp. 1546-54.

15. S. E. Morison, F. Merk, F. Friedel, *Dissent in Three American Wars* (Cambridge, Mass.: Harvard Univ. Press, 1970), pp. 3-31; Robert McCaughey, *Josiah Quincy: The Last Federalist* (Cambridge, Mass.: Harvard Univ. Press, 1974), pp. 71-83.

16. King to Christopher Gore, 17 July 1812, in *The Life and Correspondence of Rufus King*, ed. Charles R. King (New York: G. P. Putnam's Sons, 1898), 5:272-73.

17. Adams to Elkenah Watson, 6 July 1812, in George Coggeshall, *History of American Privateers and Letters of Marque* (New York: 1856), pp. xl-xli; Lawrence Kaplan, ed., "A New Englander Defends the War of 1812: Senator Varnum to Judge Thacher," *Mid-America*, 46 (1964), 277-78; King to Christopher Gore, 11 July 1814, *Correspondence of King*, 5:397.

18. Donald R. Hickey, ed., "A Dissenting Voice: Matthew Lyon on the Conquest of Canada," *KHSR*, 76 (1978), 45-52; Randolph, *AC*, 12th Cong., 1st Sess., pp. 441, 447; Nelson, p. 499.

19. Myron E. Wehtje, "Opposition in Virginia to the War of 1812," *VMHB*, 78 (1970), 65-86; John E. Talmadge, "Georgia's Federalist Press and the War of 1812," *JSH*, 19 (1953), 488-500; Sarah E. Lemmon, "Dissent in North Carolina during the War of 1812," *North Carolina Historical Review*, 49 (1972), 103-118;

Edward Brynn, "Patterns of Dissent: Vermont's Opposition to the War of 1812," *Vermont History*, 40 (1972), 10-27.

20. *AC*, 12th Cong., 1st Sess., pp. 253-54, 259-61, 300, 1478-79.

21. Taggart, *ibid.*, pp. 1638-74; *Address of Members of the House of Representatives of the Congress to their Constituents on the Subject of the War with Great Britain* (Alexandria: S. Snowdon, 1812).

22. Brigham, *AC*, 12th Cong., 2d Sess., p. 512; Quincy, pp. 542-48.

23. King, *ibid.*, 13th Cong., 2d Sess., p. 931; Shipherd, pp. 1019-30.

24. Cunningham, *Letters*, 2:794, 800, 809; Paul Woehrmann, "National Response to the Sack of Washington," *Maryland Historical Magazine*, 66 (1971), 223-60; Donald R. Hickey, "New England's Defense Problems and the Genesis of the Hartford Convention," *NEQ*, 50 (1977), 587-604.

25. Grundy, *AC*, 12th Cong., 1st Sess., pp. 426-27; Harper, p. 657; Bradley, 3d Sess., pp. 413-14.

26. Hull's Order, E. A. Cruikshank, ed., *Documents Relating to the Invasion of Canada and the Surrender of Detroit 1812* (Ottawa: The Canadian Archives, 1912), pp. 35, 37; Madison to Dearborn, 7 Oct. 1812, *TWJM*, 8:218: Madison, "Preparatory Sketch for Alexander J. Dallas's Exposition on the Causes and Character of the War," *MP*.

27. Monroe to John Taylor, 13 June 1812, *WJM*, 5:205-12; to Jonathan Russell, 26 June 1812, *ibid.*, 212-13; to American Plenipotentiaries, 14 Feb. 1814, *ibid.*, 370; to Albert Gallatin, 5 May 1813, *ibid.*, 352; Cabinet, June 1814, *TWJM*, 8:280-81.

28. Monroe to American ministers, 23 June 1813, *WJM*, 5:367-68; 370-72; to same in *DC:CR*, 1:216-18, and 648, 654.

29. *AC*, 12th Cong., 1st Sess., p. 744.

30. *Ibid.*, 13th Cong., 2d Sess., pp. 1357-58.

31. Jefferson to Charles Pinckney, 12 Feb. 1812, Andrew A. Lipscomb and Albert Bergh, eds., *The Writings of Thomas Jefferson* (Washington, D.C.: Thomas Jefferson Memorial Association, 1903), 18:272; Monroe to Jefferson and Henry Clay, 17 Sept. 1812, *WJM*, 5:220-23; King to King, 11 Feb. 1815, *Correspondence of King*, 5:466.

32. Russell to James Monroe, 3 Feb. 1812, *DC:CR*, 1:610; Calhoun, *AC*, 13th Cong., 2d Sess., p. 1694.

33. Nagel, *Sacred Trust*, p. 22; Adams to Abigail Adams, 18 Feb. 1813, *WJQA*, 4:436-37.

34. Jefferson to Madison, 19 June 1812, *MP*; Grundy, *AC*, 13th Cong., 1st Sess., pp. 226-27; Edward Carter, II, "Mathew Carey and 'The Olive Branch,' 1814-1818," *PMHB*, 89 (1965), 407-9.

35. Madison to Jefferson, 17 Aug. 1812, *TWJM*, 8:210; Monroe to Henry Clay, 17 Sept. 1812, *WJM*, 5:223.

36. Jackson, "Division Orders," and to Mrs. Jackson, 18 Jan. 1813, *CAJ*, 1:220-22, 272.

37. Hull in Cruikshank, *Documents*, pp. 35, 37; *Military Monitor*, pp. 15, 96, 283-84, 346.

38. *AC*, 12th Cong., 1st Sess., pp. 220-22, 266-67.

39. Voting, *ibid.*, pp. 267-71, 324-26. The Federalists split in New England and the Republicans split in the Middle states on the Gregg-Pope resolutions.

The Middle states favored striking "war" from the bill. New England favored
Giles's motion two-to-one, whereas the Middle states split. In all three cases, the
South and West provided the majority vote for war.

40. *Ibid.*, pp. 832, 841-44, 877-81, 912-19.

41. *Military Monitor*, pp. 321-24; *ASP: FR*, 3:726-30; Charles Ingersoll,
*Historical Sketch of the Second War between the United States of America and
Great Britain* (Philadelphia: J. B. Lippincott, 1853), Second Series, 1:83-114;
Robin Fabel, "The Laws of War in the 1812 Conflict," *Journal of American
Studies*, 14 (1980), 199-218.

42. *Military Monitor*, p. 15; Cochrane-Monroe correspondence in *DC:CR*,
1:624-26; congressional report, *ASP: FR*, 3:751-52.

43. *AC*, 12th Cong., 2d Sess., pp. 151-55, 1145-46, 1326-63; 13th Cong., 1st
Sess., pp. 489-92, 2239-48; 3d Sess., pp. 802-3, 1624, 1645-47.

44. John K. Mahon, *The War of 1812* (Gainesville: Univ. of Florida Press,
1972), pp. 263-64; John Brannan, comp., *Official Letters of the Military and
Naval Officers of the United States During the War with Great Britain*
(Washington, D.C.: Way and Gideon, 1823), pp. 244-46.

45. *CMP*, 1:509-10.

46. Robert Asprey, *War in the Shadows: The Guerrilla in History* (New York:
Doubleday, 1974), 1:139-45.

47. Jefferson to Madison, 17 Apr. 1812, *WTJ*, 11:235; Madison to Jefferson, 24
Apr. 1812, *MP*.

48. King, *Correspondence of King*, 5:420, 468; Fred Engelman, *The Peace of
Christmas Eve* (London: Hart Davis, 1962); Bradford Perkins, *Castlereagh and
Adams: England and the United States 1812-1823* (Berkeley and Los Angeles:
Univ. of California Press, 1964).

49. *PHC*, 1:841-42, 855, 933, 938, 1007.

50. Story to N. Williams, 22 Feb. 1815, cited in Irving Brant, *James Madison
Commander in Chief 1812-1836* (Indianapolis: Bobbs Merrill, 1961), pp. 378-79;
Madison to Richard Rush and Rush to Madison, 15 Feb. 1815, *MP*; William A.
Burwell to Madison, 22 Feb. 1815, *MP*.

51. Monroe to Military Committee of Senate, 22 Feb. 1815, *WJM*, 5:321-22;
Jefferson to Thomas Leiper, 12 June 1815, *WTJ*, 11:479; Pickens, Cunningham,
Letters, 2:912.

52. *AC*, 13th Cong., 3d Sess., pp. 1159-61.

53. Roberts cited in Roger Brown, *The Republic in Peril: 1812* (New York:
Columbia Univ. Press, 1964), pp. 190-91; Coggeshall, *History of Privateers*, p.
398.

54. Henry Wheaton, *Some Account of the Life, Writings, and Speeches of
William Pinckney* (New York: J. W. Palmer, 1826), p. 135.

55. Madison, "Preparatory Sketch," *MP*; The "Exposition" appeared for 10
Feb. 1815, *AC*, 13th Cong., 3d Sess., pp. 1416-79, and in pamphlet form; *TWJM*,
8:332-34.

56. Madison to Congress, 15 Feb. 1815, *CMP*, 1:538.

57. Adams to Mercy Warren, 17 Aug. 1814, *Warren-Adams Letters*, 2:396;
Monroe to Military Committee of Senate, 22 Feb. 1815, *WJM*, 5:324; *AC*, 13th
Cong., 3d Sess., pp. 1197-98, 1236.

7. EMERGENCE OF THE AMERICAN WAR MYTH

1. Bradford Perkins, *Castlereagh and Adams: England and the United States 1812-1823* (Berkeley and Los Angeles: Univ. of California Press, 1964); Samuel Flagg Bemis, *John Quincy Adams and the Foundations of American Foreign Policy* (New York: Alfred Knopf, 1949).

2. William A. Williams, *The Contours of American History* (Cleveland: World Publishing Co., 1961), pp. 182-335; Robert Remini, *Andrew Jackson and the Course of American Empire 1767-1821* (New York: Harper and Row, 1977), chap. 19.

3. *CMP*, 1:565.

4. Peter Brock, *Pacifism in Europe to 1914* (Princeton: Princeton Univ. Press, 1972), pp. 367-407.

5. Peter Brock, *Pacifism in the United States: From the Colonial Era to the First World War* (Princeton: Princeton Univ. Press, 1968), chap. 8.

6. Worcester, *A Solemn Review of the Custom of War and Seven Numbers of the Friend of Peace*, pp. 21-30.

7. *Ibid.*

8. *Ibid.*, pp. 3-6.

9. *The Moral Advocate*, no. 1, 1-2, no. 2, 17; Quincy's speech in no. 3, 41-45, no. 4, 51-56, no. 5, 68-71.

10. *AC*, 16th Cong., 1st Sess., pp. 851, 737, 2524-47; 14th Cong., 2d Sess., pp. 93-96.

11. Charles Francis Adams, ed., *Memoirs of John Quincy Adams* (Philadelphia: J. B. Lippincott, 1874-77), 6:164-65.

12. Gallatin to Matthew Lyon, 7 May 1816, *WAG*, 1:700; Madison to Charles Ingersoll, 4 Jan. 1818, *TWJM*, 8:407.

13. Clay, *AC*, 14th Cong., 1st Sess., pp. 781-84; Richard Johnson, *ibid.*, pp. 446-47; Hayne, 18th Cong., 1st Sess., p. 221.

14. Jay to John Murray, 12 Oct. 1816, *CPPJJ*, 4:391-93; 414-16; Monroe to Congress, 16 Nov. 1818, *CMP*, 1:610, 638; Adams to Don Luis de Onis, 23 July 1818, *WJQA*, 6:386-94.

15. Madison, *CMP*, 1:551; Monroe, *ibid.*, 576-77.

16. *CMP*, 1:763, 791-92; Adams, *WJQA*, 6:38; Calhoun, *PJC*, 1:315-24; 3:461-72; 5:480-90; 8:284.

17. *DC:CR*, 1:247-48, 259, 790-91; *TWJM*, 8:418.

18. Harper, *AC*, 14th Cong., 1st Sess., pp. 283-92; Clay, *ibid.*, p. 787.

19. Mason, *ibid.*, p. 126; Johnson, *ibid.*, 15th Cong., 1st Sess., pp. 889-92.

20. Jackson, "Proclamation," 29 May 1818, *CAJ*, 2:375, and 385-86; Johnson, *AC*, 15th Cong., 1st Sess., pp. 1564-65.

21. Madison to Monroe, 6 Aug. 1816, *TWJM*, 8:357, and *CMP*, 1:539, 547-48, 560.

22. *CMP*, 1:582-83, 592-94; *WJM*, 6:33; Richard G. Lowe, "American Seizure of Amelia Island," *Florida Historical Quarterly*, 45 (1966), 18-30.

23. Monroe to Jefferson, May 1820, *WJM*, 6:119, 312-13.

24. Adams, *Memoirs*, 4:437-39; to Hugh Nelson, 22 Apr. 1823, *WJM*, 6:353; and in *WJQA*, 6:372-73.

25. *PHC*, 2:513-14, 768-69, 771.

26. Jackson to James Monroe, 20 June 1820, *CAJ*, 3:28.

27. Madison, *CMP*, 1:564; Monroe, *ibid.*, 791.

28. Smith, *AC*, 15th Cong., 1st Sess., pp. 1543-44; Sanford, 16th Cong., 1st Sess., p. 545; Trimble, pp. 1756-68.

29. Albert K. Weinberg, *Manifest Destiny: A Study of Nationalist Expansion in American History* (Baltimore: The Johns Hopkins Univ. Press, 1935), pp. 49-62; Charles A. Lofgren, "Force and Diplomacy 1846-1848: The View from Washington," *MA*, 31 (1967), 57-64.

30. Bemis, *John Quincy Adams*, pp. 295-98.

31. Monroe, *CMP*, 1:582, 627-28, 786-87; "Sketch of Instructions for Agents for South America," 24 Mar. 1819, *WJM*, 5:92-102; Adams to Aquirre, 27 Aug. 1818, *WJQA*, 6:447.

32. *PHC*, 2:115-56, 291, 403, 409, 517-19, 768-69.

33. Sharp, *AC*, 14th Cong., 2d Sess., p. 730; Floyd, 15th Cong., 1st Sess., pp. 1546-55; Charles C. Griffin, *The United States and the Disruption of the Spanish Empire 1810-1822* (New York: Columbia Univ. Press, 1937), pp. 124-60.

34. George B. Dyer and Charlotte L. Dyer, "The Beginnings of a United States Strategic Intelligence System in Latin America 1809-1826," *MA*, 14 (1950), 65-83.

35. King, *AC*, 14th Cong., 1st Sess., pp. 809-11; Cunningham, *Letters*, 3:1016, 1019-20, 1037-38.

36. Monroe to Congress, 3 Dec. 1822, *CMP*, 1:762, 763; Adams to Jefferson, 28 Dec. 1823, *AJL*, 2:602; Bancroft, "Journals," 4 July 1821, M. A. DeWolfe Howe, ed., *The Life and Letters of George Bancroft* (New York: G. P. Putnam's Sons, 1908), 1:109.

37. Webster, *AC*, 18th Cong., 1st Sess., pp. 1086-99; Poinsett, pp. 1104-11; Cary, pp. 1131-32; Wood, pp. 1132-38.

38. Adams to Nelson, 28 Apr. 1823, *WJQA*, 7:370-71; to Everett, 31 Jan. 1822, *ibid.*, 201; to Mr. Luriottis, 18 Aug. 1823, *ASP:FR*, 5:257.

39. Jefferson, *Writings*, 13:119; *WJQA*, 7:487-88.

40. Monroe, *CMP*, 1:661; Adams, *WJQA*, 7:50-51.

41. Madison to Monroe, 30 Oct. 1823, *WJM*, 6:394-95; Gatlin, Cunningham, *Letters*, 3:1200-1201.

42. Ammon, *Monroe*, pp. 478-92.

43. Monroe to Jefferson, 17 Oct. 1823, *WJM*, 6:325; Jefferson to Monroe, 24 Oct. 1823, *ibid.*, 391-92.

44. Monroe's Message, *CMP*, 1:787; to Jefferson, Dec. 1823, Worthington C. Ford, "Genesis of the Monroe Doctrine," Massachusetts Historical Society, *Proceedings*, 15 (1901-02), 412.

45. *AC*, 14th Cong., 1st Sess., p. 666.

46. *WJQA*, 5:472-87; 6:238-40; *DC:CR*, 1:732-34.

47. Monroe to Congress, 25 Mar. 1818, *CMP*, 1:600-601; Calhoun to Jackson, 26 Dec. 1817, *PJC*, 2:25-26, 40.

48. Monroe to Jackson, 19 July 1818, *WJM*, 6:55-61; and "Orders," *PJC*, 2:8, 20; Jackson, *CAJ*, 2:345-46, 384.

49. Adams to Onis, 23 July 1818, *WJQA*, 6:386-94.

50. Lacock, *AC*, 15th Cong., 2d Sess., pp. 262-68.

51. Nelson, *ibid.*, pp. 516-18; Johnson, pp. 520-27.

52.   Smyth, *ibid.*, pp. 678-90; Barbour, pp. 766-79; Mercer, p. 823; Rhea, p. 867.

53.   Fuller, *ibid.*, pp. 990-1006; voting, pp. 1132-36.

54.   Maury Baker, "The Spanish War Scare of 1816," *Mid-America*, 45 (1963), 67-78; Monroe to John Quincy Adams, 10 Dec. 1815, *DC: ILAN*, 1:18-19.

55.   *CMP*, 1:626-27; Calhoun and planning in *PJC*, 4:217, 316-17, 426-27, 499, 505.

56.   Jackson, *CAJ*, 3:1, 7; Adams to Lowndes, 16, 21 Dec. 1819, *WJQA*, 6:560-63; "Resolution," 9 Mar. 1820, *AC*, 16th Cong., 1st Sess., pp. 1619-20.

57.   Monroe, *CMP*, 1:658-59; Jackson to John Quincy Adams, 17 July 1821, *CAJ*, 3:105.

58.   Cuthbert, *AC*, 18th Cong., 1st Sess., p. 1168.

59.   Wood, *ibid.*, p. 1138; Cuthbert, p. 1167.

8. LEGACIES AND LEGENDS: AN AMERICAN VIEW OF WAR

1.   Michael Walzer, *Just and Unjust Wars: A Moral Argument with Historical Illustrations* (New York: Basic Books, 1977), pp. 61-62, 132, 207-22.

2.   Charles A. Lofgren, "Force and Diplomacy: The View from Washington 1846-1848," *MA*, 31 (1967), 57-64; Norman A Graebner, ed., *Manifest Destiny*, (Indianapolis: Bobbs-Merrill, 1968), pp. 160-98.

3.   Ernest Lee Tuveson, *Redeemer Nation: The Idea of America's Millennial Role* (Chicago: Univ. of Chicago Press, 1968), pp. 186-214; George Frederickson, *The Inner Civil War: Northern Intellectuals and the Crisis of the Union* (New York: Harper and Row, 1965), part ii.

4.   Baron Henri de Jomini, *The Art of War*, trans. G. H. Mendell and W. P. Craighill (Philadelphia: J. B. Lippincott, 1862), pp. 11-13, 23, 30-31; Grady McWhiney, "Jefferson Davis and the Art of War," *Civil War History*, 21 (1974), 101-12; Thomas C. Leonard, *Above the Battle: War Making in America from Appomatox to Versailles* (New York: Oxford Univ. Press, 1978).

5.   Karl von Clausewitz, *On War*, ed. Peter Paret and Michael Howard (Princeton: Princeton Univ. Press, 1976), pp. 27-44, 75-123.

6.   Charles R. Beitz and Theodore Herman, eds., *Peace and War* (San Francisco: W. H. Freeman, 1973); Martin A. Nettleship et al., eds., *War, Its Causes and Correlates* (The Hague: Martinus Nijhoff, 1975); and L. L. Farrar, Jr., ed., *War: A Historical, Political and Social Study* (Santa Barbara: ABC-Clio Press, 1978).

7.   Michael Howard, *War in European History* (London: Oxford Univ. Press, 1976); John Nef, *War and Human Progress: An Essay on the Rise of Industrial Civilization* (New York: W. W. Norton, 1963); Theodore Ropp, *War in the Modern World* (Durham: Duke Univ. Press, 1959).

8.   Michael Howard, *War and the Liberal Conscience* (New Brunswick: Rutgers Univ. Press, 1978), pp. 11-34; Nef, *War and Human Progress*, pp. 302-28.

9.   *Ibid.*, pp. 329-56.

10. David L. Axeen, "Romantics and Civilizers: American Attitudes Toward War, 1898-1902" (Ph.D. diss., Yale University, 1969).

11. Alexis de Tocqueville, *Democracy in America*, ed., Philips Bradley (New York: Random House, 1954), 1:177-78; 2:279-302; Emory Upton, *The Military Policy of the United States* (Washington, D.C.: Government Printing Office, 1904), pp. 30-31, 35, 60-61; C. H. Hamlin, *The War Myth in United States History* (New York: Vanguard Press, 1937).

12. Thomas A. Bailey, *The Man in the Street: The Impact of American Public Opinion on Foreign Policy* (New York: Macmillan, 1948), pp. 76-87; Dexter Perkins, "The American Attitude Towards War," *Yale Review*, 38 (1948), 234-52.

13. T. B. Kittredge, "National Peace Objectives and War Aims from 1775-1955," *Marine Corps Gazette*, 40 (1956), 8-19; Robert Osgood, *Limited War: The Challenge to American Strategy* (Chicago: Univ. of Chicago Press, 1957), chaps. 1-2.

14. Samuel P. Huntington, *The Soldier and the State: The Theory and Politics of Civil-Military Relations* (Cambridge, Mass.: Harvard Univ. Press, 1957), pp. 143-56, 194-96.

15. Edward McNall Burns, *The American Idea of Mission* (New Brunswick: Rutgers Univ. Press, 1957), pp. 235-38.

16. Walter Millis, *Arms and Men: A Study in American Military History* (New York: G. P. Putnam's Sons, 1956), pp. 13, 22-34, 58.

17. Laurence Epstein, "The American Philosophy of War, 1945-1967" (Ph.D. diss., University of Southern California, 1967), developed case studies on the Nuremburg Trials, the use of the atomic bomb on Japan, the formation of the United Nations, the development of containment, the Korean and Vietnam wars.

18. Tuveson, *Redeemer Nation*, pp. 124-25, 195-96, 214.

19. John Spanier, *American Foreign Policy Since World War II* (7th ed. rev.; New York: Praeger Publishers, 1977), chap. 1.

20. Reginald C. Stuart, *The Half-way Pacifist: Thomas Jefferson's View of War* (Toronto: Univ. of Toronto Press, 1978); Lofgren, "Force and Diplomacy"; Richard Kohn, *Eagle and Sword: The Beginnings of the Military Establishment in America* (New York: Free Press, 1975), suggest the significance of the force and policy theme in American history.

21. Bernard Brodie, *War and Politics* (New York: Macmillan, 1973).

BIBLIOGRAPHICAL ESSAY

The material for this study comes from the voluminous printed sources for the Colonial, Revolutionary, and Early National periods of American History. Certain manuscript collections proved essential for filling gaps nevertheless: *The John Adams Papers*, the *James Madison Papers*, the *Papers of the Continental Congress*, the *American Periodical Series*, and Clifford K. Shipton, ed., *Early American Imprints* (Worcester, Mass.: American Antiquarian Society). Readers can consult each chapter for the principal sources which apply to the topics covered. Wherever possible, this study builds upon the research and insights of historians who have mined and sifted the history of the age of the Revolutionary generation. A list of works consulted that did not lend themselves to direct citation follows this essay.

The major biographical treatments of the Revolutionary leaders are good starting points. James T. Flexner has condensed his multivolume study of George Washington in *Washington: The Indispensable Man* (Boston: Little, Brown, 1969). Page Smith treats *John Adams* (New York: Doubleday, 1962), 2 vols.; and the definitive study of Thomas Jefferson is Dumas Malone, *Jefferson and His Time* (Boston: Little, Brown, 1948-81), 7 vols. Merrill D. Peterson, *Thomas Jefferson and the New Nation* (New York: Oxford Univ. Press, 1972), has the best one-volume treatment. For Jefferson's great friend and colleague, see Irving Brant, *James Madison* (Indianapolis: Bobbs Merrill, 1941-61), 6 vols. Ralph Ketcham, *James Madison: A Biography* (New York: Macmillan 1971), included other material and is not as favorable to the subject. For Jefferson's rival see Broadus Mitchell, *Alexander Hamilton: A Concise Biography* (New York: Oxford Univ. Press, 1976). Harry Ammon, *James Monroe: The Quest for National Identity* (New York: McGraw Hill, 1971); Samuel Flagg Bemis, *John Quincy Adams and the Foundations of American Foreign Policy* (New York: Alfred Knopf, 1949); David Freeman Hawke, *Paine* (New York: Harper and Row, 1975), and Carl Van Doren, *Benjamin Franklin* (New York: Garden City Publishing Co., 1945), cover the other major figures.

The theme of war has a vast bibliography which daunts the neophyte. Basic introductions are still Quincy Wright, *A Study of War* (Chicago:

Univ. of Chicago Press, 1942), 2 vols., and Theodore Ropp, *War in the Modern World* (Durham: Duke Univ. Press, 1959). But John U. Nef, *War and Human Progress: An Essay on the Rise of Industrial Civilization* (New York: W. W. Norton, 1963), is indispensable. Two brief surveys by an expert are Michael Howard, *War in European History* (London: Oxford Univ. Press, 1976), and *War and the Liberal Conscience* (New Brunswick: Rutgers Univ. Press, 1978). Many disciplines have made important contributions to our understanding of human conflict and a cross-section can be found in Leon Bramson and George W. Goethals, eds., *War: Studies from Psychology, Sociology, Anthropology* (New York: Basic Books, 1968); Martin A. Nettleship et al., eds., *War, Its Causes and Correlates* (The Hague: Martinus Nijhoff, 1975); and L. L. Farrar, Jr., ed., *War: A Historical, Political and Social Study* (Santa Barbara: ABC-Clio Press, 1978).

Several studies in military history were helpful. In particular see Edward Meade Earle, ed., *Makers of Modern Strategy: Military Thought from Machiavelli to Hitler* (Princeton: Princeton Univ. Press, 1941), which has seminal essays on important eighteenth-century figures. Samuel P. Huntington, *The Soldier and the State: The Theory and Politics of Civil-Military Relations* (Cambridge, Mass.: Harvard Univ. Press, 1957), is also helpful because Huntington tries to establish American views of war in the context of American national liberal ideology. Hoffman Nickerson, *The Armed Horde: A Study of the Rise, Survival, and Decline of the Mass Army* (New York: G. P. Putman's Sons, 1940), covers an important theme, as does Alfred Vagts, *A History of Militarism: Civilian and Military* (New York: Meridian Books, 1967, rev. ed.), who is vital for eighteenth-century limited-war concepts.

Many books treat the moral dimension of war in both historical and contemporary terms. Those most pertinent to the present study were Roland Bainton, *Christian Attitudes Toward War and Peace* (New York: Abingdon Press, 1960); James T. Johnson, *Ideology, Reason, and the Limitation of War: Religious and Secular Concepts 1200-1740* (Princeton: Princeton Univ. Press, 1975); and two books by Michael Walzer, *Just and Unjust Wars: A Moral Argument with Historical Illustrations* (New York: Basic Books, 1977), and his earlier *Revolution of the Saints: A Study in the Origins of Radical Politics* (Cambridge, Mass.: Harvard Univ. Press, 1965), which has an insightful section on war and English Puritan thought. The pacifist temperament emerges in Elizabeth V. Souleyman, *The Vision of World Peace in Seventeenth and Eighteenth-Century France* (New York: G. P. Putnam's Sons, 1941); and Peter Brock, *Pacifism in Europe to 1914* (Princeton: Princeton Univ. Press, 1972). Richard Cox treats a figure important for Americans in *Locke on War and Peace* (Oxford: The Clarendon Press, 1960).

Background for the legal perspective on war came from Arthur Nussbaum, *A Concise History of the Law of Nations* (New York: Macmillan, 1954). But supplement this with Sydney Bailey, *Prohibitions and Restraints in War* (London: Oxford Univ. Press, 1972); F. H. Hinsley, *Power and the Pursuit of Peace: Theory and Practice in the History of Relations Between States* (Cambridge: The University Press, 1967); Richard Shelly Hartigan, "Noncombatant Immunity: Reflections on Its Origin and Present Status," *Review of Politics*, 29 (1967), 204-20; and Michael Howard, ed., *Restraints on War: Studies in the Limitation of Armed Conflict* (Oxford: Oxford Univ. Press, 1979). Valuable insights into European traditions leading into the early modern period are in M. H. Keen, *The Laws of War in the Late Middle Ages* (London: Routledge and K. Paul, 1965). Theoretical treatments provide another dimension for this theme, and readers should consult Stanley Hoffman, *The State of War: Essays on the Theory and Practice of International Politics* (New York: Frederick A. Praeger, 1965), and Kenneth Waltz, *Man, the State and War: A Theoretical Analysis* (New York: Columbia Univ. Press, 1959).

Several studies provide a composite picture of war in the eighteenth century. In particular, see the works by Souleyman, *Vision of World Peace*, Nef, *War and Human Progress*, and chapters in Michael Howard's books. Sir George N. Clark, *War and Society in the Seventeenth Century* (Cambridge: The University Press, 1958), provides a setting for the rise of the limited-war mentality. Carl J. Friedrich, *Inevitable Peace* (Cambridge: Mass.: Harvard Univ. Press, 1948), concentrates on Immanuel Kant; Hans Speier, "Militarism in the Eighteenth Century," in Speier, *Social Order and the Risks of War* (Cambridge, Mass.: Harvard Univ. Press, 1969), pp. 230-52, supplements Vagts's book on militarism; and the documents and commentary in Geoffrey Symcox, ed., *War, Diplomacy and Imperialism 1618-1763* (New York: Harper and Row, 1973), provide a comprehensive survey. The link between European and American thought regarding international relations emerged first in Felix Gilbert's *To the Farewell Address: Ideas of Early American Foreign Policy* (Princeton: Princeton Univ. Press, 1961).

Over the past fifteen years, the intellectual atmosphere in which the Revolutionary generation learned, lived, and worked has been comprehensively developed. Bernard Bailyn, *The Ideological Origins of the American Revolution* (Cambridge, Mass.: Harvard Univ. Press, 1967), is a seminal study. Valuable antecedents are Edward McNall Burns, "The Philosophy of History of the Founding Fathers," *Historian*, 16 (1954), 142-68; Ralph L. Ketcham, "James Madison and the Nature of Man," *Journal of the History of Ideas*, 19 (1958), 62-76; and Adrienne Koch,

Power, Morals, and the Founding Fathers: Essays in the Interpretation of the American Enlightenment (Ithaca: Cornell Univ. Press, 1961). On the Enlightenment see Peter Gay, *The Enlightenment: An Interpretation* (New York: Alfred Knopf, 1969), 2 vols.; and Henry May, *The Enlightenment in America* (New York: Oxford Univ. Press, 1976). Recent studies that provide insight into their subjects are H. Trevor Colbourn, *The Lamp of Experience: Whig History and the Intellectual Origins of the American Revolution* (Chapel Hill: Univ. of North Carolina Press, 1965); Howard Trivers, "Universalism in the Thought of the Founding Fathers," *Virginia Quarterly Review*, 52 (1976), 448-62; Paul C. Nagel, *This Sacred Trust: American Nationality 1798-1898* (New York: Oxford Univ. Press, 1971); and Gerald Stourzh, *Alexander Hamilton and the Idea of Republican Government* (Stanford: Stanford Univ. Press, 1970).

Three older works were important for appreciating the intellectual climate of the time: Benjamin F. Wright, *American Interpretations of Natural Law: A Study in the Historical Process of Political Thought* (Cambridge, Mass.: Harvard Univ. Press, 1931); Charles Mullett, *Fundamental Law and the American Revolution 1760-1776* (New York: Columbia Univ. Press, 1933); and James J. Walsh, *Education of the Founding Fathers of the Republic: Scholasticism in the Colonial Colleges* (New York: Fordham Univ. Press, 1935).

As American republicanism developed within the context of independent statehood following the Revolution, eighteenth-century ideas about international relations and war and peace emerged. These were inextricably interwoven with American ideology. For examples of scholars who address this ideology and reflect American attitudes toward war, see Norman K. Risjord, *The Old Republicans: Southern Conservatism in the Age of Jefferson* (New York: Columbia Univ. Press, 1965); Gordon S. Wood, *The Creation of the American Republic 1776-1787* (Chapel Hill: Univ. of North Carolina Press, 1969); Richard Buel, Jr., *Securing the Revolution: Ideology in American Politics 1789-1815* (Ithaca: Cornell Univ. Press, 1972); Richard Hofstadter, *The Idea of a Party System: The Rise of Legitimate Opposition in the United States 1780-1840* (Berkeley and Los Angeles: Univ. of California Press, 1972); Robert E. Shalhope, "Toward a Republican Synthesis: The Emergence of an Understanding of Republicanism in American Historiography," *William and Mary Quarterly*, 3d series, 29 (1972), 49-80; and Lance Banning, *The Jeffersonian Persuasion: Evolution of a Party Ideology* (Ithaca: Cornell Univ. Press, 1978).

The literature on American attitudes toward war is not extensive. Pacifism has received some treatment. The best works are by Peter Brock, especially *Pacifism in the United States: From the Colonial Era to the*

First World War (Princeton: Princeton Univ. Press, 1968). Merle Curti's older books are still useful and easier reading than Brock's encyclopedic treatments. See Curti's *The American Peace Crusade, 1815-1860* (Durham: Duke Univ. Press, 1929), and *Peace or War: The American Struggle 1636-1936* (New York: W. W. Norton, 1936). Other titles are eclectic in coverage. William Gribbin, *The Churches Militant: The War of 1812 and American Religion* (New Haven: Yale Univ. Press, 1973); Thomas C. Leonard, *Above the Battle: War Making in America from Appomatox to Versailles* (New York: Oxford Univ. Press, 1978); and John E. Ferling, *A Wilderness of Miseries: War and Warriors in Early America* (Westport, Conn.: Greenwood Press, 1980), are useful. So is Samuel Eliot Morison, Frederick Merk, and Frank Friedel, *Dissent in Three American Wars* (Cambridge, Mass.: Harvard Univ. Press, 1970). Merlo J. Pusey, *The Way We Go To War* (Boston: Houghton Mifflin, 1971), reflected the Vietnam influence on studies of American attitudes toward war-making in the United States. So did Abraham Sofaer, *War, Foreign Affairs, and Constitutional Power: The Origins* (Cambridge: Mass.: Harvard Univ. Press, 1976). My own contribution to the literature is *The Half-way Pacifist: Thomas Jefferson's View of War* (Toronto: Univ. of Toronto Press, 1978).

There are several helpful journal articles: Jon A. T. Alexander, "Colonial New England Preaching on War as Illustrated in Massachusetts Artillery Election Sermons," *Journal of Church and State*, 17 (1975), 423-42; Arthur H. Buffinton, "The Puritan View of War," Colonial Society of Massachusetts, Publications, 28 (1930-33), 67-86; Charles Lofgren, "War Making under the Constitution: The Original Understanding," *Yale Law Journal*, 81 (1972), 672-702; Lofgren, "Force and Diplomacy: The View from Washington 1846-1848," *Military Affairs*, 31 (1967), 57-64; Dexter Perkins, "The American Attitude Towards War," *Yale Review*, 38 (1948), 234-52.

Two dissertations of note which are not directly applicable to the present study are David L. Axeen, "Romantics and Civilizers: American Attitudes Toward War, 1898-1902" (Ph.D. diss., Yale University, 1969), and Laurence Epstein, "The American Philosophy of War, 1945-1967" (Ph.D. diss., University of Southern California, 1967).

Military history, despite its frequently restricted focus, provided many studies which broadened the base of this essay into American attitudes toward war. For example, Lawrence D. Cress, "The Standing Army, the Militia, and the New Republic: Changing Attitudes Toward the Military in American Society, 1768-1820" (Ph.D. diss., University of Virginia, 1976), and Marcus Cunliffe, *Soldiers and Civilians: The Martial Spirit in America 1775-1865* (Boston: Little, Brown, 1968) illuminate the position of the military in American society at the time.

226

Douglas E. Leach, *Arms for Empire: A Military History of the British Colonies in North America 1607-1763* (New York: Macmillan, 1973), Robert L. Davidson, *War Comes to Quaker Pennsylvania 1682-1756* (New York: Columbia Univ. Press, 1957), I. K. Steele, *Guerrillas and Grenadiers: The Struggle for Canada 1689-1760* (Toronto: Ryerson Press, 1969), and Harry Ward, *"Unite or Die:" Intercolony Relations 1690-1763* (Port Washington, N.Y.: Kennikat Press, 1971), cover the colonial period.

For the Revolution see Don R. Higginbotham, *The War of American Independence: Military Attitudes, Policies, and Practice 1763-1789* (New York: Macmillan, 1971); Orville T. Murphy, "The American Revolutionary War and the Concept of Levee en Masse," *Military Affairs*, 23 (1959), 13-20; John Shy, *A People Numerous and Armed: Reflections on the Military Struggle for Independence* (New York: Oxford Univ. Press, 1976); and Russell Weigley, *The Partisan War: The South Carolina Campaigns of 1780-1782* (Columbia, S.C.: Univ. of South Carolina Press, 1970).

The period following 1783 has many fine studies. Especially important are Russell F. Weigley, *The American Way of War: A History of United States Military Strategy and Policy* (New York: Macmillan, 1971), and Walter Millis, *Arms and Men: A Study in American Military History* (New York: G. P. Putnam's Sons, 1956). More specific studies are Richard Kohn, *Eagle and Sword: The Beginnings of the Military Establishment in America 1783-1802* (New York: Free Press, 1975), and Craig Symonds, *Navalists and Antinavalists: The Naval Policy Debate in the United States 1785-1827* (Newark: Univ. of Delaware Press, 1980).

The theme of force and policy through the period covered by the present study can best be followed in the literature on expansionism. William Ricketson, "A Puritan Approach to Manifest Destiny: Case Studies from Artillery Election Sermons" (Ph.D. diss., University of Georgia, 1965), probes colonial New Englanders. Richard W. Van Alstyne traces the theme from the colonial era through the nineteenth century in *The Rising American Empire* (New York: Oxford Univ. Press, 1960). The basic work is still Albert K. Weinberg, *Manifest Destiny: A Study of Nationalist Expansion in American History* (Baltimore: The Johns Hopkins Univ. Press, 1935). James A. Field, Jr., *America and the Mediterranean World, 1776-1882* (Princeton: Princeton Univ. Press, 1969), interweaves ideology, trade, missionary work, and nonterritorial expansion. John A. Logan, *No Transfer: An American Security Principle* (New Haven: Yale Univ. Press, 1961), isolates a strategic theme. Alexander De Conde, *This Affair of Louisiana* (Baton Rouge: Louisiana State Univ. Press, 1976), covers America's first major territorial acquisition after the Revolution, and one which arguably established the leading Jeffersonians on the road to further ambitions in this regard. William A. Williams, *The Contours of American History* (Cleveland: World Publishing, 1961), presents the most persuasive economic-determinist argument.

Expansionism is also a theme in Charles C. Griffin, *The United States and the Disruption of the Spanish Empire 1810-1822* (New York: Columbia Univ. Press, 1937); Reginald Horsman, *Expansion and American Indian Policy 1783-1812* (East Lansing: Michigan State Univ. Press, 1967), which covers the northwest; and Robert V. Remini, *Andrew Jackson and the Course of American Empire 1767-1821* (New York: Harper and Row, 1977), which covers both Jackson and the southwest.

Finally, this study rests upon the considerable body of secondary literature in American Foreign Relations from 1776 to 1823. General works of note are Charles G. Fenwick, *The Neutrality Laws of the United States* (Baltimore: The Johns Hopkins Univ. Press, 1913); D. A. Graber, *Crisis Diplomacy: A History of U.S. Intervention Policies and Practices* (Washington, D.C.: Public Affairs Press, 1959); Morrell Heald and Lawrence S. Kaplan, *Culture and Diplomacy: The American Experience* (Westport, Conn.: Greenwood Press, 1977); Louis J. Halle, *Dream and Reality: Aspects of American Foreign Policy* (Westport, Conn.: Greenwood Press, 1973). Surveys of the period are Paul Varg, *Foreign Policies of the Founding Fathers* (East Lansing: Michigan State Univ. Press, 1963); Lawrence S. Kaplan, *Colonies into Nation: American Diplomacy, 1763-1801* (New York: Macmillan, 1968); and the essays in Samuel Flagg Bemis, ed., *The American Secretaries of State and their Diplomacy* (New York: Alfred Knopf, 1927), vols. 1-4. The colonial background is in Max Savelle, *The Origins of American Diplomacy: The International History of Anglo-America 1492-1763* (New York: Macmillan, 1967), and Gerald Stourzh, *Benjamin Franklin and American Foreign Policy* (Chicago: Univ. of Chicago Press, 1959).

The foreign policy of the American Revolution has several fine studies. Good essays can be found in Lawrence S. Kaplan, ed., *The American Revolution and "A Candid World"* (Kent, Ohio: Kent State Univ. Press, 1977); William Stinchcomb, *The American Revolution and the French Alliance* (Syracuse: Syracuse Univ. Press, 1969); and Richard B. Morris, *The Peacemakers: The Great Powers and American Independence* (New York: Harper and Row, 1965). Frederick W. Marks III, *Independence on Trial: Foreign Affairs and the Making of the Constitution* (Baton Rouge: Louisiana State Univ. Press, 1973), covers a generally neglected area.

The 1790s and beyond is awash in important works which explore most aspects of foreign policy. Alexander De Conde, *Entangling Alliances: Politics and Diplomacy Under George Washington* (Durham: Duke Univ. Press, 1958), and *The Quasi-War: The Politics and Diplomacy of the Undeclared War with France 1797-1801* (New York: Charles Scribners, 1966), cover the 1790s thoroughly. Also essential is Bradford Perkins's trilogy, *The First Rapprochement: England and the United States 1794-1805* (Philadelphia: Univ. of Pennsylvania Press, 1955); *Prologue to War: England and the United States 1805-1812* (Berkeley and Los Angeles: Univ. of California Press, 1961); and *Castlereagh and Adams: England and the United States 1812-1823* (Berkeley and Los Angeles: Univ. of California Press, 1964).

Several studies emphasize the ideological and political context of the second struggle with Great Britain in 1812. See Roger H. Brown, *The Republic in Peril: 1812* (New York: Columbia Univ. Press, 1964), and Robert Rutland, *Madison's Alternatives: The Jeffersonian Republicans and the Coming of War 1805-1812* (Philadelphia: J. B. Lippincott, 1975), which is intended as a text for university teaching, but which has an important analysis of the movement toward war in terms of attitudes toward military conflict and international relations. The significant material on the causes of the War of 1812 lies in journal articles. The basic historiography to its date of publication is Warren H. Goodman, "The Origins of the War of 1812: A Survey of Changing Interpretations," *Mississippi Valley Historical Review,* 28 (1941-42), 171-86. The most important developments in this literature are Margaret K. Latimer, "South Carolina — A Protagonist of the War of 1812," *American Historical Review,* 61 (1956), 914-29; Norman K. Risjord, "1812: Conservatives, War Hawks and the Nation's Honor," *William and Mary Quarterly,* 3d series, 18 (1961), 192-211; J. C. A. Stagg, "James Madison and the Malcontents: The Political Origins of the War of 1812," *ibid.,* 23 (1976), 557-85; Harry Fritz, "The War Hawks of 1812: Party Leadership in the Twelfth Congress," *Capitol Studies,* 5 (1977), 25-42; Rudolph Bell, "Mr. Madison's War and Long-Term Congressional Voting Behavior," *William and Mary Quarterly,* 3d series, 36 (1979), 373-95; J. C. A. Stagg, "James Madison and the Coercion of Great Britain: Canada, the West Indies, and the War of 1812," *ibid.,* 38 (1981), 3-34. The moral-legal restraints on Americans during the conflict emerge in Robin F. A. Fabell "The Laws of War in the 1812 Conflict," *Journal of American Studies,* 14 (1980), 199-218.

Apart from the considerable attention paid to the diplomatic and intellectual origins of the Monroe Doctrine, the period after 1815 is not so well served as the period before. The studies by Bemis on John Quincy Adams, Perkins on Anglo-American relations, and Griffin on American dabbling in the Spanish imperial difficulties were all helpful. So too was Edward Tatum, *The United States and Europe 1815-1823: A Study in the Background of the Monroe Doctrine* (Berkeley and Los Angeles:

Univ. of California Press, 1936). Good on their specific topics are Carlton B. Smith, "Congressional Attitudes Toward Military Preparedness During the Monroe Administration," *Military Affairs,* 40 (1976), 22-25; Charles Griffin, "Privateering from Baltimore During the Spanish American Wars for Independence," *Maryland Historical Magazine,* 35 (1940), 1-25; and Edward Meade Earle, "American Interest in the Greek Cause, 1821-1827," *American Historical Review,* 33 (1927), 44-63.

OTHER WORKS CONSULTED

PRIMARY COLLECTIONS

Brigham, Clarence, ed. "Letters of Abijah Bigelow, Member of Congress, to his Wife, 1810-1815," *Proceedings of the American Antiquarian Society*, 40 (1930).

Brown, Everett S., ed. *William Plumer's Memorandum of Proceedings in the United States Senate 1803-1807*. New York: Da Capo Press, 1969.

Chinard, Gilbert, ed. *The Letters of Lafayette and Jefferson*. Baltimore: The Johns Hopkins Univ. Press, 1929.

Corner, George W., ed. *The Autobiography of Benjamin Rush*. Princeton: Princeton Univ. Press, 1948.

Dwight, Theodore. *History of the Hartford Convention with a Review of the policy of the United States Government which led to the War of 1812*. New York: N. and J. White, 1833.

Knopf, Richard C., ed. *The National Intelligencer Reports the War of 1812 in the Northwest*. Columbus: Ohio Historical Society, 1958.

Locke, John. *Concerning Civil Government: Second Essay*. Chicago: Encyclopaedia Britannica, 1952.

Marsh, Philip, ed. *A Freneau Sampler*. New York: Scarecrow Press, 1963.

Moore, Frank, comp. *Songs and Ballads of the American Revolution*. Port Washington, N.Y.: Kennikat Press, 1964; f.p. 1885.

Pettee, Fred L., ed. *The Poems of Philip Freneau*. Princeton: The University Library, 1902-7. Vols. 1-3.

Riley, Patrick, ed. *The Political Writings of Leibniz*. Cambridge: The University Press, 1972.

BOOKS

Akers, Charles. *Called Unto Liberty: A Life of Jonathan Mayhew 1720-1766*. Cambridge, Mass.: Harvard Univ. Press, 1964.

Ambrose, Stephen E., and Barber, James A., eds. *The Military and American Society: Essays and Readings*. New York: Free Press, 1972.

Ammon, Harry. *The Genet Mission*. New York: W. W. Norton, 1973.

Brooks, Philip C. *Diplomacy of the Borderlands: The Adams-Onis Treaty of 1819.* Berkeley and Los Angeles: Univ. of California Press, 1939.

Brown, Wallace. *The Good Americans: The Loyalists in the American Revolution.* New York: William Morrow, 1969.

Buck, Philip. *The Politics of Mercantilism.* New York: H. Holt and Company, 1942.

Burns, Edward McNall. *James Madison: Philosopher of the Constitution.* New York: Octagon Books, 1968.

Caulder, Anna. *American Commerce as Affected by the Wars of the French Revolution and Napoleon 1793-1812.* Philadelphia: Univ. of Pennsylvania Press, 1932.

Clarfield, Gerald. *Timothy Pickering and American Diplomacy 1795-1800.* Columbia: Univ. of Missouri Press, 1969.

Combs, Gerald A. *The Jay Treaty: Political Battleground of the Founding Fathers.* Berkeley and Los Angeles: Univ. of California Press, 1970.

Cunningham, Noble. *The Jeffersonian-Republicans in Power: Party Operations 1801-1809.* Chapel Hill: Univ. of North Carolina Press, 1963.

Dabney, William. *After Saratoga: The Story of the Convention Army.* Albuquerque: Univ. of New Mexico Press, 1954.

Davis, Joseph. *Sectionalism in American Politics 1774-1787.* Madison: Univ. of Wisconsin Press, 1977.

Eagleton, Thomas F. *War and Presidential Power: A Chronicle of Congressional Surrender,* New York: Liveright, 1974.

Fischer, David Hackett. *The Revolution of American Conservatism: The Federalist Party in the Era of Jeffersonian Democracy.* New York: Harper and Row, 1956.

Foner, Philip. *Morale Education in the American Army.* New York: International Publishers, 1944.

Goetzmann, William. *When the Eagle Screamed: The Romantic Horizon in American Diplomacy 1800-1860.* New York: John Wiley, 1966.

Graber, Doris A. *Public Opinion, the President and Foreign Policy: Four Case Studies from the Formative Years.* New York: Holt, Rinehart and Winston, 1968.

Grob, Fritz. *The Relativity of War and Peace: A Study of Law, History and Politics.* New Haven: Yale Univ. Press, 1949.

Gross, Robert A. *The Minutemen and their World.* New York: Hill and Wang, 1976.

Gruber, Ira. *The Howe Brothers and the American Revolution.* Chapel Hill: Univ. of North Carolina Press, 1972.

Hill, Peter P. *William Vans Murray Federalist Diplomat: the Shaping of the Peace with France 1797-1801.* Syracuse: Syracuse Univ. Press, 1971.

Horsman, Reginald. *The War of 1812.* London: Eyre and Spottiswoode, 1969.

Howard, Michael, ed. *Restraints on War: Studies in the Limitation of Armed Conflict.* Oxford: Oxford Univ. Press, 1979.

Hurst, James W. *The Law of Treason in the United States: Collected Essays.* Westport, Conn.: Greenwood Press, 1971.

Irwin, Ray. *The Diplomatic Relations of the United States with the Barbary Powers 1776-1816.* Chapel Hill: Univ. of North Carolina Press, 1931.

Johnstone, Robert M., Jr. *Jefferson and the Presidency: Leadership in the Young Republic.* Ithaca: Cornell Univ. Press, 1978.

Keenleyside, Hugh. *Canada and the United States: Some Aspects of their Historical Relations.* Port Washington, N.Y.: Kennikat Press, 1952.

Library of Congress Symposia on the American Revolution. *The Development of a Revolutionary Mentality.* Washington, D.C.: Library of Congress, 1972.

Livermore, Shaw, Jr. *The Twilight of Federalism: The Disintegration of the Federalist Party 1815-1830.* Princeton: Princeton Univ. Press, 1962.

Lydon, James G. *Pirates, Privateers and Profits.* Upper Saddle River, N.J. The Gregg Press, 1970.

Maurice, J. F. *Hostilities Without Declaration of War.* London: H. M. Stationary Office, 1883.

May, Ernest R. *The Making of the Monroe Doctrine.* Cambridge, Mass.: Harvard Univ. Press, 1975.

———, ed. *The Ultimate Decision: The President as Commander in Chief.* New York: G. Braziller, 1960.

McElwee, William. *The Art of War from Waterloo to Mons.* London: Wiedenfeld and Nicolson, 1974.

McInnis, Edgar. *The Unguarded Frontier: A History of Canadian-American Relations.* New York: Doubleday, 1942.

Morison, Samuel Eliot. *By Land and Sea: Essays and Addresses.* New York: Alfred Knopf, 1953.

Peckham, Howard. *The Colonial Wars 1689-1762.* Chicago: Univ. of Chicago Press, 1964.

Perkins, Dexter. *The Monroe Doctrine 1823-1826.* Cambridge, Mass.: Harvard Univ. Press, 1927.

Philips, A. W., and Reede, A. H. *Neutrality: Its History, Economics and Law.* New York: Columbia Univ. Press, 1932. Vol. 2.

Royster, Charles. *A Revolutionary People at War: The Continental Army and American Character, 1775-1783.* Chapel Hill: Univ. of North Carolina Press, 1979.

Sapio, Victor. *Pennsylvania and the War of 1812.* Lexington: Univ. Press of Kentucky, 1970.

Schwoerer, Lois G. *"No Standing Armies!" The Antiarmy Ideology in Seventeenth Century England.* Baltimore: The Johns Hopkins Univ. Press, 1974.

Sears, Louis M. *George Washington and the French Revolution.* Detroit: Wayne State Univ. Press, 1960.

Sheehan, Bernard. *Seeds of Extinction: Jeffersonian Philanthropy and the American Indian.* Chapel Hill: Univ. of North Carolina Press, 1973.

Smelser, Marshall. *The Congress Founds the Navy 1787-1798.* Notre Dame: Univ. of Notre Dame Press, 1959.

Sorel, Albert. *Europe Under the Old Regime.* Trans. Francis Herrich. New York: Harper and Row, 1964.

Ward, Harry. *The Department of War, 1781-1795.* Pittsburgh: Univ. of Pittsburgh Press, 1962.

Whitaker, Arthur P. *The Spanish-American Frontier 1783-1795.* Lincoln: Univ. of Nebraska Press, 1969; f.p. 1927.

_____. *The Mississippi Question 1795-1803: A Study in Trade, Politics and Diplomacy.* New York: D. Appleton Century Crofts, 1934.

_____. *The United States and the Independence of Latin America 1800-1830.* Baltimore: The Johns Hopkins Univ. Press, 1941.

Williams, Glyndwr. *The Expansion of Europe in the Eighteenth Century: Overseas Rivalry, Discovery, and Exploration.* London: Blandford, 1966.

Woodward, E. L. *War and Peace in Europe 1815-1870.* New York: Archon Books, 1963.

Wright, J. Leitch. *Britain and the American Frontier 1783-1815.* Athens: Univ. of Georgia Press, 1975.

Zaslow, Morris, ed. *The Defended Border: Upper Canada and the War of 1812.* Toronto: Macmillan Co. of Canada, 1964.

ARTICLES

Amerman, Richard H. "Treatment of American Prisoners During the Revolution," New Jersey Historical Society, *Proceedings,* 78 (1960), 257-75.

Anderson, Olive. "The Treatment of Prisoners of War in Britain During the American War of Independence," Institute of Historical Research, *Bulletin,* 28 (1955), 63-83.

Anderson, William G. "John Adams, the Navy, and the Quasi-War with France," *AN,* 30 (1970), 117-32.

Barlow, William R. "Ohio's Congressmen and the War of 1812," *Ohio History*, 72 (1963), 175-94, 257-59.

Bernard, M. "The Growth of Laws and Usages of War," *Oxford Essays*, 2 (1856).

Berquist, Harold E. "John Quincy Adams and the Promulgation of the Monroe Doctrine, October-December 1823," *EIHC* (1975), 37-52.

Boyd, Julian P. "The Disputed Authorship of the Declaration on the Causes and Necessity for Taking Up Arms, 1775," *PMHB*, 74 (1950), 51-73.

Brant, Irving. "Madison and the War of 1812," *VMHB*, 74 (1966), 51-67.

Brown, Roger H. "The War Hawks of 1812: An Historiographical Myth," *IMH*, 60 (1964), 139-51.

————. "A Vermont Republican Urges War: Royall Tyler, 1812, and the Safety of Republican Government," *Vermont History*, 36 (1968), 13-18.

Campbell, Randolph B. "The Case of the 'Three Friends,' " *VMHB*, 74 (1966), 190-209.

Carr, James A. "John Adams and the Barbary Problem: The Myth and the Record," *AN*, 26 (1966), 229-57.

Cohen, Ronald D. "New England and New France: External Relations and Internal Disagreements Among the Puritans," *EIHC*, 108 (1972), 252-71.

Copp, Walter. "Nova Scotian Trade During the War of 1812," *Canadian Historical Review*, 18 (1937), 141-55.

Cowdrey, H. F. J. "The Peace and Truce of God in the Eleventh Century," *Past and Present*, 46 (1970), 42-67.

Crary, Catherine. "Forfeited Loyalist Lands in the Western District of New York — Albany and Tryon Counties," *New York History*, 35 (1954), 239-58.

Cress, Lawrence. "Republican Liberty and National Security: American Military Policy as an Ideological Problem 1783-1789," *WMQ*, 38 (1981), 73-96.

Dietz, Anthony. "The Use of Cartel Vessels During the War of 1812," *AN*, 28 (1968), 165-94.

Dion, Leon. "Natural Law and Manifest Destiny in the Era of the American Revolution," *Canadian Journal of Economics and Political Science*, 23 (1957), 227-47.

Donahoe, Bernard, and Smelser, Marshall. "The Congressional Power to Raise Armies: The Constitutional and Ratifying Conventions, 1787-1788," *RP*, 33 (1971), 202-11.

Earle, Edward Meade. "Early American Policy Concerning Ottoman Minorities," *PSQ*, 42 (1927), 337-67.

Ferguson, E. James. "The Nationalists of 1781-1783 and the Economic Interpretation of the Constitution," *JAH*, 56 (1969), 241-61.

Fisher, Robert. "The Western Prologue to the War of 1812," *Missouri Historical Review*, 30 (1936), 267-81.

Forbes, John D. "European Wars and Boston Trade, 1783-1815," *NEQ*, 11 (1938), 709-30.

Forman, Sidney. "Why the United States Military Academy was Established in 1802," *MA*, 29 (1965), 16-28.

Gates, Charles. "The West in American Diplomacy, 1812-1815," *MVHR*, 26 (1940), 499-510.

Gribbin, William. "The War of 1812 and American Presbyterianism: Religion and Politics During the Second War with Britain," *Journal of Presbyterian History*, 47 (1969), 320-39.

Gronet, Richard W. "United States and the Invasion of Texas 1810-1814," *Americas*, 25 (1969), 281-306.

Hatch, Nathan O. "The Origins of Civil Millennialism in America: New England Clergymen, War with France, and the Revolution," *WMQ*, 31 (1974), 407-30.

Hickey, Donald R. "Federalist Defense Policy in the Age of Jefferson, 1801-1812," *MA*, 45 (1981), 63-70.

Horsman, Reginald. "Who Were the War Hawks?" *IMH*, 60 (1964), 121-36.

———. "Western War Aims 1811-1812," *IMH*, 53 (1957), 1-18.

Howe, John R., Jr. "Republican Thought and the Political Violence of the 1790s," *American Quarterly*, 19 (1967), 147-65.

Johnson, Leland. "The Suspense was Hell: The Senate Vote for War in 1812," *IMH*, 65 (1969), 246-67.

Johnson, Ludwell. "The Business of War: Trading with the Enemy in English and American Law," *Proceedings of the American Philosophical Society*, 118 (1974), 459-68.

Kaplan, Lawrence. "France and Madison's Decision for War, 1812," *MVHR*, 50 (1964), 652-71.

———. "France and the War of 1812," *JAH*, 57 (1970), 36-47.

Kaufman, Martin. "War Sentiment in Western Pennsylvania: 1812," *Pennsylvania History*, 31 (1964), 439-40.

Ketcham, Ralph. "James Madison: The Unimperial President," *VQR*, 54 (1978), 116-36.

Kramer, Leonard. "Muskets in the Pulpit: 1776-1783," Presbyterian Historical Society, *Journal*, 31 (1953), 229-44; 32 (1954), 37-51.

Laub, Herbert. "The Problem of Armed Invasion of the Northwest During the American Revolution," *VMHB*, 42 (1934), 18-27, 132-44.

MacLeod, Julia. "Jefferson and the Navy: A Defense," *HLQ*, 8 (1945), 170-76.

Mannix, Richard. "Gallatin, Jefferson, and the Embargo of 1808,"
    Diplomatic History, 3 (1979), 151-72.
Marks, Frederick W., III. "Foreign Affairs: A Winning Issue in the
    Campaign for the Ratification of the United States Constitution,"
    PSQ, 86 (1971), 444-69.
Martel, J. S. "A Side Light on Federalist Strategy During the War of
    1812," *AHR*, 43 (1938), 553-66.
McCoy, Drew. "Benjamin Franklin's Vision of a Republican Political
    Economy for America," *WMQ*, 35 (1978), 605-28.
Millett, Allan. "American Military History: Over the Top," in *The State
    of American History*, ed. Herbert J. Bass. Chicago: Quadrangle
    Books, 1970, pp. 157-82.
Morse, Sidney. "State or Continental Privateers?" *AHR*, 52 (1946),
    68-73.
Pencak, William. "Warfare and Political Change in Mid-Eighteenth-
    Century Massachusetts," *Journal of Imperial Commonwealth His-
    tory*, 8 (1980), 51-73.
Peterson, Merrill. "Thomas Jefferson and Commercial Policy 1783-
    1793," *WMQ*, 22 (1965), 584-610.
Reveley, W. Taylor, III. "Constitutional Allocation of War Powers
    Between the President and Congress: 1787-1788," *Virginia Journal of
    International Law*, 15 (1974), 73-147.
Roberts, Michael. "The Military Revolution, 1560-1660," in Roberts,
    Essays in Swedish History. Minneapolis: Univ. of Minnesota Press,
    1967. Pp. 195-225.
Robinson, Ralph. "Retaliation for the Treatment of Prisoners in the
    War of 1812," *AHR*, 49 (1943), 65-70.
Savageau, David. "The United States Navy and Its 'Half War' Prisoners
    1798-1801," *AN*, 31 (1971), 159-76.
Scanlon, James. "The Federalist and Human Nature," *RP*, 21 (1959),
    657-77.
Shea, William. "Virginia at War 1644-1646," *MA*, 41 (1977), 142-47.
Smith, Abbot. "Mr. Madison's War: An Unsuccessful Experiment in the
    Conduct of National Policy," *PSQ*, 57 (1942), 236-41.
Smith, Theodore. "War Guilt in 1812," Massachusetts Historical
    Society, *Proceedings*, 64 (1913), 319-45.
Stagg, J. C. A. "The Coming of the War of 1812: The View from the
    Presidency," *Quarterly Journal of the Library of Congress*, 37 (1980),
    223-41.
Tolles, Frederick B. "Unofficial Ambassador: George Logan's Mission
    to France, 1798," *WMQ*, 7 (1950), 3-25.
Upton, James. "The Shakers as Pacifists in the Period Between 1812 and
    the Civil War," *Filson Club Historical Quarterly*, 47 (1973), 267-83.

Walker, William, Jr. "Martial Sons: Tennessee Enthusiasm for the War of 1812," *Tennessee Historical Quarterly,* 20 (1961), 22-25.

Wiltse, Charles. "The Authorship of the War Report of 1812," *AHR,* 49 (1944), 253-59.

Wright, Louis. "The Founding Fathers and 'Splendid Isolation,' " *HLQ,* 6 (1943), 173-96.

DISSERTATIONS

Dietz, Anthony. "The Prisoner of War in the United States During the War of 1812," the American University, 1964.

Hickey, Donald. "The Federalists and the War of 1812," University of Illinois at Urbana-Champaign, 1972.

Johnson, Warren. "The Contents of American Colonial Newspapers Relative to International Affairs, 1704-1763," University of Washington, 1962.

Rutman, Darrett. "A Militant New World 1607-1640," University of Virginia, 1959.

Spivak, Burton. "Jefferson, England, and the Embargo: Trading Wealth and Republican Values in the Shaping of American Diplomacy 1804-1809," University of Virginia, 1976.

Trask, Kelly. "In the Pursuit of Shadows: A Study of Collective Hope and Despair in Provincial Massachusetts During the Era of the Seven Years War, 1748-1764," University of Minnesota, 1971.

White, John Todd. "Standing Armies in Time of War: Republican Theory and Military Practice During the American Revolution," George Washington University, 1978.

INDEX

242

INDEX

Louisiana Purchase (1803), 72, 106, 116-
18, 161
Lowndes, William, 154, 178
Loyalism, 18, 24, 26, 30-31, 44, 55-58, 98
Lyon, Matthew, 105, 113, 130

Madison, James, 2, 5, 28, 38, 58, 62, 64-65,
72, 77, 98, 106-7, 110, 120, 112, 125, 132,
160, 187; and Algiers (1815), 160-61; and
economic coercion, 47, 89-90, 111-12;
and expansion, 58, 99-101; and force
and policy, 34, 60, 64, 117, 147, 150, 155,
163; and French Revolution, 78; and
limited-war mentality, 58, 124, 128,
134, 142-44; and war myth, 64, 69, 151,
157; and War of 1812, 137-38, 142, 157,
162
Manifest Destiny, 55, 100, 123, 133-35,
164, 184
"Manifesto to Canadians," 22
Marque and reprisal, letters, 15, 27, 60-62,
139
Marshall, John, 63
Mason, George, 34
Mason, Jeremiah, 159
Mason, Thomas, 20
Massachusetts General Court, 15
Massachusetts Peace Society, 152
Mathews, John, 31
McClenachan, William, 12
McClure, George, 141
McHenry, James, 62
McKean, Thomas, 63
Mexican War (1846), 164, 180, 184
Military Monitor and American Register,
138, 140
Military Philosophical Society, 98
Militia, 29, 31, 101-2, 118, 120, 157
Millis, Walter, 190
Miranda, Francisco de, 88, 100
Mississippi River, 58, 70-76, 98, 104, 116-
17; and Spanish closure (1802), 102,
105-6, 110
Mitchell, Samuel, 113
Model Treaty (1776), 44-45
Monarchism, 3, 42; and republicanism,
168; and war, 5, 8, 36, 47, 104, 228
Monroe, James, 47, 49, 60, 106, 125-26,
148, 160-61, 164, 172, 174; and force and
policy, 110, 117, 147, 150; and Latin
American revolutions, 166; and lim-
ited-war mentality, 102, 156-57, 178;

and neutrality, 84, 165-69; and Span-
ish-American relations, 161, 177-78;
and War of 1812, 137, 140, 144
Montesquieu, Baron, 5, 8, 11-12
Moral Advocate, 153
Morocco, 52
Morris, Gouverneur, 30, 77, 102
Morris, Robert, 14, 20, 23, 26
Murray, William Vans, 89

Napoleonic Wars, 65, 94, 96, 127, 142, 149,
185
National Intelligencer, 128
Nationalism, American, xii, 17, 22, 24, 32,
49, 59, 67, 70, 79-81, 84, 92-93, 96, 105-6,
112-14, 119, 124-25, 135, 145, 148-50,
155, 160, 169-70; and limited-war mentality, 45, 66, 76, 85, 178, 181; and
pacifism, 151-55; and republicanism,
103-4, 132, 150-51, 171; Romantic, 17,
54, 100, 121, 123, 117, 132, 138; and war,
70, 119, 136, 180, 187; and war myth,
155, 159; and War of 1812, 124, 144
Navy, United States, 70, 83, 113, 115, 157
Nelson, Hugh, 130, 132, 169
Nelson, Thomas, 175
Neutrality and American policy, 45, 74,
77, 84-85, 96, 164; in 1793, 33, 71, 75-78,
84-85, 184; and Latin American rebels,
165-69; Laws (1818), 167
New England, 34; and War of 1812, 125,
129-30, 137
New Netherland, 12
New Orleans, Battle of (1814), 150, 157
Newburgh conspiracy, 50
Newenham, Sir Edward, 46
Nicholas, Wilson Cary 107, 114
Nonintercourse, 108, 112-13; Non-inter-
course Act (1809), 107, 113-14
Nootka Sound Affair, 68, 75, 83, 85
North American Review, 168
North Carolina, 29
Northwest Ordinance (1787), 57
Northwest Posts, 58-59, 70, 74, 78
Nova Scotia, 15

Old Testament and War, 6
The Olive Branch, 137
Olive Branch Petition, 22
Onis, Don Luis de, 174
Orders in Council, 114, 124-25, 132-34
Oregon, 162, 164, 184

Reginald C. Stuart is a Canadian scholar with a Ph.D. from the University of Florida. He is Associate Professor of History at the University of Prince Edward Island and is the author of *The Half-Way Pacifist: Thomas Jefferson's View of the War* and numerous articles in his twin fields of interest — war studies and the early National period of U.S. history.